IBM RISC System/6000

Further Titles in the IBM McGraw-Hill Series

Open Systems and IBM: Integration and Convergence
Pamela Gray   ISBN 0-07-707750-4

OS/2 Presentation Manager Programming: Hints and Tips
Bryan Goodyer   ISBN 0-07-707776-8

Introduction to MVS Systems Programming
David Elder-Vass   ISBN 0-07-707767-9

IBM RISC System/6000 User Guide
Mike Leaver and Hardev Sanghera   ISBN 0-07-707687-7

PC User's Guide: Simple Steps to Powerful Personal Computing
Peter Turner   ISBN 0-07-707421-1

Dynamic Factory Automation: Creating Flexible Systems For Competitive
Manufacturing
Alastair Ross   ISBN 0-07-707440-8

Details of these and other titles in the series are available from:

The Product Manager, Professional Books
McGraw-Hill Book Company Europe
Shoppenhangers Road, Maidenhead, Berkshire, SL6 2QL
Telephone: 0628 23432 Fax: 0628 770224

Clive Harris

IBM RISC System/6000

McGRAW-HILL BOOK COMPANY

London · New York · St Louis · San Francisco · Auckland
Bogotá · Caracas · Hamburg · Lisbon · Madrid · Mexico
Milan · Montreal · New Delhi · Panama · Paris · San Juan
São Paulo · Singapore · Sydney · Tokyo · Toronto

Published by
McGRAW-HILL Book Company Europe
Shoppenhangers Road, Maidenhead, Berkshire, SL6 2QL, England
Telephone 0628 23432
Fax 0628 770224

British Library Cataloguing in Publication Data

Harris, Clive
   IBM RISC System/6000. — (IBM McGraw-Hill
   Series)
   I. Title II. Series
   004.165

   ISBN 0-07-707668-0

Library of Congress Cataloging-in-Publication Data

Harris, Clive
   The IBM RISC System/6000 / Clive Harris.
      p.   cm. — (The IBM McGraw-Hill series)
   Includes index.
   ISBN 0-07-707668-0
   1. IBM RISC System/6000 computers. 2. Business-Data processing.
   I. Title. II. Series
   QA76.8.I25975H37 1993
   004.165 — dc20   92-32089
                                                      CIP

1234 CUP 9543

Typeset by Alden Multimedia Ltd, Northampton
and printed and bound in Great Britain at the University Press Cambridge

Contents

Foreword

The IBM McGraw-Hill Series

IBM UK and McGraw-Hill Europe have worked together to publish this series of books about information technology and its use in business, industry and the public sector.

The series provides an up-to-date and authoritative insight into the wide range of products and services available, and offers strategic business advice. Some of the books have a technical bias, others are written from a broader business perspective. What they have in common is that their authors—some from IBM, some independent consultants—are experts in their field.

Apart from assisting where possible with the accuracy of the writing, IBM UK has not sought to inhibit the editorial freedom of the series, and therefore the views expressed in the books are those of the authors, and not necessarily those of IBM.

Where IBM has lent its expertise is in assisting McGraw-Hill to identify potential titles whose publication would help advance knowledge and increase awareness of computing topics. Hopefully these titles will also serve to widen the debate about the important information technology issues of today and of the future—such as open systems, networking, and the use of technology to give companies a competitive edge in their market.

IBM UK is pleased to be associated with McGraw-Hill in this series.

Sir Anthony Cleaver
Chairman
IBM United Kingdom Limited

Foreword

Trademarks

AIX, IBM, Micro Channel, Netview, OS/2, OS/400, Operating System/2, Personal System/2, PS/2, PROFS, Proprinter, Quickwriter, Quietwriter, RT, RT PC, RT Personal Computer and Systems Application Architecture are registered trademarks of International Business Machines Corporation.

AIXwindows, Application System/400, AS/400, Enterprise System/9370, ES/3090, ExecJet, graPHIGS, Impactwriter, InfoExplorer, Presentation Manager, RISC System/6000, SAA, System/370, System/390, VM/XA and Xstation Manager are trademarks of International Business Machines Corporation.

Apollo is a registered trademark of Apollo Computer, Inc. Network Computing System and NCS are trademarks of Apollo Computer, Inc.

AT&T is a registered trademark of American Telephone & Telegraph.

Display PostScript is a trademark of Adobe Corporation.

GL is a trademark and Silicon Graphics is a registered trademark of Silicon Graphics Inc.

Hayes is a registered trademark and Smartmodem 1200, Smartmodem 2400 and V-Series 9600 are trademarks of Hayes Corporation.

HP and LaserJet Series II are trademarks of Hewlett-Packard Inc.

INed is a trademark of Interactive Systems Corporation.

INGRES is a registered trademark of the Ingres Corporation, Inc.

Intel is a registered trademark of the Intel Corporation. 386 and 486 are trademarks of Intel.

Microsoft and XENIX are registered trademarks of Microsoft Corporation.

Motorola is a registered trademark of Motorola Corporation. 68000, 68020 and 68030 are trademarks of Motorola.

NextStep is a trademark of NeXT Inc.

OSF, OSF/1, OSF/Motif and Motif are trademarks of the Open Software Foundation, Inc.

PostScript is a trademark of Adobe Systems, Inc.

Racal-Vadic is a trademark of RACALVADIC Corporation.

SQL*PLUS, SQL*REPORT, SQL*MENU, SQL*FORMS, and **SQL*NET** are trademarks of Oracle Corporation.

SPECmark is a trademark of Standard Performance Evaluation Corporation.

Sun is a registered trademark and **Network File System, NFS, ONC, PC-NFS, SunOS,** and **SPARC** are trademarks of Sun Microsystems, Inc.

Telebit is a registered trademark and **Trailblazer Plus** is a trademark of Telebit Corporation.

UNIX is a registered trademark of UNIX System Laboratories, Inc.

VAX is a trademark and **DEC** is a registered trademark of Digital Equipment Corporation.

X Window System is a trademark of the Massachusetts Institute of Technology.

X/Open is a trademark of X/Open Company, Ltd in the UK and other countries.

/usr/group is a trademark of UniForum.

Acknowledgements

I would like to thank the many people who have helped and assisted in the production of this book. I certainly would not have been able to complete it without their help.

Firstly, I would like to thank the many individuals in IBM who helped me to gather information from various sources throughout IBM, in particular Ron Beal, Jon Barnes, Valerie Sangwine, Bill Sandve, Terry Critchley and John Barron. I would also like to thank the staff of McGraw-Hill for their advice and help in preparing the book. Special thanks go to Andrew Ware and Jacqueline Harbor.

Introduction

This book is written for executives, decision makers and users in any organization that uses IT, many of whom are considering moving applications or running applications under UNIX. In particular, there is a lot of interest in the RISC System/6000 from IBM. This book discusses the UNIX and Open Systems market-place and how the RISC System/6000 or RS/6000 is designed to fit into that environment, and also how to position the RS/6000 in relation to other UNIX systems and in relation to other IBM systems —specifically SAA (System Application Architecture) systems.

This book should prove equally interesting and useful to people with either little or no knowledge of UNIX or alternatively, a reasonable knowledge of UNIX systems. It will provide a useful reference source for understanding the capabilities of the RS/6000.

The book firstly discusses the meaning of Open Systems and looks at the relevant standards such as POSIX, X/Open and the UNIX based consortiums.

The next chapter looks at UNIX as an operating system, discusses its history, and the reasons why it is becoming more popular. There are a number of very different market-places and requirements for UNIX systems, these will be discussed. The basic concepts of some of the associated areas will be explained. For example, there is a section on Local Area Networks and how these are typically used in a UNIX environment.

Chapter 3 looks at AIX, which is IBM's implementation of UNIX. It compares AIX with traditional UNIX implementations and describes some of the additional features available in AIX.

The next chapter looks in detail at the RS/6000 hardware. It describes the various models and their capabilities and looks at each of the related hardware areas, such as disk, tapes, displays, etc. There is a section describing the processor architecture of the RS/6000.

Finally, the last chapter looks at a number of the related aspects. Topics such as market channels and support are discussed, and how AIX relates to IBM's proprietary architecture, Systems Application Architecture (SAA).

This book is meant to be easy to read and wherever possible jargon is not used. It should prove useful to readers who do not have a detailed background in UNIX systems and it will explain the basics of many of these areas. Equally, the reader who already knows UNIX will find the detailed information on the RS/6000 and its capabilities useful.

This is a market-place that is moving forward very rapidly. New machines and models are announced and older models are outdated very quickly. This book will discuss models and products in some areas, but the reader will need to be aware that prices and configurations of machines will change. This book discusses mainly principles and architectures and, therefore, the reader will find most of this book will remain valid even though specific details will change.

1
IBM and Open Systems

1.1   Definition of an Open System

There is a lot of discussion these days about Open Systems. Many people have a very different understanding of what is meant by an 'Open System'. It is important to realize at the outset that an Open System does not necessarily mean a UNIX system.

POSIX have defined an Open System Environment. The description is as follows:

> Open Systems Environment: The comprehensive set of interfaces, services and supporting formats, plus user aspects, for interoperability or for portability of applications, data or people, as specified by information technology standards and profiles.

This definition is also used by the European Workshop on Operating Systems and is the one adopted by IBM.

In addition, POSIX in the same document define an Open System as follows:

> Open System: A system that implements sufficient open specifications for interfaces, services and supporting formats to enable properly engineered applications software:
>
> - to be ported with minimal changes across a wide range of systems
> - to interoperate with other applications on local and remote systems
> - to interact with users in a style that facilitates user portability

This definition of an Open System is likely to be adopted by many standard setting bodies as it sums up the important aspects of an Open System in simple terms.

In summary, we can define an Open System in this way:

- *Interoperability*.   The ability for the system to successfully communicate with other open systems. This should allow users to log on and use applications and transfer or share data and resources.

- *Portability.* This should allow not just easy porting of applications from one Open System to another, but also the ability to port all of the data. Users should also be able to use a system intuitively without extensive retraining. For example, I can get into a car which is not my own and drive it without any problems, although I might spend a little time finding out details such as how to turn on the lights. If the clutch and brake pedal positions were reversed, however, I would have great problems in driving the car. Because all cars tend to use these accepted standards, it makes it much easier for users to move from one to another. The same principle should apply to a user moving from one Open System to another.

- *Standards conformance.* For any system to be deemed an Open System, it must conform to the relevant industry standards. There are a number of operating systems around that provide interoperability and portability even though many people would class them as proprietary systems. In some cases, the standards and specifications for the system are defined by the manufacturer. Examples include MVS (an IBM mainframe operating system) and VMS from DEC. These provide many of the functions of an Open System. However, their futures are governed by those manufacturers.

Software portability is a topic that needs discussing. Many organizations would like the ability to run applications on different platforms. In an Open Systems world, it would be possible to 'port' an application easily to a different system. This typically would involve re-compiling the application. In a truly Open environment the high level code will be the same for all platforms. In practice today, this is not always the case. In the UNIX world many applications can be ported to another UNIX platform with only minor changes, but some applications—particularly graphical technical applications—require extensive changes. This situation is getting easier with the evolving and emerging standards that are discussed in this chapter.

If different hardware architectures are to be employed, then the machine level code on different platforms will be different. This means that binary compatibility is not so easy, although it is not impossible if some intermediate level of code is used. In practice, users do not seem as interested in binary compatibility across platforms as in the ability to re-compile easily on the new platform.

Interoperability between systems can typically be achieved by using common functions, for example, adopting the same high level programming

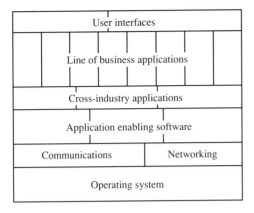

Figure 1.1. A typical customer model.

languages (ANSI standard C, COBOL or FORTRAN) or using common communications protocols (e.g. TCP/IP or OSI).

It is worth noting that proprietary does not necessarily mean bad. There are many proprietary system installed with customers who are very happy with them. These systems will clearly continue to be marketed and supported and the customers' investments will be protected. What we are seeing, however, is that these systems are frequently conforming to the Open Systems standards—such as the IBM AS/400 being POSIX compliant. This trend will continue, with the OS/400 operating system on the AS/400 and the MVS operating system for the IBM System/390 becoming more open and complying with the Open System standards. In September 1991 IBM made a number of major announcements relating to Open Systems. These included:

- POSIX 1003.1 on MVS/ESA
- POSIX 1003.1 and 1003.2 on OS/400
- Elements of OSF/DCE on all SAA platforms and the AIX family
- AIX/ESA will be built on the OSF/1 operating system
- AIX Version 3 will conform fully to OSF/1
- AIX family to include a CICS Transaction Processing Monitor
- AIX SystemView products will support OSF/DME

You will see that once we start discussing standards and Open Systems, we start running into jargon such as OSF, DCE, DME, POSIX, etc. Before we go any further we will need to discuss the various standards and organizations, and look in more detail at some of them.

The standards that exist are related to many different aspects of a computer system. Figure 1.1 shows a typical customer model with the various components. Most of the existing standards are related to the interface between the operating system and other applications. The standards over

time will almost certainly extend to cover other interfaces between
components of this model.

1.2   The Open Systems standards

This section discusses the various standards that are important in the Open
Systems arena and what all these standards mean for users of these systems.
Standards and specifications play a key role in facilitating open systems
portability and interoperability.

Some customers question whether AIX from IBM is 'standard' and some
customers question IBM's commitment to Open Systems in general. I hope
this chapter will show you that IBM provides an operating system in AIX
that complies with all the relevant standards. In addition, I hope you will see
that IBM is fully committed to Open Systems.

You will realize by now that a UNIX system and an Open System are not
necessarily the same thing. UNIX is an example of an Open System. UNIX
is, of course, a registered trademark and therefore all other manufacturers
and suppliers of 'UNIX-like' systems have to call them different names. For
example DEC has ULTRIX, Sun has SunOS, Hewlett-Packard has HP-UX
and Domain OS and IBM has AIX. In all, there are more than 400 different
versions of UNIX-based operating systems around. What is important is that
the operating system conforms to the relevant standards.

These standards can be divided into three categories:

- Authority (*ex cathedra, ad baculum*). These are standards that are defined
  by formal standards setting bodies such as ISO, ANSI or IEEE. Such
  standards include POSIX, and take the form of 'you WILL do things this
  way'.
- Consensus (*de jure*). Meaning 'by law'. This type of standard comes about
  from a group that has power or 'clout' of some kind, often a consortium
  or industry association, and these standards take the form of 'WE will do
  things this way'.
- Trends (*de facto*). These standards come about because many users
  choose to do things in a particular way. They are informal standards but
  can lead to more formal standards. The originating vendor or group may
  foster adoption by licensing source code for a nominal fee. Others may
  only publish specifications. *De facto* standards may include industry
  specifications such as X/Open's XPG3 (see below), vendor specifications
  such as Network File System (NFS) or System V Interface Definition
  (SVID), or popular implementations such as 4.3 BSD.

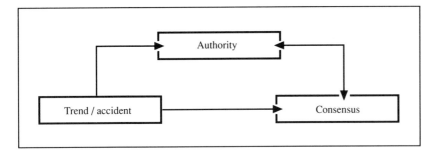

Figure 1.2. The cycle of standards.

One kind of standard can lead over a period of time to another and cycles such as in Fig. 1.2 can often occur.

Standards organizations can be categorized as follows:

- Formal development organizations such as the American National Standards Institute (ANSI) and the International Standards Organization (ISO).
- Government organizations such as NIST (National Institute of Standards and Technology) and FIPS (Federal Information Processing Standard).
- Technology implementation consortia such as the Open Software Foundation (OSF).
- Interface definition consortia such as X/Open.

There are, firstly, the Formal Industry Standards Bodies which I will now describe. Clearly any operating system in the Open Systems world should comply with these. I will then discuss other relevant standards setting organizations.

1.2.1 POSIX

The POSIX standards originate from UNIX, but do not actually mention UNIX as being required. The standards are set by the Institute of Electrical and Electronics Engineers (IEEE) and define a Portable Operating System Interface (POSIX). These standards are supported by numerous vendors, users and other interested parties.

The original POSIX standard was introduced in 1989, and, although at the moment there is only one standard over a period of time a suite of these standards will be developed. The present standard is actually based on work that was done by the International Unix User Group (/usr/group) which is now known as UniForum.

Table 1.1. POSIX working groups

Working group	Description
1003.0	Guide to POSIX Open Systems environment
1003.1	System Interface
1003.2	Shell and Utilities
1003.3	Test Methods
1003.4	Real Time and Extensions
1003.5	Ada Language Bindings
1003.6	Security
1003.7	System Administration
1003.8	Transparent File Access
1003.9	FORTRAN Language Bindings
1003.10	Supercomputing AEP
1003.11	Transaction Processing AEP
1003.12	Protocol Independent
1003.13	Real Time AEPs
1003.14	Multiprocessing AEP
1003.15	Batch Services
1003.16	C Language Binding
1003.17	Directory Services API

There are a number of working groups working on POSIX standards within the IEEE technical committee on operating systems.

- P1003 looking at operating systems
- P1201 investigating Graphical User Interfaces (GUI)
- P1224 covering OSI (Open Systems Interconnect) Communications

Some of the different POSIX working groups are shown in Table 1.1. The work of these committees tends to be longer-term work and, at the moment, not many of the working groups have a finalized published standard. The most important of the completed standards at present is the one defined by the 1003.1 group relating to the system interface. The full published standard is known as IEEE Std 1003.1-1990: System Application Program Interface. This is also an international standard called ISO/IEC 9945:1-1990.

IEEE Std 1003.3-1991 is also a finalized, published standard. When operating systems are quoted as being POSIX compliant, it means that they conform to this 1003.1 standard.

The review groups typically number 200 to 300 people and balloting requires 75 per cent approval. Although this process can take several years to produce a standard, the end product is an ANSI/ISO standard that is almost always adopted by hardware and software vendors. For marketing reasons, suppliers find these standards virtually mandatory.

As mentioned earlier, the POSIX standards do not only apply to UNIX systems. IBM has announced that the AS/400 and its OS/400 operating system will be POSIX compliant, and also that IBM's popular mainframe operating system MVS will comply with the POSIX standards.

The intention is that any application written to run on a POSIX-compliant system can be ported to any other system that is also POSIX-compliant. This would typically involve re-compiling the application on the new platform.

A system may have functions over and above the POSIX standards. As long as these functions do not conflict with the POSIX standards then this should not be a problem. However, users need to be careful that they do not use any of these extra functions that might compromise the portability of their applications.

The POSIX standard allows variations within specified limits. Some standards (such as FIPS 151-1) are specific 'versions' of the POSIX standard. This specifies particular parameters or options from within those allowed by POSIX 1003.1.

1.2.2   X/Open

The X/Open organization is an international consortium of vendors. It was founded in 1984. The members change from time to time, but there are many members from the US, Europe and Japan. Members include IBM, DEC, Hewlett-Packard, Open Software Foundation (OSF), and UNIX International (UI). At this time, X/Open has 21 major shareholders and approximately 80 other companies are members. This number is growing rapidly.

X/Open is a world-wide, independent open systems organization dedicated to developing an open, multi-vendor Common Applications Environment (CAE) achieved through close cooperation between users, vendors and standards organizations world-wide. X/Open defines a Common Applications Environment (CAE) which also conforms to the ANSI and ISO standards.

Vendors can test the portability of applications that run on their operating systems using the X/Open suite of tests. This is known as the X/Open Portability Guide. The latest version is Version 3. This is commonly known as XPG3. Most UNIX-like operating systems, including AIX Version 3, conform to XPG3 specifications. XPG3 has three separate levels as shown in Table 1.2. In recent times, X/Open has moved to be more of a user organization. The intention is that requirements will be driven more by users than by vendors. X/Open have published a 'road-map' defining how the organization will respond to market requirements. X/Open intends to release 50 or so publications up to the end of 1993 covering issues in five key areas:

Table 1.2. X/Open XPG3 levels

XPG3 level	Defines
Base level	System Calls and Libraries Commands and Utilities C Language Internationalization
Extensions	Window Manager Terminal Interfaces Network Transparent Interface (XTI) PC Inter-networking ISAM and SQL Database Interfaces COBOL, FORTRAN 77, and PASCAL Languages
Optional	Source Code Transfer Inter-process Communications Ada Language

- Coexistence, interoperability and integration
- Applications support
- Human computer interaction
- Data interchange and access
- Systems management and administration

1.2.3   Open Software Foundation

In October 1987, AT&T announced that it had signed a deal with Sun Microsystems, including an undertaking that AT&T would use Sun's proprietary SPARC processor in its machines and incorporate Sun's UNIX implementation into UNIX System V.4. AT&T also took the opportunity to acquire some shares in Sun.

The reaction of a number of suppliers, including IBM, was to group together to form a consortium, the Open Software Foundation (OSF), which is non-profit making. The Open Software Foundation is an international organization created to define specifications, develop leadership software, and make available an open, portable application environment.

In contrast to the IEEE (POSIX) and X/Open, the OSF develops code. This code is made available to members of the OSF. To make it easier for users to mix and match computers and software from different suppliers, the OSF addresses the following needs:

Portability   The ability to use application software on computers from multiple vendors.

Interoperability   The ability to have computers from different vendors work together.

Scalability   The capability to use the same software environment on many classes of computers, from personal computers to supercomputers.

The foundation is incorporated as a non-profit, industry-supported organization. It consists of a software development company and a research institute to fund and oversee research that advances the foundation's technology.

Foundation membership is open to computer hardware and software suppliers, educational institutions, government agencies, and other interested organizations world wide. The foundation has broad industry backing and initially had 90 million US dollars of funding to begin operations. Initial funding for OSF was provided by the following sponsors:

- IBM
- Digital Equipment Corporation
- Apollo Computer Inc
- Hewlett-Packard Company
- Groupe Bull
- Nixdorf Computer AG
- Siemens Aktiengesellschaft

Members attend regular foundation meetings, submit technologies for evaluation, recommend initiatives, participate in user groups, review specifications, and provide input.

Open Software Foundation activities

- Adopt existing standards and propose new standards based on industry acceptance of specific software features.
- Define and publish specifications for the OSF application environment, operating system, and subsystems.
- Establish a formal, open process for soliciting input on new software developments.
- Develop and distribute source code for an OSF operating system and subsystems. (The foundation will not develop hardware or application software.)
- License source code and provide maintenance and enhancements.
- Develop verification methods and test for establishing compatibility with relevant standards and OSF specifications.
- Communicate the benefits of open systems, including OSF offerings.
- Fund and oversee research to support future offerings.
- Develop a hardware-independent software format for mass distribution of applications.

OSF guiding principles

- Offerings based on relevant industry standards
- Open process to actively solicit inputs and technology
- Timely, vendor-neutral decision process
- Early and equal access to specifications and continuing development
- Hardware-independent implementations
- Reasonable, stable licensing terms
- Technical innovation through university/research participation

OSF standards support

The foundation is a powerful complement to international standards organizations, and supports the mission of those organizations. Where relevant standards exist, the foundation will support them. The foundation may also provide technology in advance of the formal establishment of standards. As necessary, the foundation will adapt these advanced technologies to meet standards as they are established.

OSF offerings

- Specification documents
- Source code
- Sublicensing rights
- Foundation services include:
  - snapshots of specifications/source during development
  - documentation
  - training
  - other services as required
- Subscription for foundation newsletters, including notification of conferences, seminars, and source code availability

Software made available by the sponsors

At the press conference introducing the Foundation, 'contributions' from the sponsoring members of the Foundation were announced.

IBM's contribution

'A future release of AIX will be used as the base for the first implementation of OSF Operating System.'

OSF process

The process used by the OSF to develop standards is to issue a Request For Technology (RFT) based on specific requirements. This is essentially an invitation for any supplier (not just OSF members) to offer their implementation for consideration by the OSF. In due course, after receiving these RFTs, the OSF announces the chosen technology based on an independent decision process.

OSF updates

Since OSF was formed Hitachi, American Express, Tandem, Barclays Bank, NEC, Unilever and many others have joined the original sponsors, and there are over 300 members. The most important products or standards that have emerged from the OSF include:

- *Motif* OSF/Motif is a graphical user interface (GUI). The Windowing system most commonly used in a UNIX environment is X Windows, which on its own does not present a usable environment. Some extra coding is needed to enable a user to re-size windows, move them around, and perform many other tasks. Motif provides these extra functions and is designed to work in much the same way as Presentation Manager which is used by the OS/2 operating system. A user who is familiar with Presentation Manager (PM) will very quickly understand Motif.

  Motif is very widely used in a UNIX environment with X Windows. At present 42 suppliers provide OSF/Motif to the world-wide computing industry including Data General, DEC, Dell, HP/Apollo, Groupe Bull, Hitachi, IBM, Intergraph, NEC, NCR, Siemens/Nixdorf, Silicon Graphics, Santa Cruz Operation, Sony, Unisys, Wang and many others. Third party organizations support Motif on hardware from vendors, such as Sun Microsystems, who have chosen to support other GUIs. Major end user organizations, such as American Airlines, Boeing, European Community, Lockheed, Marriott Corporation, NASA, Shell Oil and many others have specified OSF/Motif.

  Approximately 70 per cent of US government requests for proposals reference OSF/Motif functionality. OSF/Motif conforms with the relevant standards in this area.

- *DCE (Distributed Computing Environment)* OSFs Distributed Computing Environment is a comprehensive, integrated set of services that supports the development, use, and maintenance of distributed applications. The availability of a uniform set of services, anywhere in the

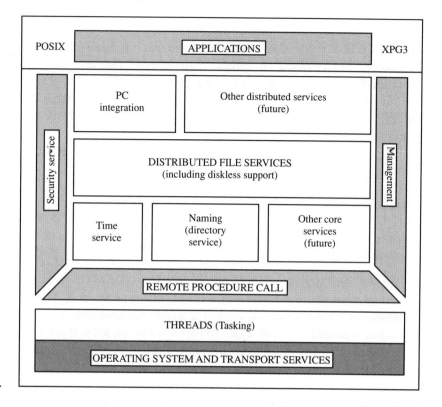

Figure 1.3. Distributed computing environment.

network, should enable applications to harness the power that tends to lie unused in many networks

The architecture of DCE is a layered model which integrates a set of eight technologies. The architecture is layered bottom-up from the most basic, or supplier services (operating system), to the highest level consumers of services (applications). To applications, the environment appears as a single logical system rather than a collection of disparate services. Figure 1.3 shows the structure of the DCE services.

The services provided by DCE include:

- Remote procedure call
- Naming (or directory) services
- Time service
- Security service

- Threads service
- Distributed file system
- Diskless support
- MS-DOS file and printer support services

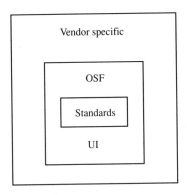

Figure 1.4. Typical structure of an open system.

The OSF is currently shipping DCE code and many suppliers will support DCE on their platforms. AIX Version 3 on the RS/6000 will support all DCE functions.

- *DME (Distributed Management Environment)*   OSF have also recently announced the technology that they will use for their Distributed Management Environment. This is a framework for Network Management of distributed networks.

The operating system OSF/1 is now generally available and has been adopted by a number of manufacturers as the basis of their offerings. Typically, a supplier such as IBM will license the OSF/1 code from the Open Software Foundation and will incorporate this into their own products. This will normally mean adding 'bells and whistles' or extra functions which will differentiate the product from others. IBM will make sure that these added functions do not conflict with the independent standards, since this could affect portability.

The operating system that is shipped to a customer normally will consist of various parts. The structure of a typical Open System is shown in Fig. 1.4.

1.2.4   *UNIX International*

UNIX International (UI) is in direct competition with the Open Software Foundation. The UI specifications are based on ATC System V.4 as the base. The group was formed to counteract the influence of the OSF and directs the development of UNIX systems. Again, the specifications conform to the POSIX and X/Open standards.

Members of UI include Sun and Amdahl. However, some of the members have also supported OSF initiatives including OSF/Motif and DCE.

UNIX International was formed primarily to be a proponent of ATC and Sun's offerings, lacking any real independent authority. When UI and AT&T

released their 'statement of joint intentions' in January of 1989, it spelled out
how the UI process would work:

> UNIX international will define the future features and functionality of
> UNIX System V through an open process, and AT&T will accept that
> direction. UI offices will be used to resolve all differences, except those which
> are inimical to ATC interests.

UNIX International has since developed a 'road-map' of features and
functions it would like in future System V releases. The road-map unarguably
suggests improvements in security, in multiprocessing capability, and in other
areas. However, the 'open process' suggests that AT&T is firmly in the
driver's seat. The pacing of the road-map development matches the capabilities, business objectives, and resource levels of ATC's UNIX software
operation (USO).

1.3   Other versions of UNIX

There are a very large number of versions of UNIX in existence now. Only
one should really be called UNIX—the product that originally came from
AT&T. Other operating systems, although based on the same principles,
should really be called UNIX-like operating systems.

What is most important now is that the operating system conforms to the
relevant standards such as POSIX, X/Open, etc. Most of the operating
systems available today do conform, and in practice porting of applications
and interoperability is possible. Some operating systems conform to OSF
specifications and some to UNIX International specifications. In practice the
difference is not great and porting between both environments is often not a
problem. It is my belief that the differences will gradually diminish further as
the OSF and UI specifications move closer together.

Most suppliers will add value to their operating system. IBM has added a
number of functions to AIX Version 3 for the RISC System/6000 and has
also removed a number of traditional UNIX limitations. It is important that
these added functions do not conflict with the standards and do not restrict
portability.

1.4   Manufacturer alliances

In addition to manufacturers joining consortiums such as UI and OSF, many
manufacturers are forming alliances. These include the ACE consortium and
the IBM/Apple alliance. All these alliances will lead to better products
reaching the market-place sooner and being more widely accepted.

ACE consortium

The Advanced Computing Environment (ACE) realigns many of the major suppliers involved with UNIX systems as well as PC systems. ACE supporters believe that hardware neutral suppliers of system software are essential to the success of creating industry standard hardware platforms. The chip-set for the hardware will be multi-sourced and based on the MIPS RISC architecture. Members include DuPont Pixel Systems, Tandem, Siemens Nixdorf, Wang, SCO, Sony, Silicon Graphics, Pyramid, Prime, Olivetti USA, DEC, Microsoft, MIPS, Compaq, CDC, NEC, Alcatel.

The intention of this consortium is to establish a limited number of platforms on which binary compatibility could be achieved. This would enable 'shrink-wrapped' applications to be distributed. Seven members, however, have currently hedged their bets, signing up for both ODT and SVR4, leaving their options open (NEC Corporation, Olivetti Systems and Networks, Prime Computer Inc., Pyramid Technology Corporation, Siemens Nixdorf Informationssysteme Ag, Sony Corporation, and Tandem Computers Inc.).

The PC platform in the initiative represents nothing new, except the NT kernel for OS/2 3.0. SCO's ODT remains the same on the X86. The major change extends both PC software systems to the MIPS family of RISC processors. The initial ODT system supporting these systems will be based upon ULTRIX/MIPS, an OSF based product from DEC. Most of the layered function likewise comes from OSF, but includes NFS and provides SVID 3 compliance. POSIX and X/Open standards will also be supported.

The new ACE consortium represents a loose business association, rather than a standards setting body. On the negative side, the ACE process of defining specifications within the group will contribute to significant discomfiture in the industry among users and vendors, as there is no mechanism to evaluate outside technology systematically. Apparently, they will operate in combination more as a single vendor offering 'added value' on top of a standards based system. The ARCS technical committee initially includes Compaq, DEC and MIPS, with Microsoft and SCO serving an advisory role, in defining hardware specifications. Microsoft essentially retains a free hand in defining OS/2 3.0; SCO and DEC will hold responsibility for Open Desktop.

IBM/Apple

In October 1991, Apple, IBM and Motorola announced intentions to work together to produce the new PowerPC family of single-chip Reduced Instruction Set Computing (RISC) microprocessors. PowerPC microprocessors will form the foundation for new high-performance, low-cost systems from Apple and IBM. Motorola will manufacture and market the technology world wide, making this new microprocessor family widely available to other systems manufacturers. Apple, IBM and Motorola will play key roles in defining the PowerPC architecture.

The PowerPC is the hardware component of the PowerOpen computing environment that was also announced by Apple, IBM and Motorola. Apple is also bringing the Macintosh operating system to the PowerPC, which will remain compatible with today's Macintosh. IBM will offer a new release of its AIX operating system for the PowerPC.

PowerPC will be based on IBM's POWER architecture and the RISC System/6000 which are discussed in more detail in Chapter 4.

The companies also intend to form a new industry organization to promote PowerPC and the PowerOpen computing environment to other manufacturers, software developers and end users.

Apple, IBM, and Motorola will work together to design the PowerPC microprocessors. Apple plans to use the PowerPC in future versions of the Macintosh personal computer. IBM will manufacture PowerPC chips for its own use in future desktop workstations and servers, which will complement the existing RISC System/6000 line and be able to share applications without modification. Motorola will supply PowerPC chips to Apple and will also market them for other systems and microprocessor applications.

IBM has also licensed its 0.5 micron complementary metal-oxide semiconductor (CMOS) process technology (used in fabricating chips) to Motorola. Motorola will be able to use this technology for PowerPC chip development.

The PowerPC design initiative will be spearheaded by a team of IBM and Motorola employees to be located in a customer design centre in Austin, Texas. More than 300 engineers (all continuing to work for their respective firms) will initially be assigned to the customer design centre project.

The goal of the team is to develop multiple PowerPC implementations, initially targeting three design points, as well as to identify requirements for future enhancements. This core team will provide strong technical coordination while quickly bringing new designs to market.

1.5   IBM's commitment to standards

With more than 2400 employees participating in standards organizations world wide, IBM's activities in these organizations include the following:

• Participation in the Portable Operating Systems for Computing Environments (POSIX) of the Institute of Electrical and Electronics Engineers (IEEE) standards working groups.

- Membership in the X/Open Company, Ltd and participation in the X/Open technical committees in the development of the X/Open Portability Guide. The X/Open Portability Guide, Issue 3 (XPG3) contains an evolving portfolio of practical industry standards and reflects the X/Open Common Applications Environment (CAE). The Common Applications Environment is built on the interfaces to UNIX operating systems and also covers other aspects required of a comprehensive applications interface.
- Founding sponsor of the Open Software Foundation. In addition, IBM participates in numerous OSF technical committees, in the development of the OSF Application Environment Specification and OSF/1 and is the system integrator for Distributed Computing Environment (DCE).

IBM is committed to being an open systems vendor and subscribes to the IEEE POSIX definition of an open systems environment:

> Open Systems Environment: The comprehensive set of interfaces, services and supporting formats, plus user aspects, for interoperability or for portability of applications, data or people, as specified by information technology standards and profiles.

AIX Version 3 for RISC System/6000 standards and de facto *standards*

Operating system
- POSIX IEEE Standard 1003.1-1988 conformance
- X/Open XPG3 branded
- IEE 754-1985 Floating Point Standard conformance
- AT&T UNIX System V (SVID Issue 2)
- 4.3 BSD Compatible

User Interface
- C, Bourne and Korn Shells
- AIXwindows Environment/6000 (based on the OSF/Motif graphical user interface)
- X Windows System X11 Release 3
- Display Postcript
- FIPS 158

Graphics
- CGI
- CGM
- GKS

Languages
- XL C—ANSI X3.159-1989, X/Open XPG3 branded
- XL FORTRAN—ISO 1539-1980(E), ANSI X3.91-1978, FIPS Pub 69, X/Open XPG3 branded.
- VS COBOL—ISO 1989-1985(H), ANSI X3.23-1985, ANSI X3.23-1974(H), FIPS Pub 21-2, X/Open XPG3 branded.
- XL Pascal—ISO 7185-1983(O), ANSI/IEEE 770X3.97-1983, FIPS Pub 109, X/Open XPG3 branded.
- Ada ISO 8652-1987, ANSI/MIL STD 1815 A-1983, FIPS Pub 119, X/Open XPG3 branded.

Communications
- TCP—RFC 793, RFC 768, MIL STD 1777
- OSI—ISO 8822/5, ISO 9945/1 1989
- Network Management—RFC 1155-8
- Mail—RFC 821, RFC 974, RFC 987, CCITT X.400(84), MIL STD 1781
- Telnet—RFC 854-8, RFC 860, RFC 1073, RFC 1091, MIL STD 1782
- File Transfer—RFC 783, RFC 822, RFC 959, MIL STD 1780, ISO 8571, ISO 8649-50
- Session—ISO 8326/7, ISO 8208, ISO 8348, ISO 8473, ISO 8878
- Time—RFC 742, RFC 868
- Name Server/domain—RFC 1032-5
- Routing—RFC 791-2, RFC 826, RFC 877, RFC 888, RFC 890, RFC 893, RFC 904, RFC 950, RFC 1038, RFC 1042, RFC 1058, MIL STD 1778
- IEEE 802.3, ISO 8802/3
- IEEE 802.5, ISO 8802/5
- X.25—(X.21, V.24, V.35)
- SCSI ANSI X3.131—1986
- RS232, RS 422, MIL 188
- NFS 4.0
- SNA LU 0, 1, 2, 3, and 6.2; PU 2.1

IBM has made a major investment in AIX, IBM's implementation of the UNIX operating system. AIX combines the best of the popular UNIX implementations and adds significant enhancements of function, quality, serviceability, data integrity and security.

IBM participates fully in industry standards efforts and with major industry consortiums. IBM is continuing to enhance AIX and to extend its capabilities with a broad portfolio of applications, as evidenced by the fact that some 750 leading independent application developers already provide more than 2500 solutions world-wide for this relatively new operating system.

2
UNIX market-place

2.1   Short history of UNIX

The history of UNIX goes back to 1968 when Ken Thompson and his colleagues in the Computer Research Group at Bell Labs were working on the MULTICS project. The MULTICS system did not take off, but Ken Thompson developed an operating system from this to enable him to run a Space Travel program on his computer. This was the first version of UNIX.

UNIX was ported to the PDP-11/20 in 1970, which was quite a task as the entire system was written in assembler. At the same time, Bell Labs were looking for a test-processing system. They selected the PDP-11/20 based UNIX system over a commercial system. It supported three concurrent users. In 1983 Ken Thompson and Dennis Ritchie rewrote UNIX in the C language which improved the robustness and reliability of the system and made it easier to support. At this stage there were roughly 25 UNIX systems in existence.

Ken and Dennis published a paper in 1974 describing the fifth edition of UNIX which caused a lot of interest in academia. Because of its low cost, a number of academic institutions used it as a teaching aid. The sixth edition was released in 1975 and was widely used. AT&T through Western Electric Co. offered licences to commercial and government users.

UNIX was gradually ported to other hardware platforms and the functionality of the operating system was increased. The philosophy of UNIX systems was being established.

A number of organizations became involved with UNIX and either used it or developed further enhancements. Bolt Baranek and Newman Inc. were involved with the US Department of Defense and the Arpanet network. They did some work in designing communications software for UNIX, subsequently enhanced by the University of California, Berkeley, Computer

20

Science Department and distributed by them. This gave UNIX its communications abilities for which is it now famed. In addition, Berkeley was chosen as the primary implementation site for the DARPA (DoD's Advanced Research Projects) development project. This large project implemented an AI and VSLI computing environment to be based on UNIX. Bell decided to let Berkeley redistribute source code, but the customer also needed to have a licence from Bell. The version of UNIX with enhancements developed by Berkeley was known as BSD, but since it was from a university environment no formal support was available for customers.

Historically, the two most important versions of UNIX were the ones described above—UNIX System V from AT&T and BSD from Berkeley. However, licensing became a problem and various UNIX-like operating systems or clones evolved. If the kernel is rewritten the vendor can avoid the high licensing costs of the original UNIX software. This led to the various organizations defining the standards that describe this kind of operating system.

The more recent growth of UNIX systems has been explosive. This has been for a number of different reasons, but it has matched the growth of powerful inexpensive desktop computers and the availability of applications, particularly for technical workstations. In the last few years UNIX has been used more and more for commercial applications and multi-user systems. With the availability of 'production' operating systems such as AIX, this is set to continue.

AIX as an operating system has been around for quite some time. AIX has been available on the PC or PS/2, on the IBM 6150 or PC RT and on the mainframe. The IBM 6150 or PC RT was the predecessor to the RS/6000. AIX Version 3 which runs on the RS/6000 conforms to the relevant independent standards, but in addition has compatibility with other versions of UNIX. Figure 2.1 shows how AIX Version 3 fits in with other versions of UNIX. It has been designed to allow users of other major UNIX versions to feel at home when using AIX.

There is a hierarchy of standards to which the AIX operating system conforms. The external, independent standards come at the top of that list. However, if there is no conflict, commands and system calls from other versions of UNIX have been included.

2.2   Benefits of UNIX

A number of organizations are now using UNIX for various reasons.

UNIX as an operating system is written in a high level language. This gives

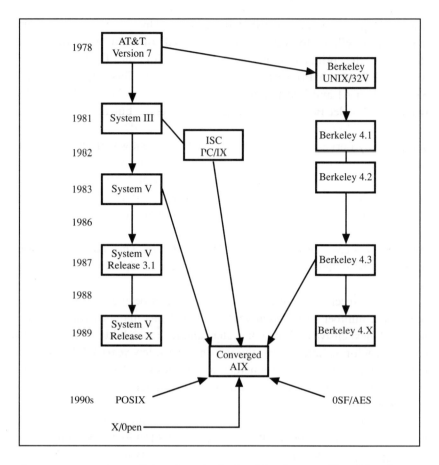

Figure 2.1. AIX positioning.

advantages over the traditional method of writing in assembler. Most importantly, the UNIX operating system is not tied to any particular hardware implementation and the operating system itself has been ported to many different hardware platforms with many different architectures.

The main reasons for the popularity of UNIX, however, are related to applications. Because of the rapid growth in the sales of UNIX platforms, software vendors are porting their applications to the UNIX world. This gives the software vendors a wider choice of platforms on which to sell their applications. In addition, it is usually very easy to port an application to run on a wide variety of UNIX platforms with their associated flavour of UNIX. This further increases the market opportunities for the software vendors.

All this leads to a large number of applications being available in the UNIX environment. The number is certainly in excess of 18 000. Some organizations choose UNIX simply because the application that they have chosen runs in this environment.

In the recent moves towards Open Systems, users are becoming aware that they can have independence in their choice of supplier. Due to the fact that all major vendors offer UNIX solutions, the market-place has become very competitive which is almost certainly to the advantage of users and purchasers. An organization does not have to feel locked in to any particular manufacturer or any specific platform. If they are not happy with the products or services from a supplier, it is much easier to go elsewhere instead.

Another important factor in the popularity of UNIX solutions is the ability to have heterogeneous operating environments. Very few organizations can claim to have only one platform for all of their applications. Typically, any organization will have a mixture of hardware platforms, software, and communications methods. Communication and interoperability between these systems can often be a nightmare.

Historically UNIX has been strong in the area of communications. The RS/6000, for example, supports a wide variety of communications protocols and connections. If a system is required that needs to communicate with systems from other manufacturers, then a UNIX solution often fits the bill. Communications involving TCP/IP also often play an important part as all major manufacturers support TCP/IP communications. TCP/IP is today's practical Open Systems method of communications.

For all of the above reasons, there has been a dramatic growth in the sales of UNIX systems. Decisions to purchase a UNIX system often fall into one of the following categories:

- An organization chooses a particular application which happens to run under UNIX. The user has no specific preference for UNIX as an operating system but has chosen the best available application.
- An organization stipulates various standards in the requirements for a system. These stipulations today might mean that UNIX is the only solution. Such organizations might include government departments that are very supportive of the drive to Open Systems.
- A particular user may like UNIX as an operating system. He may have had experience with UNIX—it is widely used in academia and he may like the flexibility offered.
- A UNIX solution may be the only possible choice. In the case of technical applications involving compute intensive performance or a high level of graphics, a UNIX application may be the only one available.

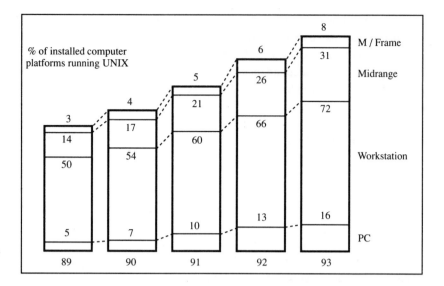

Figure 2.2. Growth of
UNIX systems.

Similarly, if a communications solution is needed, a UNIX solution may be
the only sensible choice.

2.3   Growth of UNIX

There are various figures relating to the world-wide growth of UNIX
systems. These figures vary somewhat, but, in general terms, the trend is that
the Open Systems market-place is growing at roughly twice the pace of the
computer industry as a whole. Clearly at the moment, the growth of UNIX
systems tend to be at the PC or mid-range end of the market. However, this
part of the market is growing rapidly compared to larger systems.

In the PC range, the proportion of machines running DOS is expected to
decrease while the number of machines running OS/2, MAC OS and UNIX
will increase. The UNIX growth will be the most explosive.

In the mini- or mid-range market, there will be a slow growth of proprietary systems and a very fast growth of UNIX systems. This will be fuelled by
the fact that all major vendors support UNIX solutions, in fact some vendors
only support UNIX and will therefore sell this very hard. Figure 2.2 shows
the predicted growth of UNIX systems.

2.4   Limitations of traditional UNIX systems

As you will now realize, UNIX comes from a background in universities. It
is an operating system that was developed by programmers, for program-

mers, and as a result there are certain perceived drawbacks to it. There is a philosophy associated with UNIX. It is a very flexible operating system but there are limitations. Users who have some experience with UNIX will often claim that UNIX has limitations such as:

- The hardware is PC type hardware and is not reliable enough to support large numbers of users.
- The UNIX operating system is not capable of being used in a production environment.
- UNIX is not easy to use.
- Storage management with large volumes of data is limited.
- Security is weak with UNIX systems.
- UNIX systems do not have sophisticated memory management.
- UNIX systems cannot run real-time applications.
- Support for UNIX systems is poor.

These claims can often be true when discussing some of the older traditional versions of UNIX, however, AIX Version 3 on the RS/6000 has been designed to overcome many of these problems.

Each of these potential areas of weakness is discussed below. AIX Version 3 has been designed to address these and therefore these are not limitations to be found when using the RS/6000. With some versions of UNIX however, these limitations can be a problem. Most of these areas are discussed in more detail later in the book.

Hardware reliability

Reliability, availability and serviceability (RAS) were an integral part of the hardware design for the RS/6000. All of the chip to chip buses have parity, and the memory bus has Error Checking and Correction (ECC). The chip data paths, including registers, register files, cache, Translation Look-aside Buffers (TLBs), and directory arrays also have parity. For main memory, double-bit detect, single-bit correct ECC, bit steering and memory 'scrubbing' are performed. Memory scrubbing is a test on memory during normal operation. Bit steering logic is designed to bypass a detected hard failure and substitutes a good spare bit for a failing bit; as a result, a memory card will continue to function even when some of the DRAMs fail. During power-up, all the CPU chips go through a self-test sequence where all the logic and memory is extensively tested. There is a hardware diagnostics package that enables diagnosis of hardware problems and isolation of faulty components. There are extensive trace and dump facilities within AIX in addition to error log facilities.

Industrial strength operating system

A large part of the AIX code has been rewritten to provide an operating system that is an industrial strength operating system capable of running in a production environment. It is easy to use, removes traditional UNIX limitations, and adds extra function.

Ease of use

UNIX commands can be complicated. The format is usually a command followed by a minus sign followed by various parameters. Examples of UNIX commands are:

- tar − cvf − file1 | dd of = /dev/rmt1
- sar − y − r 2 20
- dd if = text.ascii of = text.ebcdic conv = ebcdic

It is not obvious to someone who is not familiar with UNIX what these commands mean. There are similarities to DOS, but UNIX is more complex with more commands and more parameters for each command. To shield the user who is new to UNIX from this, the RS/6000 has implemented various functions within AIX. The most important of these is the Systems Management Interface Tool (SMIT). This is a menu-driven system that provides a very comprehensive way of performing systems administration on the RS/6000.

Almost all system administration and system management functions can be performed through these menus. For a user who does not know UNIX commands, this can be invaluable. If a user already knows the appropriate commands these can be used. In fact, within the menus, a function key can be pressed to show the appropriate command at the point of performing a particular task and so the commands can be learned as the user operates the system.

Figure 2.3 shows some of the typical tasks that a systems administrator would have have to carry out on a UNIX system that does not have a tool such as SMIT. These tasks would involve changing parameters by editing files, running complex UNIX commands and sometimes running UNIX shell scripts. These tasks on a traditional UNIX system would almost certainly have to be performed by a highly skilled UNIX systems programmer. By

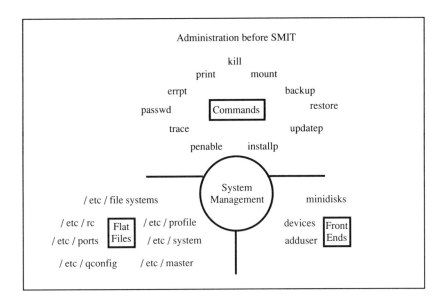

Figure 2.3. Administration before SMIT.

using SMIT on the RS/6000 these tasks can be carried out by a person with little UNIX experience using the menu-driven interface. In addition, the RS/6000 would not need to be shut down and re-booted to perform many of these tasks—they could be carried out dynamically. There are other ways in which the RS/6000 with AIX has been designed to be easy to use and these are discussed in later chapters.

Storage management

AIX Version 3 has a number of advanced features in the area of storage management. Typically, UNIX systems have had to be shut down to perform many tasks—including adding devices and changing sizes of resources such as a filesystem. AIX provides the Logical Volume Manager (LVM) which will be discussed in more detail later. This enables filesystems to be dynamically increased in size 'on the fly' without shutting the system down. In addition, the standard filesystem under AIX is a journalled filesystem. This protects the integrity of the filesystem in the event of things such as power failures. AIX also provides the ability to 'mirror' logical volumes.

Security

A range of functions that address data integrity and controlled access have been incorporated into the AIX operating system. AIX Version 3 satisfies C2 level security as defined by the National Computer Security Centre (NCSC). IBM intends to submit AIX Version 3 for B level evaluation.

Virtual memory

The RS/6000 was designed with a very large virtual memory management scheme. The AIX virtual memory management is very sophisticated. It is performance oriented and it also offers the 'single-level store' concept similar to that used on the IBM System/38 and AS/400. The hardware architecture allows for a virtual address space of 2 to the power of 52 although the virtual address space implemented today in the software is 2 to the power of 48 (or 256 terabytes).

Real-time capability

The RS/6000 with AIX provides an extended real-time execution environment which allows it to support real-time applications as well as time-sharing applications.

The real-time support includes:

- Priority control and scheduling of multiple processes for execution.
- Pre-emptive priority dispatching of 'ready-to-execute' processes.
- A pre-emptable kernel for bounded context switch latency.
- Timer control for privileged time-based operations based on the use of the RS/6000 hardware timer which has a resolution equal to ten times the processor cycle time.
- Facilities for direct control of virtual memory which allow a program to pin/lock itself and its data into memory. This prevents critical programs or data from being paged to disk.

Support

IBM attempts to provide a very high level of support for the RS/6000 through various programs. These are discussed later in this book.

2.5   Technical workstation and commercial markets

There are very distinct market-places in the UNIX world. UNIX traditionally came from a university and technical background and has a very high presence in areas involving technical workstations.

A technical workstation is typically a system that has only one user. The system is used for applications that require a lot of intensive computing resources—such as mathematical modelling, finite element analysis and other applications of that type. This is usually known as numeric intensive computing (NIC) or compute intensive. A particular machine needs to be designed to run this kind of workload efficiently. The RS/6000, for example, has an integrated floating point processor to enable NIC applications to perform well.

Technical workstations do not always require this high performance with regard to the processor. Some applications are graphical—such as Computer Aided Design (CAD) or visualization applications. These do not neccessarily need a fast processor but often need the ability to display complex graphics quickly. The performance of the graphics adapters (2D or 3D) will be the key here.

In this market-place, Sun Microsystems has a large market share. A number of other manufacturers including IBM have realized that this is an important and growing market and have brought out products to compete. This is now a very competitive environment. IBM intends to compete strongly in this market-place and this was the reason for the RS/6000 family being announced.

Another very different UNIX market-place is that for commercial applications or multi-user computing. As explained earlier, a technical workstation typically has only one user, although in some circumstances other screens such as Xstations may be attached to the system. In the case of a commercial UNIX system, a large number of users will be attached to the system—perhaps hundreds—and the applications will often be database applications or other commercial applications.

This market-place is also growing very fast because of the drive towards Open Systems. The players in this market are often very different and the requirements of a system are different. Here, disk I/O, communications performance, and overall system performance are as important as the CPU performance or graphics performance.

No one particular manufacturer has a large market share but IBM with AIX features well in this commercial arena.

The RS/6000 has been specifically designed from the outset to perform in three separate environments: technical workstations, multi-user commercial systems, and LAN server systems.

As a technical workstation, the RS/6000 has an integrated floating point processor and a range of high performance graphics adapters. As a commercial system the RS/6000 can attach hundreds of ASCII screens through multi-port adapters, can have large amounts of memory, has a wide range of very fast disks and disk-subsystems, and has a totally balanced system design to support large workloads. The RS/6000 can be used as a LAN server due to its large capacity and wide range of communications abilities.

For all of these requirements the same basic RS/6000 models are used. However, they can be configured in many different ways with many different adapters, disks and memory sizes. Some of these systems will be called POWERservers whereas some will be called POWERstations depending on how they are configured. It is important to realize that these are the same RS/6000 models and, by changing the internal configuration of devices, an RS/6000 can be a POWERstation or a POWERserver.

The term POWER (Performance Optimization With Enhanced RISC) describes the RS/6000 architecture which will be discussed in a later chapter. For example, an RS/6000 model 350 that is configured with a graphics adapter, a graphics screen, memory and disk, to be used to run a CAD application, will be a POWERstation as it will be used as a technical workstation, whereas the same model 350 of RS/6000 configured with a 64 port adapter, 64 ASCII screens, memory and disk, used to run a database application, will be called a POWERserver.

2.6   Performance and benchmarking

One of the most widely discussed topics in the UNIX world is performance. It also has a lot of jargon associated with it. In essence it is not complicated but there are often a number of misconceptions.

In most cases, a user is interested in how a particular application that he wants to use will perform on a specific hardware platform. In an ideal world, he would actually run this application on the machine and measure the results, but there are often problems associated with this. For example:

- The application may not yet be written.
- The data that the application uses may not be available.
- The exact scenario cannot be reproduced in terms of number of users using the system concurrently, and the networking structure cannot be replicated.
- The correct configuration of machine is not available.

Therefore as an alternative, users look at the results of 'standard' benchmarks that have been run to simulate a real workload on a particular machine. There are a number of these standard benchmarks and the most common ones will be discussed in this chapter.

Benchmarks

A benchmark is a set of jobs, tasks or transactions to compare the 'capacity' of systems doing various types of work. This 'capacity' can take the form of:

- Fixed point or integer instructions per second (MIPS)
- Floating point operations per second (FLOPS—usually expressed as KFLOPS or MFLOPS)
- Throughput of transactions or batch jobs per unit time
- Response time for a transaction or time to run a job
- Scripts executed per unit time for workloads such as TSO or Office
- Some mixtures of these
- Others, including real customer workloads

They are, in the main, created to be close to the type of user workload they are meant to represent, but do not necessarily show what throughput might be obtained by any particular user and his specific workload.

The following is a list of some of the major performance elements of interest to UNIX system users:

- Fixed point or integer performance (commercial workloads)
- Floating-point performance (scientific workloads)
- I/O performance (DASD)
- I/O performance (communications)
- Graphics performance
- X Windows performance

In general, real workloads are composed of mixtures of these elements. Real workloads usually have significant interaction with the operating system whereas some benchmarks can run in isolation from the operating system. There are a variety of benchmarks designed to measure system performance in many of these areas, both singly and in combination. Performance measurements on tapes, printers and other peripheral devices are *not* discussed in this book. It is perhaps appropriate to discuss these performance elements in a little more detail before looking at the benchmarks themselves.

Fixed point or integer performance

Fixed point numbers are defined with a number of digits before and after the decimal place fixed throughout the program execution. For example: 312.046279 (III.DDDDDD). Integer numbers are the special case where there is no decimal point. Fixed point numbers are limited to a relatively small range because of the fixed position of the decimal point.

Floating point performance

Floating point representation came out of the need to represent a wide range of numbers with a reasonable number of digits. Floating point numbers are described by a mantissa and an exponential field. The decimal place is 'moved' by changing the value of the exponential field. Examples are:

- 1.23456 + E06 is 1,234,560
- 1.23456 − E02 is 0.0123456

I/O performance—DASD

Disk I/O performance is usually tested using programs which read and write records at various block sizes to or from disks. Measurements can take the form of elapsed time for doing a fixed number of reads/writes or the access times for various retrieval and update activities.

An example would be writing 10 000 4 K blocks to a disk and reading them back twice to simulate the observed pattern of more reads than writes to typical files and databases. However, the results obtained from such tests will depend on whether the disk I/Os are random or sequential accesses to files. It is also possible to get results which are in excess of those which would be observed in real life if the test or benchmark file is much smaller than the production file. Much of the test file could reside in main storage during the benchmark run.

I/O performance—communications

Communications performance can be measured in two basic ways:

1　Overall end-to-end times for file transfer, transaction shipping, remote file access and so on.
2　Speeds of individual elements of the system, e.g. the number of frames per second that an X.25 adapter can support.

There are few, if any, standard benchmarks in this area and customers usually perform their own tests.

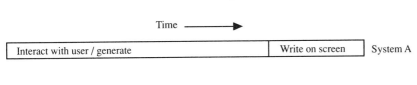

Figure 2.4. End-to-end performance time.

Graphics performance

Graphics performance is often taken to mean the speed at which the workstation graphics hardware can draw on the screen once the data is handed to the adapter. Sometimes it is interpreted as the speed at which the CPU can handle the user requests to generate graphics output and get it onto the screen for viewing.

Question: Which workstation is the best graphics performer?

Answer: Depends on your viewpoint.

Normally performance for graphics is quoted in raw 'draw' speed, but it must be remembered that for any real application running the job is the only real test of graphics end-to-end performance (see Fig. 2.4).

The two main ways of writing to graphics screens are low level code, sometimes at device command level, and higher level code such as PHIGS, GKS or GL. These may be used in conjunction with a windowing system.

The thrust in graphics hardware development is to put more manipulation function in the adapter cards and do less with software in the CPU. The fact still remains that having a nominally faster graphics adapter/card does not necessarily mean the best overall graphics performance.

Some types of graphics performance metrics are covered later in this chapter dealing with actual benchmarks.

X Windows performance

The performance of an X Windows system or an X-terminal is even more difficult to define than graphics performance. The performance parameters involved in using X Windows are:

• The CPU/adapter speed and buffer size of the X-terminal
• The efficiency of the 'windowing' software (MOTIF, Openlook, etc.)
• The speed of the 'host' processor
• The speed of the network 'feeding' the X-terminal
• The utilization of the network

Despite these issues, attempts are being made to develop such benchmarks and some of these are covered later.

Table 2.1. MIPS ratings for an
IBM processor

MIPS	Which processor
1.4	?
5.0	?
8.0	?
10.2	?
13.1	?
20.0	?
40.0	?

Benchmark metrics

In any benchmark, it is important to state exactly what the test is measuring,
under what conditions, how the results are to be presented, and what *inter-
pretation* can be placed on them. This is necessary to allow a fair comparison
of results for different machines. For example, Table 2.1 shows results for
'millions of instructions per second', or MIPS, for some IBM processors.
Question: Which IBM CPUs are represented here?
The answer in all cases is the IBM 3081D. The reason for the variation in
answers for 'MIPS' ratings is the fact that the instruction mixes are different
in each case. The 'big MIPS' results could be accounted for by a mix of fast
register-to-register instructions, whereas the 'low MIPS' results can be
accounted for as mixes of complex or diagnostic instructions.

Similarly, floating point measurements expressing 'millions of floating
point instructions per second' (MFLOPS) can be misleading since there are
a range of floating point calculations and some CPUs have hardwired
multiply or divide instructions. Benchmarks concentrating on these 'fast'
calculations can show artificially high results for MFLOPS which might not
be achieved when running realistic numerically intensive programs with a
wide range of computational operations.

It is these anomalies which have given rise to carefully defined benchmarks
with stated metrics to measure workstation performance in various types of
workload. It is important to understand not only the figures produced by any
given benchmark, but also its limitations.

UNIX benchmark types

In the following discussions the boxes shown at the beginning of the sections
represent the system functions tested by the benchmark. The legends are
shown in Fig. 2.5. In this chapter *multi-tasking* is used to define a set of tasks
running in a system without external terminal I/O. This mode of operation

Figure 2.5. UNIX benchmark types.

is usually initiated by a program within the system itself. A multi-tasking operation might be a single simulated user initiating many tasks or multiple simulated users doing multiple tasks. If the number of tasks in both cases is the same, then the system resources consumed should be the same. The basic difference is that the scheduler might do a little more work in the multi-user case.

The term *multi-user* is used in the case of tasks being initiated externally, either via real users at terminals or another system (e.g. a PS/2) acting as a 'driver'.

I will now discuss some of the more common 'standard' benchmarks that are often used in the UNIX environment.

Integer or fixed-point benchmarks

Dhrystone benchmark

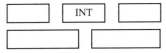

The Dhrystone benchmark is a test of C compiler maturity, processor perform-ance, and, to some degree, processor architecture. It is a compute bound program which utilizes no system calls, and thus can be run without an operating system.

There are at present two versions. The latest version, V2, is available as one 'C' version split into three parts. The two source code parts are to be compiled separately so that optimizing compilers are prevented from moving code out of the measurement loop. Limitations of the benchmark include:

- There are two versions which can give different results for the same system.
- It is a 'synthetic' benchmark that does no particular job.
- It can be sensitive to run-time parameters.
- It is compiler dependent.
- It can generally run in the high-speed cache of a workstation and so really measures the speed of the cache and not the whole memory and CPU.
- There is no 'central control' body to oversee the benchmark.

Despite these limitations, this benchmark is often quoted as a measure of integer performance. Results are quoted in thousands of Dhrystones per second, where high is good.

Derivation of MIPS rating from Dhrystones: Often, systems quote a 'MIPS' figure along with a Dhrystone rating. This 'MIPS' number is not the same as the one discussed previously. It is the figure derived from the fact that the VAX 11/780 is rated at about 1760 Dhrystones and is often rated as 'a 1 MIPS' machine by DEC and users. This we can call a 'VAX MIPS' and this is the rating called 'MIPS' quoted in workstation performance—it is not the same as the IBM 'RPP' number although it is possible to relate the two to some extent. Thus: (VAX) MIPS = Dhrystones (Version 1.1) I1760

Floating-point benchmarks

Whetstone benchmark

The Whetstone benchmark can be performed in both single and double precision floating point formats, with the results being tabulated in Whetstone instructions per second. The higher this number, the better the floating-point performance of a computer system. It tests a combination of computer floating-point processing power and compiler maturity.

The floating-point functions included in the Whetstone benchmark are convergent series, trigonometric functions, and transcendental functions. The benchmark, however, has some limitations:

- It is a 'synthetic' benchmark that calculates no specific result.
- There is no check on the correctness of the results of computations.
- It is compiler dependent.
- It can generally run in the high-speed cache of a workstation and so really measures the speed of the cache and not the whole memory and CPU.
- Figures may be quoted for single or double precision. Some workstations have single precision figures up to several times their double precision figures. IBM single and double precision figures tend to be very close to each other.
- There is no 'central control' body to oversee the benchmark.

Despite these limitations, it is often quoted as a measure of floating-point performance. Both the Whetstone and Dhrystone benchmarks are seen as less useful than the SPEC 1.0 benchmark described later.

LINPACK benchmark

FPT		

The LINPACK benchmark is an example of a real work benchmark which uses a linear programming problem to test machine performance. LINPACK solves dense systems of linear equations with a high percentage of floating point operations. A 'dense' system is one in which few of the elements of the vector or matrix arrays are zero.

The programming problem is standardized so that results from a variety of machines can be meaningfully compared. The innermost computational loops of the LINPACK benchmark are isolated into subroutines called the 'Basic Linear Algebra Subroutines', or BLAS for short. Since most of the floating-point work is carried out by the BLAS, the overall performance of the workstation as measured by LINPACK will be highly dependent on the implementation of BLAS. The three basic implementations of BLAS are:

1   *Coded BLAS*—These are coded in machine language for the workstation in question.
2   *Rolled BLAS*—These are coded in FORTRAN for machines with vector capability.
3   *Unrolled BLAS*—These are coded in FORTRAN for scalar machines.

For use with supercomputers there are versions called Extended BLAS or Level 2 BLAS but they need not concern a discussion on workstation performance.

Some factors to note about LINPACK are:

•   It has reasonable 'central' control and ownership.
•   It can be compiler and cache dependent (particularly the BLAS).
•   It can be quoted in single or double precision forms.
•   It is generally accepted as a good measure of the floating-point perform-ance of a workstation and other systems.

The results of the LINPACK benchmark are reported in units of MFLOPS (millions of floating operations per second) or KFLOPS (thousands of floating operations per second). The larger this number, the better the floating-point performance.

The Argonne National Laboratory report, which is updated about every five or six months, contains data on about 100 machines from Crays to IBM PCs and includes several of the more popular workstations (Sun, Apollo, RS/6000). There are several types of LINPACK runs listed, in particular figures for single precision and double precision may show some machines to be much worse at the latter than the former, in some cases by a factor of up to two.

Livermore Loops

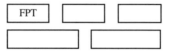

The Livermore Loops benchmarks were developed by the Lawrence Livermore Laboratory in the US. The primary purpose of these 'tests' is to evaluate the performance of computers with vector and/or parallel processing capabilities.

The benchmark consists of 24 Livermore FORTRAN Kernels (LFKs) which represent types of computational work found on large-scale scientific processors. The Kernels contain a wide range of FORTRAN coding practices and floating-point operations. A MFLOPS rating is obtained by assigning weights to the different types of floating point measurements.

The LFK loops are highly vectorizable and hence are often used in tests on vectorizing compilers and their development. This type of work is not generally applicable to workstations. The major use of Livermore Loops can be summarized as:

- A test of FORTRAN compiler development and maturity in terms of code optimization.
- A test of compiler accuracy.
- A test of the speed of different types of floating-point operations in the hardware of a processor.
- A test of the intrinsic speed of floating-point operations when the loops are re-coded in machine language.

The only useful measurement from the LFKs applicable to workstations is the MFLOPS rating, which in general will not be the same as the LINPACK MFLOPS rating.

Mixed measurement benchmarks

Khornerstone benchmark

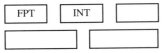

This benchmark was created by Workstation Laboratories. It consists of a balanced mix of floating point tests, integer (fixed point) tests, and disk I/O tests and uses 21 separate programs coded in C and FORTRAN. They are run separately and then together and the 'Khornerstone' rating obtained is derived thus:

- 20 per cent of the value is based on disk performance
- 27 per cent of the value is based on integer performance
- 23 per cent of the value is based on floating point performance
- 30 per cent of the value is based on the total time taken to execute the entire set of tests

The mix is meant to represent a typical single-user workload on a PC or workstation and the results are expressed in units of thousands of Khornerstones per second. Large numbers indicate better performance.

Some features of the Khornerstone benchmark are:

- It is a composite benchmark
- It is single user
- It is operating system dependent
- It can be cache dependent
- It is widely accepted

This is sometimes referred to as the 'Tested Mettle' benchmark after the name of a report which outlines performance of various workstations, which includes Whetstones, Dhrystones and LINPACK as well as Khornerstone ratings.

SPEC benchmark

The Systems Performance Evaluation Cooperative (SPEC) announced the availability of Release 1.0 of the SPEC benchmark suite on 2 October 1989. Release 1.0, which consists of 10 engineering and scientific benchmarks, is

Table 2.2. Release 1.0 SPEC benchmark suite

Program	Type of benchmark	Language	Performance measure
gcc	Eng. (GNU compiler)	C	I
espresso	Eng. (PLA simulator)	C	I
spice 2g6	Eng. (ECAD-Analog Circuit simulation)	F	F
doduc	Sci. (Reactor physics)	F	F
nasa	Sci. (Synthetic –7 kernels)	F	F
li	Eng. (LISP)	C	I
eqntott	Eng. (Boolean)	C	I
matrix300	Sci. (Monte Carlo)	F	F
fpppp	Sci. (Quantum chemistry)	F	F
tomcatv	Sci. (Fluid dynamics)	F	F

Notes:
C = C language, F = FORTRAN (language)
I = Integer, F = Floating point (performance measure)

endorsed by 12 of the leading computer system vendors (including IBM) as a common means of measuring computing system performance, particularly workstations.

Release 1.0 is a complex set of benchmarks that measure CPU-intensive (integer and floating-point) computation associated with engineering and scientific applications. In total, release 1.0 consists of over 150 000 lines of C and FORTRAN code and a high-end technical workstation or minicomputer would require up to three hours to execute the complete series of benchmarks.

The size and complexity of the SPEC Benchmark Suite, drawn from real application sources, make it a meaningful test of engineering and scientific performance and eliminate the 'cache' resident aspects of some other benchmarks discussed previously. Future suites will measure other important aspects of system performance, such as disk, graphics, and communications. The 1.0 SPEC benchmark may replace existing common measures of workstation performance, viz:

- Whetstones (floating point)
- Dhrystones (integer)
- Khornerstones (floating point, integer parts)
- LINPACK (floating point linear equations)
- BYTE (floating point, integer parts)

SPEC metrics: The parameters used in the SPEC 1.0 benchmark are:

- SPEC Reference Machine—VAX 11/780
- SPEC Reference Time—The elapsed time in seconds that it takes the reference machine to run a SPEC job.

- SPECratio—The ratio of the time taken by the reference machine to run a SPEC job divided by the time taken by the system under test to run the same job.

$$SPECratio = Time\ taken\ by\ VAX\ 11/780/Time\ taken\ by\ test\ system$$

- SPECmark—The geometric mean of the 10 SPECratios.

$$SPECmark = 10th\ root\ of\ (SPECratio1\ \times\ SPECratio2\ \times\ \dots$$
$$\times\ SPECratio10)$$

SPEC 1.0 compares the performance of systems running single copies of the benchmark programs. In real life, there are likely to be many jobs running simultaneously on a uni- or multi-processor system. SPEC have accordingly developed a new metric call SPECthruput. Multiple copies of each of the 10 SPEC 1.0 benchmarks are run and the new metric calculated as follows:

- Start $K*N$ copies of SPEC benchmark i (i = 1 to 10), N = number of CPUs on system, K = number of jobs per processor (K = 2).
- Measure the elapsed time ($E(i)$) to complete.
- Compute the thoughput ratio $TR(i) = R(i)/E(i)$, where $R(i)$ is the throughput reference time (VAX 11/780).
- Calculate the geometric mean of the 10 throughput ratios $TR(i)$

$$SPECthruput = 10th\ root\ of\ (SPECthruput1\ \times\ \dots$$

$$\times\ SPECthruput10)$$

$$Aggregate\ thruput = Number\ of\ CPUs\ (N)\ \times\ SPECthruput$$

SPEC integer and floating point breakdown: Sometimes the individual integer and floating point SPECratios and SPECmarks may be quoted. The SPECmarks are calculated by taking the sixth root of the product of the six floating point measurements and the fourth root for the integer measurements.

SPEC is essentially a composite benchmark. It is likely that SPEC will also use the individual components SPECfp, the floating point measure derived from the six floating point programs in the same way SPECmark is derived, and SPECint the integer element derived from the other four programs.

AIM benchmarks

The AIM benchmarks are C programs used by AIM Technology to compare the performance of Unix Systems. There are several AIM benchmark suites:

- AIM Application Benchmark Suite II
- AIM Multi-User Benchmark Suite III
- AIM Workstation Benchmark Suite V
- AIM X Windows Benchmark Suite X
- AIM Milestone Benchmark

Multiple versions of the benchmarks exist.

AIM Technology, based in California, has performance reports based on the above benchmarks. AIM Performance Report (used until June 1990) uses older versions of Suite II and Suite III; AIM Performance Report II uses newer versions of Suite II and Suite III, plus the new Milestone benchmark.

AIM Technology also has other performance related software offerings:

- AIM NETWORK File Manager for Sun NFS
- AIM Disk Tuner, Job Scheduler, Job Accounting

AIM II benchmark

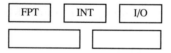

The AIM II Suite was introduced in 1984 to test the performance of different parts of a UNIX system simulating a single user. This means a single program performs the whole suite sequentially. Using a program to analyse a 'Results' database, it is possible to:

- Assess the performance of a single system under various use conditions.
- Measure the performance of multiple UNIX systems using a variety of application mixes.
- Compare the performance of up to 20 systems at a time.

AIM II uses 38 functional tests which consist of different types of operation (disk I/O, Pipes, etc.) usually in combinations.

Functional tests: These tests are the basic building blocks of AIM II. For the older AIM Performance Report, the functional tests are used in combination to evaluate performance for functional mixes and application mixes.

Users can select and weight application mixes (for a charge) and run tests representing their own workload, e.g. 20 per cent word processing, 10 per cent spreadsheet, 70 per cent accounting.

This might be done to compare several systems running the same (weighted) application mix. In addition, a user can compare different (weighted) application mixes on a single system.

Multi-tasking benchmarks

In this document, 'multi-tasking' means a single user executing multiple tasks simultaneously. 'Multi-user' means multiple users executing a single or multiple tasks generated by external terminal I/O, either via real terminals and users or a terminal emulator. In either case, the system then has to handle character I/O which impacts the performance of a system.

AIM III benchmark

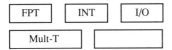

Currently there are two versions of AIM Suite III—1.4 and 3.0. Version 1.4 is used for the old AIM Performance Report, and Version 3.0 is used in the newer AIM Performance Report II.

AIM Suite III Versions 1.4 and 3.0 contain all of the same tests, although the tests themselves have changed slightly. The disk tests do more reading and writing to disk, and others have been improved so that optimizers will not affect their operation. For Version 1.4, some of the tests were eliminated by optimization at compile time and therefore were compiled without optimization. For Version 3, all tests are optimized. The following description applies to both versions.

AIM Suite III is a multi-tasking system level benchmark. No external interactive users are simulated in the default mix which is used for the performance reports. The benchmark exercises functions from both the engineering/scientific and the commercial environments. It is very CPU intensive and emulates a large user load but does no terminal I/O.

AIM Suite III is made up of 31 tests. The tests are C programs that stress specific functions of a system. Tasks are created to load a system. The greater the number of users simulated, the greater the number of tasks that are started. Each task runs all of the tests in a random order. The exact tests differ from Version 1.4 to 3.0. Users can select and weight functional tests to suit their own needs. However, AIM Suite III defaults to the following:

- 20 per cent RAM
- 10 per cent Float
- 10 per cent Pipe
- 20 per cent Logic
- 20 per cent Disk
- 20 per cent Math

This is called the AIM standard mix and is used for the performance reports.

Interpreting AIM III Version 1.4 benchmark data
Two metrics are used in the original AIM performance reports for relative system performance positioning.

- *Performance rating:* The percentage of power that the system under test has compared to the Standard AIM System (SAS), a DEC VAX 11/780 running Ultrix. It is a measure of 'raw processing power' relative to the SAS.
- *User load rating:* This is a measure of system throughput, excluding terminal overhead. It is the maximum number of simulated users that can be supported before response time becomes unacceptable. The response time cut off is 1.2 jobs/minute/user. One 'User Load', or one 'simulated user' is one process that executes all 31 of the tests, one at a time. One 'job' is one of the 31 tests.

The 'performance rating' is similar to the 'AIMS' rating on the new APR II, but they are not directly comparable. Also note that this 'user load rating' is not directly comparable to the 'maximum user load' for APR II. The new report uses a response time cut off of 1 job/minute/user instead of 1.2, and the new Suite III Version 3.0 is slightly heavier (i.e. harder to run—Version 3.0 is more demanding for a given user load). The standard AIM System has a user load rating of 12 and a performance index of 100.

Interpreting AIM III Version 3.0 benchmark data
Three of the metrics presented on the first page of the AIM Performance Report II are for relative system performance positioning and come from AIM III Version 3. A chart is also included showing system throughput for varying user load levels. The following descriptions are from the APR II.

- *AIMs:* The AIM Performance Rating—reflects the overall performance of the system measured in AIM Multiuser Performance Units. A DEC VAX 11/780 (SAS) typically rates 1 AIM.
- *User Loads:* Maximum User Load—indicates the multi-tasking user load where the system's performance could become unacceptable, i.e. less than 1 job/minute/user load. The User Loads for the SAS is 9. One User Load, or one 'simulated user' is one process that executes all 31 of the tests, one at a time. One 'job' is one test, so each User Load runs 31 jobs at each level of testing.

- *Jobs/Minute*: Maximum Throughput—the point at which the system is able to process the most jobs per minute.
- *System Throughput graph*: The total amount of work the system processes per minute at various user loads. Graphed as jobs/minute, it shows how many jobs (or tests) a system can complete a minute as a function of the number of simulated users.

The AIMs rating is similar to the 'Performance Rating' from the original APR, but they are different and not directly comparable. This is due to differences in Suite III versions.

Note that this Maximum User Load rating is not directly comparable to the 'User Load Rating' for the original APR. The new report uses a response time cut-off of 1 job/minute/user instead of 1.2, and the new Suite III Version 3.0 is slightly heavier (i.e. the old User Load rating for the SAS is 12, and the new User Load rating for the SAS is 9).

The User Load rating may not be appropriate for determining the number of users a given system can support. The two metrics do not necessarily reflect identical relative performance ratios between two given systems because the formulas and data used to arrive at these metrics are different.

Generally, AIM III results should not be used to represent a given customer's real application unless it can be shown that the customer's application and these tests exercise similar functions in approximately the same proportion.

The AIM III Suite can also exercise the following resources:

- TTY (simulates the actions of on-line users)
- Tape read/write
- Line printer
- Virtual memory use—allocates as much virtual storage as a system will give it (20 MB maximum!) and changes memory locations such that little locality of reference is possible and paging results.
- Database Calls

These resources can be exercised singly or in combination. Additionally, users can add any test written in C.

Some points to note about AIM III:

- It is a multi-user, multi-tasking benchmark with possible simulated terminal I/O but no real terminal I/O.
- AIM III release 1.4 may not take full advantage of compiler optimization techniques. This limitation is removed in Version 3.0 of AIM III.

- It has the following advantages:
  - It is portable to most UNIX implementations.
  - It has a large database of results for several vendors' systems.
  - It is regulated by AIM technology.

Neal Nelson benchmark

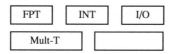

The Neal Nelson benchmark is a product of Neal Nelson & Associates aimed at measuring performance in a variety of commercial environments. It is, like the AIM benchmark, a multi-tasking rather than multi-user set of tests. Neal Nelson offer a variety of performance tests and services, the main one being the Business Benchmark.

Other services and tests available are:

- Business Benchmark Reports
- Business Benchmark Source Code
- Benchmark Services
- A Remote Terminal Emulator (RTE) and Software
- Multi-User Benchmark with RTE for UnixWorld
- An RPG Benchmark

The Business Benchmark is available in C, Basic, FORTRAN and other languages.

The Business Benchmark

The Business Benchmark consists of 18 separate test programs ranging from very specific tests (e.g. 64-bit arithmetic) to composite tasks. These tests can be grouped to exercise a system doing work similar to tasks such as:

- Word Processing
- Spreadsheet
- Database management
- Engineering and scientific
- Programming and application development

The Neal Nelson Business Benchmark:

- Runs 1 to 100 copies of the 18 test jobs, stressing the system with an increasing load.

- Runs on Unix systems only.
- Has disk I/O buffers artificially fixed at 6 Mb.
- Is multi-tasking, not multi-user.
- Has no terminal I/O either real or simulated.

The Neal Nelson benchmarks measure times for the various tasks in seconds and so low values mean higher performance.

Business Benchmark reports

Each of the 18 tests of the Business Benchmark is reported separately. The report of each test consists of a response time graph and a bar chart showing the percentage difference in response time for two systems being compared. The reports must be purchased directly from Neal Nelson & Associates.

The UnixWorld/Neal Nelson & Associates Benchmark

The UnixWorld/Neal Nelson & Associates (UW/NNA) Benchmark is run by NNA and the results are published in UnixWorld magazine. The benchmark requires a remote terminal emulator and runs UNIX commands on the system under test (SUT). From 1 to 16 users are simulated. No application software like an RDBMS or word processor is used.

For publication, Neal Nelson combines the results from his numerous tests into four general categories:

- Integer performance
- Floating point performance
- Disk performance
- Disk cache performance

Multi-user benchmarks

It may be useful to recall the difference between Internal Throughput Rate (ITR) and External Throughput Rate (ETR).

They are defined as follows:

$$ITR = \frac{\text{Transactions/second}}{\text{Processor Busy Time}} \qquad ETR = \frac{\text{Transactions/second}}{\text{Elapsed Time}}$$

ITR effectively measures the transactions per CPU second in an unconstrained environment, viz., enough memory, DAD, etc., to drive the CPU to high utilizations.

ETR effectively measures the transaction throughput rate of the whole system and is not necessarily a measure of processor performance. The ITR measurement described above will provide this measure for a single system or, in the case of two or more systems, a comparison.

RAMP-C benchmark

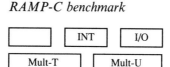

RAMP-C is an IBM synthetic benchmark, essentially measuring Internal Throughput Rate (ITR).

- It represents commercial interactive work
- It is written in COBOL and is proprietary to IBM although it is specified in great detail in generally available publications
- It exercises the full range of system resources:
  - Full screen terminal I/O
  - Disk I/O (indexed not relational)
  - Processor and main storage
- It has four transaction types
  - Simple
  - Average
  - Complex
  - Very complex

The RAMP-C benchmark workload allows uniform commercial performance comparisons between systems of differing architectures. The RAMP-C application is divided into four types of transactions or 'classes'. Each class consists of many separately compiled programs designed to execute a single transaction each time one is requested. Each RAMP-C workstation executes only one program. The programs are set up interactively so that a request is a simple return from the workstation to the system. For execution purposes, a RAMP-C work load is defined as a combination of classes, or a 'mixture'. For this mixture, the number of transactions from each class comprises a certain percentage of the total number of transactions. To help maintain this mixture, each workstation is assigned a constant key and think time depending on which class of program is being run on that workstation.

The RTE driver in RAMP-C provides the following data:

- Throughput in a given time period
- Actual average key-think time

- Average response time
- 90th percentile response time

From this data, two values are derived:

- Total system throughput at 70 per cent CPU utilization (RAMP-C transactions per hour)
- Average response time over all workstations and all transactions at that throughput

RAMP-C results are expressed in thousands of transactions/hour.

Running the system up to 70 per cent utilization means supplying whatever other resources are needed to achieve this (memory, disk, etc.), in other words, a balanced system. This means the RAMP-C tests are assessing the system capacity for processing transactions at a normally accepted limit for CPU utilization.

TPC-A benchmark

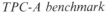
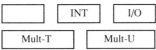

This benchmark is produced and owned by the Transaction Processing Performance Council (TPC) and was designed to eliminate some of the inconsistencies and loopholes in other multi-user benchmarks. A key design factor is that the environment should be similar to that found in real, operational commercial systems. This includes requirements for recovery, consistency and so on which have an effect on systems performance since they take system resources to implement. TPC-A and TPC-B effectively replace the debit/credit varieties of benchmark. TPC-B is outlined later in this chapter.

The TPC benchmark A exercises system resources needed to perform tasks associated with on-line transaction processing (OLTP) with database update activity. This OLTP environment is characterized by:

- Multiple on-line terminal sessions
- Significant disk I/O
- Moderate system and application execution time
- Transaction integrity

The TPC-A workload is designed to represent a bank teller system, similar to debit/credit but with constraints and different metrics.

- Transaction/second (tps)

- Subject to a response time constraint
- The associated cost per transaction/second

The benchmark can be run on a local area network or a wide area network (tpsA-Local, tpsA-Wide)

The TPC-A Standard contains rules, definitions and descriptions for:

- Transaction and terminal profiles
- Transaction system properties
- Logical database design
- Scaling rules
- Distribution, partitioning and message generation
- Response time
- Duration of test
- System under test (SUT), driver and communications definition
- Pricing of system
- Full disclosure
- Audit

The simulation of terminals is done by a Remote Terminal Emulator which is outside the SUT.

TPC-A response time constraint: 90 per cent of all transactions started and completed in steady state during the measurement interval must have a response time of less than two seconds. The response time is defined as:

The time before the first byte of the transaction leaves the RTE until the time after the last byte of the response arrives at the RTE.

The reported tps rating must be measured and not interpolated or extrapolated.

The TPC-A benchmark requires a graphical report displaying the frequency distribution of response times from 0 to 20 seconds at least. The response time axis must have at least 20 1-second intervals. In addition, the maximum and average values of response time must be reported.

Test system properties: The atomicity, consistency, isolation and durability (ACID) properties of transaction processing systems must be supported by the SUT running TPC-A. These properties (not 100 per cent enforceable) are:

- *Atomicity*—Atomicity of a transaction means that the system will perform either all the individual operations of the transaction or none of them and will ensure that no partially completed operation leaves any effect on the data.

● *Consistency*—is the property of an application that requires any execution of a transaction to take the database from one consistent state to another.

● *Isolation*—operations of current transactions must yield results which are indistinguishable from the results which would be obtained by forcing each transaction to be serially executed to completion in some order. This is also called serializability.

● *Durability*—The tested system must guarantee the ability to preserve the effects of committed transactions and ensure database consistency after recovery from:

    – permanent irrecoverable failure of database, tables, logs, etc.
    – system crash or hang requiring re-boot/re-IPL to recover
    – failure of all or part of memory (loss of contents)

There are still some areas of OLTP not defined by TPC-A but the benchmark is closer to 'real life' transaction processing than debit/credit and some other benchmarks.

TPC-B benchmark

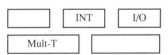

The TPC-B benchmark was defined by the TPC as a follow-on to the TP1 benchmark. It is identical to the TPC-A benchmark with the following notable exceptions:

● The transaction profile does not contain terminal I/O.
● Internal response time ('residence time') is used in place of external response time.
● No think time or keying time ('cycle time') is required.
● Terminals need not be simulated or priced.

It is important to remember that the characteristics and metrics of TPC-B are very different from TPC-A.

Graphics benchmarks

Graphics benchmarks measure the speed of particular graphics operation rather than an idealized instruction mix. The actual application performance

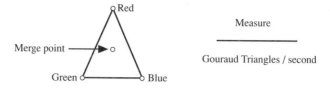

Figure 2.6. Intensity interpolated shading.

is difficult to estimate from such figures however. Some of the 'benchmarks' used are:

Characters/second: This is the speed at which bit-mapped characters are moved from the character ROM to the screen RAM. On systems with many fonts, this figure is not meaningful since the fonts have to be retrieved as well as displayed.

BitBLT: Bit BLock Transfer in millions of pixels per second. A common operation in GUIs or 2D graphics is to move a block of (picture) bits from one part of the screen to another, e.g. cut and paste. This speed can depend on a number of factors and there are no defined standards (metrics) for measuring the BitBLT rate unambiguously.

2D vectors/second: or how quickly 2D lines can be drawn. When comparing quoted figures, it is important to remember that the rates can vary significantly depending on the length of the line drawn, the orientation of the line, and whether it is drawn as part of a polyline or as a simple line.

In an application, lines pass through a number of stages before they are actually drawn. They are transformed from an idealized (world) coordinate system to the device coordinate system, scaled and clipped to an area on the screen. Other things to note therefore are whether or not the line is transformed, sealed, or clipped. The apparent performance of some adapters can be increased by up to 50 per cent if none of these operations are carried out prior to drawing.

3D vectors/second: The factors affecting 2D draw rates also apply to 3D. Additional factors are whether the line is drawn with perspective, and whether hidden line removal is carried out. Again, the moral is as before.

Shaded polygons/second: Solid models are usually composed of many small 3D segments. This 'benchmark' measures how many segments are drawn and shaded per second. A typical solid model comprises 10 K to 30 K polygons. A special case of this type of shading are Gouraud Triangles which are triangles drawn with the three primary colours starting at the vertices and merging at the centre (see Fig. 2.6). This is often called 'Intensity Interpolated Shading' which aims to eliminate intensity discontinuities.

GPC benchmarks

The Graphics Performance Characterization (GPC) benchmarks have been created by the GPC Committee which is administered by the National Computer Graphics Association. The GPC committee includes members from Alliant Computer Systems, Digital Equipment Corporation, DuPont Pixel Systems Ltd, Evans & Sutherland, Hewlett-Packard/Apollo, IBM, Intergraph, Megatek, Prime Computer, Silicon Graphics Inc., Sun Microsystems, and Tektronix. New members have been joining the sub-committee as the benchmark gains acceptance.

In order to perform a GPC benchmark, all vendors must port the central program to their workstation. This program, called the Picture Level Benchmark (PLB) program then accepts geometry that has been taken from any user application. This geometry must first be reformatted to the Benchmark Interchange Format (BIF).

The PLB accepts graphics functions and then executes these functions on the geometry from the BIF. For example, if an architect is trying to select a graphics system that will allow him to walk through a computer-generated building, the geometry of the building created in any CAD program is extracted and reformatted to comply with the BIF. The PLB is then fed the motion commands to move through the building, and the GPC benchmark will test how fast the graphics on a specific workstation will 'walk' through the building. The same BIF can then be carried to another vendor's workstation or simply the same vendor's workstation with more graphics hardware and software for comparison. In addition to watching the benchmark run, a written report called the Benchmark Reporting Format (BRF) has been designed to provide a common written report, listing configuration as well as performance information.

Currently, initial alpha GPC benchmarks have been run by Digital Equipment Corporation, Evans & Sutherland, Hewlett-Packard/Apollo, IBM, Silicon Graphics Inc., and Sun Microsystems. Three BIF files have been created and have been titled, pc_board, sys_chassis, and cyl_head. These BIF files represent a printed circuit board, a three-dimensional wire-frame representation of a computer chassis and a solid model of a cylinder head from a four cylinder automobile engine. For each of the three initial BIF files a GPCmark can be derived. The resulting GPCmarks are not combined because the fundamental purpose is to compare specific graphics hardware and software with real life applications.

Interest in the GPC benchmarks has already been significant, with several large customers expressing interest in using GPC benchmarks with work-station procurements.

Xstation benchmarks

Xstation performance is difficult to define and measure for the reasons given before. In spite of this, there are several emerging benchmarks designed for this purpose.

x11perf: A suite of public domain programs for X-server performance tuning. It measures a wide range of operations and displays the results. x11perf measures window manager performance as well as traditional graphics performance and includes benchmarks for:

- The time it takes to create and map windows, e.g. at startup time.
- Mapping an existing set of windows on the screen, e.g. when you de-iconify an application.
- Rearranging windows, e.g. moving windows around to find the one you want.
- Graphics performance such as Copyplane and scrolling.

The x11perf benchmarks do not seek to produce a single number ('HeXStones') to represent X Windows performance. They rather seek to analyse the strengths and weaknesses of a server in various areas of operation. For repeatable results, x11perf is run using a local connection on a freshly started server. Each test is run five times to check for consistency of results.

xbench/xstones: xbench is similar to x11perf and is aimed at the server. It attempts to give a 'feel' for the x-server performance by outputting a number of graphics commands, and measures the time taken to put them on the screen. It is a useful tool for comparing different server implementations and for measuring tuning effects.

Each test is run three times and the best rating, not the average, is taken to minimize the effect of demons or other background processes.

The benchmark includes the following operations:

- lines (horizontal, vertical, dashed, and wide)
- rectangles (filled, unfilled)
- arcs
- bitBLTS
- character output

The xstones benchmark is a weighted composite figure which is intended as an overall benchmark but, as the benchmark author pointed out, it is only meaningful if the composition happens to match the application in question. No account is taken of networking.

gem: Gemstones (or Xwinstones) are a set of graphics benchmarks for X Windows shipped with the X11.4 distribution tape. They allow the user to specify a range of benchmark tests—possibly thousands.

Gemstones provides standard scripts that exercise the benchmark options in specific combinations. They are a useful tool for users to identify the specific strengths and weaknesses of their X11 implementation. The tests do not test the performance of window management functions nor measure CPU loads.

2.6.1 RS/6000 performance data

Table 2.3 shows the current data for RS/6000 performance. Clearly the current models and their performance are constantly changing and up-to-date information can always be obtained from IBM.

2.6.2 RS/6000 performance versus competition

Figure 2.7 shows that the RS/6000 stands up very well when compared with representative competitive products. It also shows SPECmark results that are a measure of performance. Figure 2.8 shows the price/performance of the RS/6000 versus competition measured using the AIM benchmark. This gives a measure of dollars per unit of AIM workload.

2.7   Local Area Networks

The UNIX world, the Local Area Network (LAN) is commonplace. Typically, the LAN will be a Token Ring LAN or an Ethernet LAN. In principle they are both similar and offer the same kind of functionality, but they differ in the way they work. PC LANs are also commonplace in the commercial world, but these tend to use LAN Manager or Novell protocols to communicate between machines. UNIX machines usually use TCP/IP to communicate. In principle, a LAN is a fast method of communicating with other local machines to provide functions such as:

- Logging into other machines
- Transferring files
- Server machines (file servers, printer servers, etc.)
- Gateways to other networks

Table 2.3. RS/6000 performance data

Desktop machines		RISC System/6000 Model					
		220	22W	22G	320H	340	350
Clock (MHz)		33	33	33	25	33	42
MIPS					37.0		
MFLOPS	SP				13.3		
	DP	6.5	6.5	6.5	11.7	14.6	18.6
SPECmark 1.0		25.9	25.9	25.9	43.4	56.5	71.4
SPECint 1.0		17.5	17.5	17.5	21.8	28.8	36.2
SPECfp 1.0		33.7	33.7	33.7	66.8	88.7	112.3
TPC-A	TPS						
	K$/TPS						
TPC-B	TPS				41.4		
	K$/TPS				2.5		

Deskside and rack machines		RISC System/6000 Model					
		520H	530H	930	550	950	560
Clock (MHz)		25	33.3	25	41.6	41.6	50
MIPS				37.0	52.2	62.2	
MFLOPS	SP		19.2	14.4	24.3	24.3	
	DP	11.5	20.2	15.4	25.6	25.6	30.5
SPECmark 1.0		43.5	59.9	46.1	75.9	75.8	89.3
SPECint 1.0		21.8	29.2	22.1	36.8	36.9	43.8
SPECfp 1.0		68.9	96.7	75.2	123.0	122.6	143.6
TPC-A	TPS		32.0		32.0	38.0	
	K$/TPS		15.7		15.9	23.2	
TPC-B	TPS		52.7		69.2	74.2	
	K$/TPS		2.7		2.8	4.5	

The TCP/IP protocols allow this in the same way as the PC products—LAN Manager, Novell, etc.

More than one protocol can run on any physical LAN at the same time, so that a Token Ring LAN could support TCP/IP protocols and Novell protocols concurrently over the same cabling. There will obviously be limitations as to which machines on the LAN can support particular protocols.

In the Technical Workstation market, Ethernet is commonly used as the LAN and TCP/IP protocols are almost always used for communications. TCP/IP provides the basic protocols and there are functions (or applications) that allow particular actions to be taken. For example:

- telnet   Remote logging into other systems
- ftp   File Transfer

In addition, once TCP/IP is running between systems, other products can often run on top of this. For example NFS (Network File System) can be

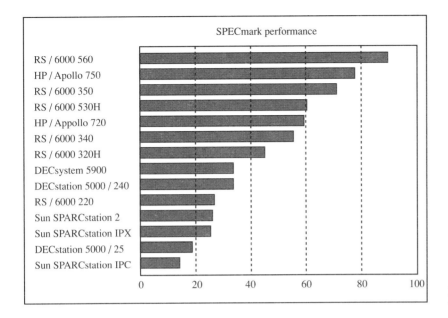

Figure 2.7. SPECmark performance.

used for sharing data on a LAN, or X Windows can be used for running remote 'windows' into other systems. NCS (Network Computing System) can also be used for sharing computing resources across a LAN.

The RS/6000 can operate equally well with Token Ring or Ethernet. AIX

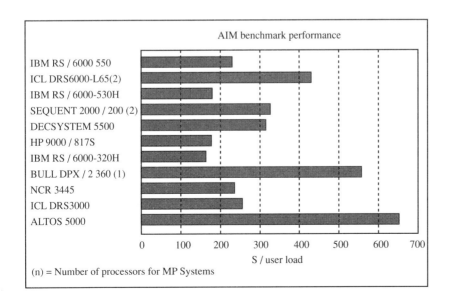

Figure 2.8. AIM benchmark.

Version 3 contains the TCP/IP, NFS and NCS support as part of the operating system and X Windows is available as an optional product.

IBM also has an agreement with Novell that will allow RS/6000s to participate in a Novell network.

PCs or PS/2s can support TCP/IP in addition to other PC communications protocols. This will be discussed in more detail later.

Although LANs were originally intended for local communications, as the name suggests, nowadays they are often used for wider communications. LANs can be bridged locally or remotely to form larger networks. The same kinds of functions can therefore be provided over a wide area, although performance will clearly depend on the type of link between the LANs. Wide area performance will not normally be as fast as the local LAN itself.

Token Ring and Ethernet

Although Token Ring and Ethernet Networks provide similar functions, they work in very different ways and there are fundamental differences between them. Token Ring is very reliable and performs well even when heavily loaded. The ring can run at 4 Megabits per second or 16 Megabits per second. Each device on the network is cabled into a Multi-Access Unit (MAU) that can also be connected to other MAUs and hence other devices. The MAU provides intelligence to allow for cases when a device on the network is faulty or there is a cabling problem. In these cases the Token Ring network will continue to function without a break. The Token Ring network is designed for reliability, resilience and availability as well as performance.

There are two kinds of Ethernet network—thick and thin. The thin Ethernet is a very simple network with very little in the way of error recovery. If a device on the network fails this can bring down the complete network. The thick Ethernet has transceivers and is more sophisticated in its design. Ethernet networks employ a collision detection mechanism. If two devices on the network transmit at the same time, then they will both back off and try again a little later (at different times). However, if the network is heavily loaded, then more collisions will occur and there will be a deterioration in performance.

2.8   Graphical User Interfaces

Traditionally UNIX systems used a very simple asynchronous (ASCII) screen to gain access to applications. Today, with faster and cheaper systems, many users take advantage of graphics on their terminal. Graphics can mean many different things but a Graphical User Interface (GUI) is essentially a windowed environment. Many users are familiar with Windows/3 from Microsoft for the PC, or Presentation Manager under OS/2 on the PS/2. These provide multiple windows on the same screen so that a number of applications can run concurrently.

In the UNIX world windows are usually provided through the X Windows interface. X Windows is an adopted standard, but differs from Windows/3 or Presentation Manager in that it is a networking interface. Windows can be opened on screens attached to other UNIX systems by communicating across a network. On its own, X Windows is not usable. A set of 'tools' for re-sizing windows, moving them and providing many other functions is needed. This is obtained by using software such as Motif, a User Interface defined by the Open Software Foundation.

X Windows with Motif is widely used as a GUI in the UNIX world and is adopted as a standard by many manufacturers. OSF/Motif has been designed to work in a very similar way to Presentation Manager, and a user moving from one interface to the other should have little difficulty. Other GUIs are available including the NextStep Interface, OpenLook and NewWave from Hewlett-Packard. Essentially, they provide the same function but in different ways.

The tools that are supplied for writing programs to run in an X Windows environment include widgets and gadgets to help the programmer easily write applications to use scroll-bars, buttons and other windowing functions.

3
UNIX from IBM—AIX

This chapter describes AIX and its functionality. As discussed earlier, AIX conforms to all of the accepted Open System standards, but also provides extra functionality that does not conflict with this. AIX has been developed by IBM in Austin, Texas in conjunction with the RS/6000 hardware to make sure that the overall system is highly optimized and performs well. There are many enhancements in AIX Version 3 that make it an outstanding operating system.

The extra functions can broadly be divided into three categories:

- Making AIX more reliable and robust so that it can be used in a production environment.
- Removing traditional restrictions and limitations within UNIX.
- Adding extra functionality that does not conflict with the standards.

A large part of the original UNIX code has been rewritten by IBM to be the basis for AIX. This has been achieved without conflicting with the all-important standards.

3.1   Overview of AIX Version 3 for the RISC System/6000

AIX Version 3 for the RS/6000 is a new version of the IBM AIX Operating System that has been restructured and enhanced to support and exploit the POWER Architecture of the RS/6000. Included are new or improved features such as: POSIX standards conformance, Berkeley Software Distribution 4.3 (4.3 BSD) compatibility, extended real-time support, enhanced virtual memory management, enhanced physical disk space management, and advanced file system and program management. Facilities designed to meet Trusted Computing Base (TCB) level C2 security support, improved system management with network install facilities, and on-line hypertext softcopy information are included. Communications and networking support includes TCP/IP, X.25, Network File System (NFS) and Network Computing System (NCS) facilities.

AIX Version 3 is a multi-tasking, demand-paged, virtual memory operating system which can operate as a single-user or multi-user system.

IBM announced and shipped AIX Version 3.2 early in 1992. This has many added advantages over Version 3.1. For example, AIX Version 3.2 supports X Window Version 11 release 4—a faster and better version of X Windows. AIX Version 3.2 has a new file tree structure that is compatible with the OSF standards, and AIX Version 3.2 also supports all of the latest models and peripherals that were also announced in January 1992.

The following sections in this chapter will describe in detail the AIX Version 3 operating system and its capabilities.

3.2   Enhanced AIX functionality

There are a number of ways in which AIX has been enhanced to provide extra functionality. Some of these are discussed below. Many of these aspects are covered in more detail in later sections of this book.

3.2.1   User interfaces

AIX Version 3 along with some associated licensed programs provides a flexible user environment through the following user interfaces:

- AIXwindows (based on the OSF/Motif user interface)
- X Window System user interface (based on MIT's Version 11, Release 4)
- XGSL (GSL Graphics Routines are fully integrated into the enhanced X Window System environment)
- GKS and graPHIGS Graphics Routine Libraries
- C, Bourne, and Korn shells

AIXwindows Environment/6000

AIXwindows Environment/6000 is a state-of-the-art graphical user interface environment for the RS/6000 using AIX Version 3.2. AIXwindows Environment/6000 consists of a base product, which is primarily for customers who require 2D graphical user interface (GUI) support, and an optional 3D graphics feature, called AIXwindows/3D, which is directed to customers using 3D technical applications.

AIXwindows Environment/6000 (Base) has received major enhancements with the addition of:

- Enhanced X-Windows support based on X Window System Version 11 Release 4
- OSF/Motif 1.1 support (including Multi Byte Character Set (MBCS) support)
- AIXwindows Desktop enhancements
- 24-bit colour visual support in Enhanced X Windows

AIXwindows/3D includes:

- Graphics Library (GL) a well known application programming interface (API) with DBCS capability, highly compatible with the GL application interface from Silicon Graphics, Inc.
- Personal graPHIGS which meets a number of ANSI/ISO standards for API.
- Graphical Kernel Systems Compatibility Option (GKS-CO contained within Personal graPHIGS).
- Initial Release of MITs PEX (3D Extension to X Windows) support.

AIXwindows Environment/6000 provides a graphical extension to AIX Version 3 for RS/6000. It is based on, and compatible with, the industry-accepted X Window System and the OSF/Motif 1.1 graphical user interface, and can interact with other AIX and other equipment manufacturer systems, implementing the X Window System and OSF/Motif interfaces. AIXwindows Environment/6000 provides a sophisticated graphical desktop (AIXwindows Desktop) that can be tailored for integrating and launching applications. The AIXwindows Environment/6000 also provides the facilities to execute and develop Enhanced X Windows applications, OSF/Motif applications and applications requiring Display PostScript support.

In addition, AIXwindows/3D provides the facilities for the execution and development of three-dimensional applications for scientific and engineering applications. These include 3D applications which are supported by graPHIGS, GL or PEX. X Window, 2D and 3D applications may be executed in adjacent X Windows.

Highlights

- X.desktop 3.0 with SBCS
- OSF/Motif 1.1 with MBCS
- Enhanced X Windows 11.4
  - AIXterm with MBCS and compound text
- Personal graPHIGS

- Graphics Library with DBCS
- PEX initial implementation server/client support

AIXwindows (OSF/Motif and AIXwindows Desktop)

The graphical user interface included in AIXwindows is based on the OSF/Motif user interface offering and has been enhanced to support internationalized applications that can handle MBCS. AIXwindows runs in the Enhanced X Windows environment. The AIXwindows user interface is comprised of the AIXwindows run-time environment and the AIXwindows application development environment.

The AIXwindows run-time environment consists of an OSF/Motif window manager and AIXwindows Desktop, a sophisticated graphical OSF/Motif-based desktop that provides an iconic view of the file system and the ability to shield the user from the low-level complexities of the AIX operating system. AIXwindows Desktop is an enhanced version of X.desktop Version 3.0. Simple file maintenance functions can be performed on the files via direct manipulation of the icons. The AIXwindows Desktop can be tailored by the user to integrate and launch applications.

The AIXwindows application development environment provides the application developer with a high-level toolkit based on OSF/Motif with MBCS support. The AIXwindows application environment consists of the following tools:

- OSF/Motif user interface toolkit (C, C+ + language bindings)
- OSF/Motif Xm library, containing user interface widgets and gadgets (windowless widgets)
- User Interface Language (UIL) and Motif Resource Manager (MRM) components
- OSF/Motif examples

The Window Manager and Xm library conform to the Inter-Client Communication Convention with support for Compound Text Interchange.

Enhanced X Windows

The Enhanced X Windows function is an enhanced version of the X Window System Version 11 Release 4, designed to increase the usability of the application processing environment. It contains:

- X11 server
- X11 clients

- X11 protocol extensions
- X11 library and toolkit (libX11.a and libXt.a)
- X11 Xamples (includes a majority of the MIT X11)

Enhanced X Windows Version 11 Release 4 is backwardly compatible with Enhanced X Windows Version 11 Release 3 and has been enhanced to provide increased functionality and improved performance. Support for X Visual types has been expanded to include visual depths of 4, 8 and 24 bits. A set of end user and application programming interfaces is provided to support both graphic and text applications. Text applications that use the system interfaces will work in a windowed environment without modification. Multi-head support is also provided, allowing the movement of the cursor between adjacent displays without having to 'hot key' between sessions or displays. Language bindings are available in X library for C and FORTRAN. The windows may contain application sessions running on the local processor or on (LAN)-connected compatible systems. AIXterm (ASCII Terminal Emulator) can support any locale installed in AIX Version 3.2 for RISC System/6000 and also supports MBCS and compound text.

A font library has been added to support a full range of code sets, styles and sizes. These are optionally installed.

Enhanced X Windows Display PostScript (DPS)

Display PostScript is supported in an X window allowing applications to output Display PostScript to a window. The Display PostScript Interpreter provides an interactive, display-oriented environment that is independent of the window system. In addition, it provides a single-image model for both display and printer data streams. Nine additional fonts have been added, for a total of 22 Adobe fonts. Additional samples have been provided to demonstrate some of the capabilities of Display PostScript.

AIXwindows/3D Feature

This includes Personal graPHIGS, GL, and PEX.

Personal graPHIGS

AIX Personal graPHIGS is a high-performance high-function 2D/3D graphical programming interface based on American National Standards Institute (ANSI) and the International Standards Organization (ISO), Programmer's Hierarchical Interactive Graphics System (PHIGS). The graPHIGS design features which exploit the advanced capabilities of the RS/6000 graphics adapters are:

- Enhanced integration with AIXwindows
- Advanced 3D modelling capabilities displayed on a high resolution 1280 × 1024 pel display
- Both an immediate (non-retained) mode and a (retained) mode interface
- Support for interactive picking of on-screen structures
- Gouraud and constant shading modes and Z-Buffer support
- Antialiasing of lines
- Primitives for curve and surface creation including triangle strip, polysphere, polyhedron edge, and Non-Uniform Rational B-Splines (NURBS)
- Rendering enhancements which include hidden line/hidden surface removal (HLHSR), multiple light source simulation, and depth cueing
- Colour index mode and direct colour specification mode
- Proportional Character Fonts which provide text fonts where character width may vary on a character-by-character basis
- DBCS support

The following standards are supported, subject to certain limitations:

- ANSI/ISO PHIGS FORTRAN language binding
- ANSI/ISO PHIGS C language binding
- Computer Graphics Metafile (CGM), a standard file format. Personal graPHIGS supports CGM as file format output only

An interactive Personal graPHIGS tutorial and other sample demonstration programs are provided.

Graphics Library

GL is designed to provide a high-performance, high function graphical interface to AIXwindows Environment/6000 graphics components for the graphics applications programmer. C language bindings are provided. GL is compatible with GL Interface from Silicon Graphics Inc., and provides a simplified porting path for many GL-based graphics workstation applications.

PEX—3D Extension to X

AIXwindows/3D feature provides the MIT (Massachusetts Institute of Technology) PEX (sample implementation) protocol in a window. This is an extension to the Enhanced X Windows server and provides an Application Programming Interface (API) to PHIGS and PHIGS Plus and utilizes the same client–server model available through the X Window System. PEX SI allows an application to access a heterogeneous network environment of AIX, non-AIX, IBM, non-IBM and UNIX systems that support PEX. Applications can be executed on one system and display the results on another system, provided the systems operate using the same PEX protocol version.

Graphics Adapter Interface (GAI) display drivers

The GAI provides a set of software services to graphics software such as GL and the Personal graPHIGS application programming interface. It is not intended as a programming interface for users. However, it is the set of software which manages the device dependencies of each display adapter, and new adapters will require a GAI display driver to communicate efficiently with other IBM software graphics packages.

The programming interface to the GAI, including but not limited to the data structures, the procedure calls and the architecture of the software, could change in subsequent releases of AIXwindows Environment/6000. This may require applications directly using the GAI programming interface to be modified in order to be updated to a subsequent release of AIX Version 3.

Command shells

The basic user interface to the UNIX operating system is the command 'shell'. Interacting with the user through the keyboard and terminal display, the shell manages the dialogue between the user and the UNIX system. In effect, the shell is the procedure language.

AIX Version 3 for the RS/6000 provides multiple command shells.

Bourne shell

The Bourne shell is the most widely used shell on UNIX operating systems, and gains its name from its developer.

C shell

The C shell was originally developed as part of the BSD implementations. Although it is similar to the Bourne shell, it differs in that commands that control the flow of the shell scripts resemble the corresponding constructs in the C language, hence the name C shell. It also provides additional built-in features for example, a history command buffer, aliasing and other convenient enhancements.

Korn shell

The Korn shell is the default shell for AIX Version 3. It is based on the *ksh* shell offered with AT&T UNIX System V Release 3. The Korn shell is an enhanced compatible superset of the Bourne shell incorporating additional features, many of which were previously available only in the C shell.

3.2.2   System management

System management is an important part of managing a computer environment, and a system's management tools and capabilities should be considered as part of an overall computer decision. Traditionally, UNIX operating systems have implemented several detached utilities to accomplish the core pieces of this task.

The RS/6000 along with AIX provides a different approach for system management, with a layered, open and extendible architecture that is integrated throughout the AIX environment. The user interface approaches tasks from an administrator's viewpoint, independent of the operating environment.

System management disciplines should handle, in a user friendly and consistent way, not only the administrative tasks at a single site, but also the more complex management of multiple systems. In multiple systems management, issues such as easy installation and updates for multiple sites, and problem determination of system and network functions from a central site become increasingly important as the number of machines grows. AIX Version 3 provides tools and facilities for both single system and multiple system management.

Logical volumes

Some operating system implementations based on AT&T UNIX System V do not offer the flexibility of AIX Version 3. In those operating systems, file space is pre-allocated for uses like paging, program products, the operating system, user files, etc. System managers (or users) must decide the size and placement of these preallocated areas (sometimes called minidisks or partitions) at installation. If one of these areas proves to be too small, a major administrative effort that may take several hours is required to reorganize the disks. And while the disks are being reorganized, the system cannot be used for productive work. Even though there may be plenty of free space in other partitions or unallocated areas of a disk many UNIX systems are incapable of using this space.

AIX V3 includes a facility named the Logical Volume Manager that addresses the above problem and others. Logical Volumes are collections of equal sized disk space (128 bytes to 256 MB each) called Physical Partitions that appear to applications and users as if they are a single area. If one of these Logical Volumes runs out of space, the administrator can simply add one or more Physical Partitions while the system is running.

Unlike traditional partitions or minidisks, Logical Volumes allow files to span physical volumes. This allows very large files (greater than can be contained on one disk) to be used without special programming. Spanned volume file support is implemented by assigning Physical Partitions on multiple physical disks to the Logical Volume.

Disks are one of the most fragile and error prone components of modern computing systems. For extremely critical data, some applications maintain two or more copies of data on separate physical disks. This technique is known as disk mirroring. The Logical Volume Manager can provide this type of safety margin transparently to applications. This feature is implemented by creating Logical Partitions which consist of from one to three Physical Partitions. When an application updates a file residing on a Logical Partition containing more than one Physical Partition, AIX V3 insures that all Physical Partitions are updated. If one of the disk drives in a Logical Partition develops a problem, applications can continue running uninterrupted.

Management of Single Systems

System Management Interface Tool

AIX Version 3 includes a system management tool called System Management Interface Tool (SMIT). SMIT is a set of menu-driven services which facilitate the performance of tasks such as installation, configuration, device-management, problem determination and storage management. The user is guided by a series of interactive menus and/or dialogues that automatically build, execute, and log commands required to accomplish selected operations, thus eliminating the need for a user to know or learn command-level syntax for system management tasks. In addition, on-line softcopy help

```
                        Systems management

Move cursor to desired item and press Enter.

 Installation and Maintenance

Devices
Physical and Logical
Security and Users
Communications Applications and Services
Spooler (Print Jobs and Printers)
Problem Determination
Performance and Resource Scheduling
System Environments and Processes
Applications
Using SMIT (information only)


 F1 = Help          F2 = Refresh      F3 = Cancel      F8 = Image
 F9 = Shell         F10 = Exit        Enter = Do
```

Figure 3.1. SMIT (systems management tool) main menu.

information is available at each level of the interface. This means on-the-spot help that is meaningful and flexible, depending on the need. Figure 3.1 shows the SMIT main menu.

On-line hypertext softcopy information

InfoExplorer, as an integral part of AIX Version 3, allows a user to access information in the on-line hypertext information base. A user can enter the hypertext information base in a variety of ways, select a desired task, and be shown the information on how to do the task. Users can set up an information window so that the information on how to do something is visible while they are doing it. Figure 3.2 shows the front screen of the InfoExplorer Hypertext system.

Install/update facilities

There are many features available to simplify installation and update of software and hardware. The AIX operating system, along with the selected licensed programs, can optionally be preloaded onto disk at the factory to save time in the initial installation.

Menu-driven installation/update facilities include:

- Support for multiple types of software distribution media (manufacturing preinstalled/preloaded hardfile, 8 mm tape cartridge, 1/4-inch tape cartridge, 3.5-inch diskette).
- Simplified installation through numerous configuration defaults and the consolidation of all interactive install questions at the beginning of the

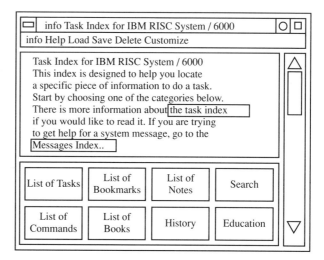

Figure 3.2. InfoExplorer.

process. Any subsequent prompting is limited to media or error handling only.

- Dynamic configuration of devices and services.
- Verification of disk space availability and automatic extension of logical volumes as needed, to reduce significantly the time that information is unavailable.
- Licensed program history information and 'vital product data' provided to help in future problem determination.

Configuration device management
A set of high-level commands is provided to support task-oriented device configuration such as the addition or removal of a device, showing a device, or changing a device.

Storage management
Several high-level commands are available to manage file systems, and logical and physical volumes of disk. A user can add a volume group of hard disks to the system, remove a volume group of hard disks, move the contents of one hard disk to another, add a logical volume, or vary a volume group on- or off-line.

Logical volumes can be extended once configured, and can span multiple physical disk units. Logical volume services also provide support for addition or removal of system physical disk units, and the ability to maintain automatically multiple copies of (or 'mirror') information at the logical volume level.

Problem determination
Facilities are included to provide users and service representatives with the ability to diagnose and correct hardware and/or software failures. These services include error messages, trace, dump, error log, update facilities for application of program fixes, and a standalone, menu-driven package for diagnosing hardware problems and isolating faulty parts.

Accounting services
AIX Version 3 can collect and process the following types of system data:

● Connect-time accounting (data collection and reports)
● Process accounting (data collection and reports)
● Disk-usage data
● Printer-usage data
● Fees for services and materials.

Management of multiple distributed systems
A distributed systems environment can mean a few RS/6000s located at one site, or multiple computers spread over a wide geographic area. Building on the capabilities just discussed for management of single systems, AIX system management provides additional capabilities for management of distributed systems.

Remote self-sufficiency
With multiples sites, one requirement is to make the end user as self-sufficient as possible. AIX Version 3 helps in this arena with the easy-to-use menu-driven interfaces of SMIT, the advanced InfoExplorer hypertext on-line documentation, and state-of-the-art user interfaces.

Easy installation and updates
Another requirement is to make multiple installations and updates as easy and accurate as possible. AIX provides several ways to accomplish this, including the software preload option, a batch file control method, or a LAN network installation method. The software preload option allows the RS/6000 to be shipped from the factory with AIX selected licensed programs already loaded on the disk.

The batch file control method goes a step beyond the preload option. It allows the central site to choose its unique installation options and load the choices to a file. The file media can then be sent to each site. The site is spared the task of choosing appropriate installation options, and the central site can be assured of a proper installation.

The LAN network installation method allows the main server in the network to update the other clients in the network automatically. The client systems IPL with a system-provided disk/diskette resident 'boot' program that contacts the central site server for download operations.

Remote operation
The central site has the ability to access a remote system and work on it as if it were local. Normal commands and problem determination functions of TCP/IP or the Host Command Facility (HCF) can be used, depending on what type of host is at the central site. TCP/IP is a common mechanism if the central site has an AIX system installed, or TCP/IP can also be used from an MVS, VM or AS/400 computer. The HCF is another tool with similar functions, available under MVS and VM. HCF is used on several IBM distributed platforms and may be chosen if these IBM systems are planned or are already in place.

TCP/IP automation
A menu and dialogue user interface are provided for TCP/IP functions. Users can configure most networks without having a detailed knowledge of specific networking configuration requirements. The tools permit installation and configuration without remaking the kernel, plus systems resource control for TCP/IP and its demons.

Network problem determination
Network problem determination can be simplified by trapping, forwarding, and reporting error conditions when they occur to the appropriate source. With tools such as the SNMP Interface and the AIX Network Management/ 6000 program, a central facility can often remedy a problem before the end user even knows there is a problem. This can create a high level of end-user satisfaction.

- *SNMP Interface Mode*: Simple Network Management Protocol (SNMP) agent support is provided in AIX Version 3 for TCP/IP networks. SNMP is a popular industry protocol for managing TCP/IP networks and provides the capability of get, set and trap and a Management Information Base (MIB). Traps such as cold start/warm start, link state changes and authentication failure can be set. It provides read/write, read-only and access denial control.
- *Netview/6000, Netview Service Point and AIX Network Management/ 6000*: The Netview/6000, Netview Service Point and AIX Network Management/6000 licensed programs provide SNMP manager support for TCP/IP networks, as well as generic alert support and other services

for a Systems Network Architecture (SNA) network with an IBM
System/370 or System/390 NetView host. The SNMP manager function
is able to respond to agent generated traps and to send get and limited set
requests to the agents.

These products are described in detail in Sec. 3.5 which discusses Network
Management on the RS/6000.

3.2.3 On-line documentation

A new approach to On-line documentation

- Resides on CD-ROM or disk
- One copy accessed by many
- Entire library up to date
- Flexible user interface

InfoExplorer, as an integral part of AIX Version 3, allows users access to
information in the on-line hypertext information base. Users can enter the
on-line hypertext information base via an index of common tasks, select the
desired task, and be shown information on how to do the task. Users can set
up an information window beside an AIX window and have the information
on how to do something visible while they are doing it. Other methods of
access into the information include selecting a particular command or subroutine from a list rather than having to recall its name, browsing in a
simulated book mode, full-text search on words/phrases/fields, plus a variety
of Boolean search specifications and user-created bookmarks. Some of the
key points are:

- Users can customize the presentation of information on their own
  screens.
- 'View graphics' facilities include zoom/pan capabilities.
- On-line publications information is also the second level of help for
  system messages.
- Information can reside on the hardfile or CD-ROM, serving one or more
  users and allows efficient up-to-date information for all users.
- The on-line 'pubs' man command is also available and provides the
  capability to view sections of the AIX Operating System Commands
  Reference and Technical Reference information.

Design

The key advantage of a hypertext approach is to move easily from one piece of information to another piece of 'related' information. In traditionally implemented on-line documentation, the concept of books, and related information as organized by 'books' were simply moved into machine readable format. A user might have access by subject, but upon gaining access to this information, the system typically would support only sequential movement through the information.

With the RS/6000 design, all words in the documentation are indexed, and information was created by subject, not organized by book. Links are provided so that a user can easily move from one link point to another, in effect, information related to a subject is easily obtained. This approach takes advantage of hypertext, in that users now have the ability to obtain complete answers to any questions they may have. The documentation for the RS/6000 was designed from the ground up with hypertext in mind.

The results are documentation written by article, not as a collection of books, and link points logically developed by related subject.

Choice of access

The InfoExplorer system provides the user with a variety of methods for obtaining information from the database. The menu-driven interface allows the user to seek information based on what the user is trying to accomplish, or the user can request information by commands. The on-line interface is available for all displays on the system, both graphic and ASCII displays. In addition, on-line user education is provided through this menu interface.

Navigation facilities

Upon entering the on-line documentation system, the user is aided in moving from one piece of information to another. All link points to related articles are highlighted, so the user can easily choose to see other information. As the user moves around, the system keeps track of this movement, so the user can easily navigate back and forth.

Where graphic information exists, it is highlighted, and the user thus has the ability to view the graphic while paging through the text. Movement can be captured in a history file, so the user can quickly return to information reviewed in the past. The user has the option of placing a 'bookmark' on key information, and through the menu-driven access can quickly review this. The system even supports the ability for the user to add annotation to the text. This is particularly helpful for installations that wish to add examples particular to their needs or standards, or to provide customized information.

While all this capability is being taken advantage of, the user, within the window manager, can be running other jobs, or actually trying in another window, what is being learned from the on-line documentation. It's like the 'open book in your lap' while trying it on the system, except you no longer need the book, nor do you need to juggle several books to cross reference information. The system does the navigation.

Some of the powerful tools provided for users to move through the on-line documentation are:

- Link points are highlighted in the text
- Graphic information is noted where applicable
- History of movement automatically kept for easy back and forth searching
- Personal annotation supported and can be shared on installation basis

The InfoExplorer search/retrieval facility on the RS/6000 is a significant advancement. Publications were not just keyed into the system, but data is written by subject. Most on-line systems give you contextual entry but then sequential paging, whereas hypertext gives you contextual entry and contextual movement once you enter on-line publications.

InfoCrafter

AIX InfoCrafter/6000, which executes on AIX Version 3.2, offers a solution for the on-line authoring and management of large libraries of information. This software product allows a choice of authoring environments that facilitate the effective construction of large libraries of information. AIX InfoCrafter/6000 is designed to increase the productivity of information developers and information users. It is a tool set that enhances internal information management, and/or as a 'value add' for application developers enabling them to provide on-line comprehensive documentation to support their software products.

AIX InfoCrafter/6000 is a set of tools that provide a batch-oriented 'build' process for compiling on-line libraries read by the InfoExplorer information retrieval software. A library may be virtually any size and may be segmented into as many as fifteen separate information bases allowing for a greater degree of modularity. These information bases may contain a variety of hypertext links, i.e. links to processes, links from text-to-text, links from text-to-art or links from text-to-system files. Articles in information bases, within the same library, may be cross-linked to improve the accessibility of information and can contain tables, text, on-line help text for applications, multiple fonts and illustrations. Authors can create navigation documents designed specifically to assist users with the retrieval of information. These navigation documents capitalize on the InfoExplorer's extensive navigational capabilities.

On the authoring side, AIX InfoCrafter/6000 can accept input from a choice of authoring environments. AIX InfoCrafter/6000 allows for usage with any of the following authoring environments that are compatible with AIX Version 3.2.

- *Interleaf* In this environment the user structures the information in Interleaf documents, using a special catalogue containing pre-defined components specifically designed for the creation of hypertext information. The author creates hypertext links using Interleaf's autonumbering and autonumber referencing features.

  Either Professional Writer or Interleaf Production (optional Interleaf packages) are required for text formats.
- *ASCII* Allows the user to insert formatting tags into ASCII documents using an editor of the author's choice. These tags format text and create hypertext links once the files have been processed by AIX InfoCrafter/ 6000.
- *FrameMaker 3.0* In this environment, the user structures the information in FrameMaker 3.0 documents saved in Maker Interchange Format (MIF). AIX InfoCrafter/6000 translates MIF to Standard Record Format (SRF) in order to build the InfoExplorer information base.

AIX InfoCrafter/6000 also accepts the following graphic formats:

- *Interleaf 5 (vector graphics)* Allows the user to create an artwork component, thereby creating an Interleaf frame using either of the following Interleaf options:
  – Professional Writer
  – Interleaf Production
- *Computer Graphics Metafile (CGM) (vector graphics)*–ANSI X3.122- 1986 and ISO 8632-3 Draft Supports the Binary Encoding of CGM. This format is recommended for vector graphics both in monochrome and in colour.
- *Tagged Image File Format (TIFF)* Class B/CCITT (bitmap/raster graphics) Allows users to use scanners to import graphics into their documents without having to reauthor existing drawings.

3.2.4   *Compiler technology and languages*

Advanced optimizing compilers

AIX V3's compilers for C, FORTRAN, and Pascal significantly contribute to performance by producing highly efficient code. These compilers produce intermediate code which is fed into a common back-end which does the optimization and code generation. And since most of AIX V3, along with its utilities and subsystems, is written in the C language, the optimizations improve overall system responsiveness and performance.

Optimization techniques implemented include:

- *Constant folding*: During compilation, the compiler may be able to determine that an expression consists entirely of values which will not change. In such cases, the compiler replaces the expression with the calculated result reducing code size and increasing execution speed.
- *Common subexpression elimination*: Frequently, programs will include duplicate calculations such as indexing a particular value in a vector. This technique saves the result from the first calculation and replaces all of the remaining duplicate calculations throughout the program with a reference to the saved result. This increases execution speed and reduces program size.
- *Dead code elimination*: Some coding techniques can produce code which is unreachable or 'dead'. The compilers remove this from the executable code to reduce its size. For example, a programmer may have a function which includes a complex series of tests. The compiler may be able to determine that a certain combination of conditions that is checked for will never be true. It removes the check and any calculations that would be executed as a result of a successful test. This can reduce code size and increase speed.
- *Code motion*: At a very low level, loops often include calculations which do not change with each iteration. 'Code motion' moves these calculations outside of the loop where they can be calculated a single time. The code inside of the loop is adjusted to become a simple reference to a precalculated result. This improves execution speed.
- *Induction variable elimination*: An induction variable is a loop variable that is exclusively modified by adding or subtracting a constant. It is often used to limit the number of loop iterations within the loop and to index array elements. The induction variable can be removed by multiplying the loop increment by the array element size and changing the end of loop test to look for a calculated end of array address. This can reduce program

size and increase speed.

- *Strength reduction*:   This means that a faster executing instruction can be substituted for a more general one. For example, when sequentially accessing an array, the array element size can be added to the last used element address rather than multiplying the index number by the element size. The RISC System/6000 even allows this optimization to be improved by providing load instructions that automatically increment or decrement the base register.

- *Efficient register allocation*:   Like most RISC systems, the RISC System/6000 implements a load/store architecture. This means that memory is accessed by load/store instructions (to/from registers) and all logic and arithmetic instructions reference registers rather than memory. This functional partitioning allows memory access to be overlapped with execution. Even though the RISC System/6000 has 32 general purpose registers, they are a scarce resource. When all registers are in use and an additional word of data needs to be accessed, the contents of one of the registers must be written to memory or 'spilled' (assuming its contents will be needed in the future). These compilers use a particularly effective algorithm for minimizing the register 'spilling' called graph colouring. The compiler first assumes an infinite number of registers and, in later operations, optimizes to the actual number of registers with the graph colouring algorithm. This can dramatically improve performance.

- *Procedure inlining*:   For short subroutines, the overhead for the call and return can account for a significant percentage of the execution time for the routine. Inlining means that the compiler copies the code within the body of the subroutine to each place where it is called (making appropriate adjustments). This increases the size of the executable but buys speed.

- *Loop unrolling*:   This technique makes one or more copies of the body of the loop code making appropriate changes to loop increments and other items. Loop overhead is thus amortized over more instructions improving performance. The increased number of instructions inside the loop also enables more opportunities for scheduling to prevent pipeline bubbles. This technique increases speed.

- *Exploit machine idioms*:   The RISC System/6000 includes some instructions that are unusual for RISC processors such as 'string move'. Many compilers on the market do not exploit all the power of the underlying architecture because their authors were unable to justify the extra investment in the compiler to recognize special cases that could use powerful instructions. These compilers do. The result is higher performance and reduced code size.

Programming languages

XL C Compiler
The XL C Compiler produces optimized object code when the optimization compiler option is specified. If no optimization is requested, compilation is faster.

STANDARDS CONFORMANCE/SOURCE CODE COMPATIBILITY
The XL C Compiler aids migration and coexistence by conforming with the C standard and providing source code compatibility with various existing compilers listed below:

- Language standards/specifications—Draft Proposed ANSI C Standard, Document Number X3J11/88-159, dated December 1988, as interpreted by IBM on 9 June 1989.
  XL C Compiler implementation for AIX systems complies with the SAA C level 2 definition, with some exceptions. The exceptions are specified in the AIX XL C Compiler/6000 User's Guide (SC09-1259).
- Source code compatibility
  The XL C Compiler is source code compatible with the languages supported by the following compilers, with some exceptions.
  – IBM RT PC C
  – IBM RT PC Advanced C Compiler
  The exceptions are specified in the XL C Compiler User's Guide (SC09-1259).

XL C Compiler provides compile time options to select which C language definition is required: ANSI mode, SAA mode, or EXTENDED mode.

OPTIMIZATION TECHNIQUES UTILIZED
When optimization is selected at compilation time by the user, the XL C Compiler performs a variety of optimizations upon the program, which may include:

- Flow of control optimization, such as:
  – Designed to eliminate unreachable code
  – Designed for straightening
  – Designed for elimination of unnecessary branches
- Value numbering

- Reassociation (subscript optimization in loops)
- Dead code elimination (i.e. removal of code which computes unused results)
- Common sub-expression elimination
- Constant folding
- Code motion for loop invariants
- Strength reduction
- Elimination of induction variables
- Elimination of redundant load/store sequences
- Store motion (moving stores out of loops)
- Global register allocation
- Instruction scheduling
- Exploitation of machine idioms

XL FORTRAN Compiler

The AIX XL FORTRAN Compiler/6000 is an optimizing compiler that executes under AIX Version 3. It produces optimized object code when the optimization compiler option is specified. If no optimization is requested, compilation is faster.

The AIX XL FORTRAN Compiler/6000 licensed program product includes the function of the AIX XL FORTRAN Run Time Environment/6000.

STANDARDS CONFORMANCE/SOURCE CODE COMPATIBILITY

The AIX XL FORTRAN Compiler/6000 aids migration and coexistence by conforming with the following FORTRAN standards and providing source code compatibility with compilers listed below:

- Industry standards
  - ANSI X3.9-1978 (Full ANSI FORTRAN 77)
  - ISO 1539-1980(E), Programming Languages, FORTRAN
  - FIPS PUB 69—FORTRAN
- Source code compatibility
  The AIX XL FORTRAN Compiler/6000 conforms with the AIX Family FORTRAN language definition.
  The AIX XL FORTRAN Compiler/6000 conforms to the IBM SAA FORTRAN CPI. Support includes optional flagging of all language elements that are not part of the IBM SAA FORTRAN CPI.
  The AIX XL FORTRAN Compiler/6000 is source code compatible with the languages supported by the following compilers with some exceptions.

– IBM VS FORTRAN
– IBM RT PC FORTRAN 77
– IBM RT PC VS FORTRAN
– IBM AIX/RT XL FORTRAN

The AIX FORTRAN/6000 User's Guide (SC09-1257) specifies the exceptions.

The AIX XL FORTRAN Compiler/6000 provides compile time options to flag extensions beyond either ANSI FORTRAN 77 or SAA FORTRAN.

OPTIMIZATION TECHNIQUES UTILIZED

When optimization is selected at compilation time by the user, the compiler performs a variety of optimizations in the same way as the XL C Compiler. Additional features included in Version 2.2 are:

- Interprocedural analysis
- Assertions on run-time expectation
- Memory management
- Enhanced inlining features

Interprocedural analysis: The inspection of called subroutines and functions provides information on relationships between arguments, returned values and global data. This can provide many of the benefits of inlining without replacing the CALL or function reference.

Assertions: Assertions provide the preprocessor with information on the run-time characteristics of a program which are not otherwise available at compilation time.

Memory management: Optimization techniques are employed to make optimal use of the data cache. This significantly reduces the effect of cache misses in many applications.

Enhanced in-lining features: New options enable a user to have more control of the in-lining process.

AIX XL FORTRAN Run Time Environment Version 2.2

Applications developed using the AIX XL FORTRAN Compiler/6000 must be bound with the AIX XL FORTRAN Run Time Environment/6000 for execution. The Run Time Environment may be bound using dynamic binding which requires that the AIX XL FORTRAN Run Time Environment/6000 be available at the time the application is executed. As an alternative, the Run Time Environment may be statically bound to the application resulting in a larger object module. This then eliminates the requirement for the AIX XL FORTRAN Run Time Environment/6000 in the execution environment.

The November 1990 update of AIX Version 3 enhanced the performance of 20 routines in the Basic Linear Algebra Subroutines (BLAS) library. To use the BLAS routines, the AIX XL FORTRAN Run Time Environment/6000 Version 2 is required at the time the application is executed. Alternatively, the Run Time Environment may be statically bound to the application resulting in a larger object module, but eliminating the requirement for the AIX XL FORTRAN Run Time Environment/6000 in the execution environment. The November 1990 update of AIX Version 3 also enhances the performance.

APL2

APL2 is a highly productive interactive language that is easy to learn and use. It provides an extensive collection of functions that can be quickly combined to solve many business problems. APL2 is widely used in diverse application areas such as commercial data processing, system design and prototyping, engineering and scientific computation, artificial intelligence, and the teaching of mathematics and other subjects.

IBM AIX (R) APL2/6000 provides a productive environment for the development and execution of applications on the RS/6000 family including Xstations. It is designed to be compatible with IBM APL2 Version 1 Release 3 which runs on IBM's host mainframe processors and APL2 for the IBM PC (APL2/PC).

- The processing speed of the RS/6000 and the expressive mathematical power of the APL2 language provide a powerful tool for rapid prototyping and working with ill-defined or constantly changing problems.
- APL2/6000 language is highly compatible with APL2 Release 3 on the host and with APL2 for the PC using the same APL2 programming language reference manual. It provides an easy path for migrating work to or from other APL2 platforms via the ')OUT' and ')IN' system commands.
- APL2/6000 Session Manager has the same look and feel as the Session Managers of the PC and host APL2 products with the added benefit of X Window System.
- APL2/6000 includes many Auxiliary Processors and distributed workspaces of the PC or host APL2 products. AP144 provides the application interface to X Window System.
- APL2 keycaps are provided.

APL2/6000 is an interpreted language rather than a compiled language, allowing a high degree of interaction with the computer.

The Session Manager exploits X Window System features such as window movement, resizing, font specification, and use of icons. Other usability features include scrolling capability, permanent session logs, statement recall, stacked input, colour control, programmed function (PF) key support, keyboard redefinition, and national language support. The user interface is consistent with APL2 Release 3 on the host and APL2/PC.

For users with PC (APL2/PC) or the host (APL2 Release 3) applications, APL2/6000 provides an easy migration path to the RS/6000. APL2 provides transportability of workspaces in transfer file format between APL2 platforms. EBCDIC/ASCII translation is performed automatically. APL2/6000 uses the same language reference manual used by the host APL2 and APL2/PC with deviations documented in the APL2/6000 User's Guide. This demonstrates compatibility of the language across the IBM APL2 platforms. APL2/6000 provides many of the Auxiliary Processors available with the PC and/or host APL2 including:

- AP100 Host System Command processor
- AP101 Input Stack processor
- AP124 Full Screen Management processor
- AP210 File I/O processor
- AP211 APL2 Common Object Library processor

APL2/6000 provides many of the common distributed workspaces and functions that are currently available on the PC and host APL2 products. It completes the range of IBM APL2 supported products from the PS/1 through the ES/9000 with Vector Facility. APL2/6000 uses standard AIX system facilities for security, auditability and accounting. APL2/6000 runs on the entire RS/6000 family of processors. A minimum configuration of 16 MB of random access storage is recommended. It is capable of exploiting the maximum memory available on the RS/6000. It requires 1 MB of virtual storage in addition to the workspace virtual storage requirements of the user's application.

APL character support requires a display that provides AIXwindows capability. In addition to supporting high-resolution graphics displays including the IBM 5081 and 6091 colour displays, APL2/6000 supports the IBM Xstation 120 through local area network attachment.

Ada

The Ada programming language is a modern, higher-order language that resulted from a development effort sponsored by the US Department of

Defense. Ada incorporates modern software engineering principles such as modularization, separate compilation and data abstraction.

A key application area for which Ada was intended is embedded system programming. As a result, Ada plays an important role in application development with defence contractors and firms in the aerospace industry. Ada has expanded into scientific and engineering applications and is expected to become a significant factor in commercial application development, especially among defence contractors and related companies.

AIX Ada/6000 Release 2 compiler has been scheduled for validation at Level 1.11 of the Ada Compiler Validation Capability (ACVC) test suite. On-line hypertext documentation is supported and binding to the GL Graphics Support Library of AIX is provided.

Ada/6000 provides the user with a source-level symbolic debugger, Ada library management tools, binder, run-time environment, profiler, Ada source formatter, cross reference lister, Ada source dependency lister and other language-specific tools. In addition, AIX Ada/6000 can be used with CASE tools from IBM Business Partners for the development of Ada software projects on the RS/6000. With the Ada/6000 compiler and run-time environment, a user may develop and execute an Ada application on an RS/6000 machine. The AIX Ada Run Time Environment is required to execute an Ada application if the Ada/6000 compiler is not installed.

Ada/6000 is supported by the on-line hypertext documentation support, using the InfoExplorer program provided with AIX Version 3. AIX Ada/ 6000 Release 2 provides a binding to the GL Graphics Support Library of AIX. With this binding, Ada programmers can build applications using the GL Library directly with the Ada programming language.

Ada/6000 executes on RS/6000 models with a minimum of 16 MB memory and 320 MB of fixed-disk storage with one display or one graphic display with keyboard or ASCII terminal. It requires AIX Version 3. In general, except for new requirements imposed by the ACVC validation level 1.11, Ada/6000 Release 2 is source code compatible with Ada/6000 Release 1.

XL Pascal Compiler

The AIX XL Pascal Compiler/6000 is an optimizing compiler that executes under AIX Version 3. It produces optimized object code when the optimization compiler option is specified. If no optimization is requested, compilation is faster. The AIX XL Pascal Compiler/6000 licensed program product includes the function of the AIX XL Pascal Run Time Environment/6000.

The AIX XL Pascal Compiler/6000 aids migration and coexistence by conforming with the following Pascal standards and providing source code compatibility with compilers listed below:

- Industry standards
  - ANSI 770X3.97-1983, American National Standard Pascal Computer Programming Language
  - ISO 7185-1983, Computer Programming Language Pascal—Level 0
  - FIPS PUB 109—Pascal
- Source code compatibility
  The AIX XL Pascal Compiler/6000 is source code compatible with System/370 VS Pascal, with some exceptions. The exceptions are specified in the AIX Pascal/6000 User's Guide (SC09-1326)

OPTIMIZATION TECHNIQUES UTILIZED

When optimization is selected at compilation time by the user, the compiler performs a variety of optimizations upon the program, which again are as described for the XL C Compiler.

AIX XL PASCAL RUN TIME ENVIRONMENT/6000

Applications developed using the AIX XL Pascal Run Time Environment/6000 must be bound with the AIX XL Pascal Run Time Environment/6000 for execution. The Run Time Environment may be bound using dynamic binding which requires that the AIX XL Pascal Run Time Environment/6000 be available at the time the application is executed. Alternatively, the Run Time Environment may be statically bound to the application resulting in a larger object module, but eliminating the requirement for the AIX XL Pascal Run Time Environment/6000 in the execution environment.

The AIX XL Pascal Run Time Environment/6000 library routines include support for the following types of functions that may be invoked by an AIX Pascal/6000 program:

- Text file data transformations between the character form found in text files and the internal data formats
- Data file access and support functions
- String manipulation functions

VS COBOL Compiler

The AIX VS COBOL Compiler/6000 offers a productive application development environment that allows for the development and execution of high-function applications for the RISC System/6000. The AIX VS COBOL Compiler/6000 aids the development and maintenance of COBOL applications targeted for compilation and execution on IBM System/370 host mainframes in the VM/CMS and MVS operating environments. The AIX VS COBOL Compiler/6000 licensed program product includes the function of the AIX VS COBOL Run Time Environment/6000.

STANDARDS CONFORMANCE/SOURCE CODE COMPATIBILITY

The AIX VS COBOL Compiler/6000 aids migration and coexistence by conforming with the following COBOL standards and providing source code compatibility with compilers listed below:

• Industry Standards
  This product is designed according to the specifications of the following Industry Standards as understood and interpreted by IBM as of June 1989:
  – ANSI X3.23-1985, ISO 1989-1985 (High Level)
  – ANSI X3.23-1974 (High Level)
  – FIPS PUB 21-2—COBOL

• Source code compatibility
  IBM AIX VS COBOL/6000 conforms to the IBM SAA COBOL CPI. Support includes optional flagging of all language elements not part of the IBM SAA COBOL CPI. Details on specific system or implementation semantics can be found in the Language Reference for IBM AIX VS COBOL/6000.

  The AIX VS COBOL Compiler/6000 is source code compatible with the languages supported by the following compilers, with some exceptions.
  – AIX PS/2 VS COBOL
  – AIX RT VS COBOL
  – IBM Personal Computer COBOL Compiler Version 1.00
  – IBM COBOL Version 2.00
  – IBM COBOL/2(TM)
  The exceptions are specified in the AIX VS COBOL/6000 Language Reference Manual (SC23-2177).
  Language syntax variants supported by AIX VS COBOL Compiler/6000 include:
  – A subset of IBM VS COBOL II syntax
  – A subset of IBM OS/VS COBOL syntax
  – IBM Personal Computer COBOL Compiler Version 1.00 and IBM COBOL Version 2.00 syntax with minor restrictions

– IBM COBOL/2
– Micro Focus (2) extensions for the IBM Personal Computer
– SAA COBOL CPI with DBCS support

AIX VS COBOL Compiler/6000 uses the indexed sequential access method (ISAM) which supports alternate keys with duplicates, multiple keys (one prime plus 63 alternates), and split keys. Both fixed length and variable length record files are supported.

AIX VS COBOL Compiler/6000 includes Animator(2), an interactive debug tool that allows isolation of program errors at the source code level while the COBOL Compiler application is executing intermediate code. The Animator provides the programmer with full control over program execution and the ability to:

- Start and stop execution including single-stepping
- Set multiple conditional or unconditional breakpoints
- Change the flow of control
- Control execution speed by single stepping through source code statements at one of ten different speeds
- Skip over subroutines or called programs
- Interrogate, modify and monitor data items
- View variables
- View source code during application execution
- View the application screen
- Use split screen to view simultaneously two different areas of the source code
- Debug called programs to supported levels of nesting

AIX VS COBOL Compiler/6000 can also generate code to support native code debugging with the symbolic debugger (DBX) included in the AIX Base Application Development Toolkit/6000, which is part of AIX Version 3.

FORMS-2 package(2) is a companion utility to the IBM AIX VS COBOL Compiler/6000 that is designed to enable the developer to create and edit data entry screens interactively. In addition it provides:

- Translation of user screen layouts into COBOL record descriptions for inclusion in IBM AIX VS COBOL/6000 application programs.
- Verification of user screen layouts in a check-out program before their incorporation in an application program.
- Retention of exact screen images of the user screens in files for subsequent editing and printing.

AIX VS COBOL Compiler/6000 also allows access to AIX functions.

Overlay syntax and fully qualified file names (including paths) are supported except the filename portion may only contain up to 14 characters. A fast sort/merge module is also included.

AIX VS COBOL RUN TIME ENVIRONMENT/6000

The AIX VS COBOL Run Time Environment/6000 contains the necessary COBOL components to execute applications that were developed with the AIX VS COBOL Compiler/6000 on another system.

- Default configuration definitions for IBM AIX VS COBOL Run Time Environment/6000 applications
- AIX VS COBOL Run Time Environment/6000 library of routines called at run-time
- Run-time error message file
- Utility to configure the keyboard definitions
- Utility to configure the display definitions

Graphics programming languages

AIX Personal graPHIGS Programming Interface/6000

GraPHIGS EXTENSIONS

IBM AIX Personal graPHIGS Programming Interface/6000 Version 2 provides extensions for PHIGS. Designated PHIGS PLUS, these include direct colour specification, more sophisticated rendering capabilities, and representation of advanced graphics primitives such as curves and surfaces. Designed to take advantage of the high-performance rendering capabilities of the RS/6000 and its family of Graphics Adapters, this version provides continuing support for applications written with IBM Personal graPHIGS Programming Interface Version 1.

The AIX Personal graPHIGS Programming Interface/6000 Version 2 application programming interface (API) is based on American Standards Institute Inc. (ANSI) and the International Standards Organization (ISO) standard with the Programmers Hierarchical Interactive Graphics System (PHIGS).

PHIGS PLUS is a designation for extensions being proposed by an *ad hoc* committee from a consortium of graphics professionals of various companies and educational institutions.

AIX Personal graPHIGS Programming Interface/6000 Version 2 is a Systems enabler of the IBM Integrated Manufacturing (CIM) Architecture.

The CIM Architecture is IBMs key direction for integrating CIM solutions in a consistent manner to assist with integration efforts.

System enablers are the fundamental CIM Architecture building blocks. AIX Personal graPHIGS Programming Interface/6000 Version 2 implements one of the programming interfaces defined by the CIM Architecture.

AIX Personal graPHIGS Programming Interface/6000 Version 2 includes design features which exploit the advanced capabilities of the RS/6000 graphics adapters.

BASE APPLICATION DEVELOPMENT TOOLKIT

The Base Application Development Toolkit is a collection of common development tools that are designed to aid a programmer's productivity on the RS/6000 and provides a key element in a Computer Aided Software Engineering (CASE) environment. The Base Application Development Toolkit includes: X development environment (XDE), source code control system (SCCS), system build facilities (MAKE), symbolic debugger (DBX), Application Development Facilities (ADF) tools, and the AIX Assembler.

X DEVELOPMENT ENVIRONMENT (XDE)

XDE provides an interactive multi-window application development environment that assists the developer to debug applications. XDE was developed using AIXwindows application development environment, based on OSF/Motif, and requires AIXwindows Environment/6000 to be installed for execution and use. XDE has the following capabilities:

- Individual windows for displaying information such as current program state, including stack traceback and accessible variables, source code, error messages, and help text.
- Ability to inspect the local environment of any function in the stack traceback. The local environment consists of the source code and variables accessible within the scope of the function.
- Structured objects (structs, unions, arrays, pointers) may be decomposed to reveal arbitrary levels of detail.
- Supports DBX symbolic debugger commands.
- Provides dynamic configuration of window visibility and layout, and user customization by assigning commands to keys and defining entries in a user-specific menu.

SOURCE CODE CONTROL SYSTEM (SCCS)

SCCS is a collection of programs that are designed to manage changes to controlled text files. It provides facilities for storing, updating, and retrieving any version of a controlled file, controls updating privileges to a file, and records who made each change, when it was made, and why it was made. SCCS assists software developers during the development, testing, and support of programs. SCCS provides commands to manipulate a repository of program files. It includes the following features:

- Stores only changes made to a file instead of unnecessarily duplicating storage of the entire changed file.
- Protects from unauthorized changes.
- Can automatically insert identifying information into source and object code modules.
- Restores files to a previous stage of development or maintenance.

SYSTEM BUILD FACILITIES (MAKE)

MAKE utilizes a set of pre-defined (and user customizable) rules and a user-defined MAKE description file to create target products. MAKE is primarily used for building up-to-date versions of programs though it can also be used for many other applications. MAKE can work with any compiler, assembler, or linker that uses a command line interface. When the target product is a program, the predefined rules will typically be language specific, and the description file will define how and when to build target programs. If a target product is changed, the MAKE command will build only those files of the target product affected by the change. MAKE can build programs from SCCS source files. Default rules are also provided for building C, FORTRAN, Pascal, Assembler, YACC, and many other files. A user can:

- Combine in a single file the instructions for creating a large program or other target product.
- Utilize macros and conditional constructs in the MAKE description file.
- Create libraries.
- Provide customized rules sets.
- Use single quotes in the MAKE description file to tell the MAKE command to interpret the quoted string literally.

SYMBOLIC DEBUGGER (DBX)

DBX is a multi-language debugger that is designed to provide the user with debugging commands that help simplify error. DBX provides the following functions:

- Support for XL C, AIX XL FORTRAN/6000, AIX VS COBOL/6000 and AIX XL Pascal/6000 languages.

- Supports source level debugging.
- Supports machine level debugging.
- Displays and modifies program variables.
- Controls the execution of the program.
- Allows access and display of the source file through an editor.
- Support for full signal handling.
- Allows setting of break and trace points with conditions.
- Allows multi-process debugging across FORK and EXEC.
- Allows attachment to and detachment from a running process.
- Provides a user tailorable environment.

APPLICATION DEVELOPMENT FACILITY TOOLS (ADF)

The ADF tools are a set of tools in the Base Application Development Toolkit that include a set of UNIX operating system commands and utilities primarily used in the software development process. These tools include:

- Program object module tools (dump, lorder, nm, ranlib, size, strip, and tsort)
- Programming utilities (asa, cb, cflow, cpp, cxref, fpr, fsplit, indent, lint, mkstr, regcmp, struct, unifdef, and xstr)
- Language utilities (bs, lex, sno, and yacc)

AIX ASSEMBLER

The AIX Assembler is provided for developers who need to generate the machine instructions directly.

Note: The Base Application Development Toolkit is part of AIX Version 3.

AIX Computer Graphics Interface Toolkit/6000

The AIX Computer Graphics Interface Toolkit/6000 provides tools for programmers or developers to help them create graphics software that remains independent of the graphic I/O devices supported. It provides a set of graphics device drivers for printers, plotters, and displays to provide device independence for programs. This device independence gives the software a greater portability and compatibility, and allows the end user a larger range of choice in the selection of supported graphics hardware. The AIX Computer Graphics Interface Toolkit/6000 also includes a set of graphics primitives that can be called by high level languages to perform functions such as displaying pie slices and drawing lines, polygons and circles.

The AIX Computer Graphics Interface Toolkit/6000 is the toolkit that provides a migration path for applications developed using the IBM RT System Graphics Development Toolkit. A number of basic and advanced functions are provided through the AIX Computer Graphics Interface Toolkit/6000 at both the device and program levels.

The CGI device drivers packaged with AIX Version 3 provide the execution support for hardcopy graphics on AIX graphics devices and screen output for the AIX Computer Graphics Interface Toolkit/6000 on the following device drivers:

- AIXwindows system driver
- Tektronix 4105 driver
- PostScript printer driver
- Proprinter data stream driver (9 wire resolution)
- Proprinter data stream driver (24 wire resolution)
- IBM 5202 Quietwriter III driver (Quietwriter data stream driver)
- HP LaserJet + driver
- IBM plotter devices driver (6180, 6182, 6184, 6186, 7372)
- Computer graphics metafile driver (binary record format)

This section is summarized in Table 3.1.

Table 3.1. Languages, toolkit and user interface summary

Name	Highlights
XL C Compiler	• Included in operating system • Produces optimized object code • Conforms to Draft ANSI C Standard, document number X3J11/88-159, dated December 1988, as interpreted by IBM on 9 June 1989 • Source code compatible, with some exceptions, with IBM RT PC C and IBM RT PC Advanced C Compiler • Implements the C interface of the Systems Application Architecture SAA CPI Level 2, with some exceptions, in the AIX environment • National Language Support, including single- and double-byte character sets

AIX XL FORTRAN Compiler/6000	• Produces optimized object code
	• Pointer support
	• Extended precision floating point
	• Option for promotion of floating-point items
	• I/O enhancements and BYTE data type
	• Optimizing preprocessor:
	  – Loop and expressions optimization
	  – Inline procedure expansion
	  – Library call generation
	  Additional features included in Version 2.2 are:
	  – Interprocedural analysis
	  – Assertions on run-time expectation
	  – Memory management
	  – Enhanced inlining features
	• Source code compatible, with some exceptions, with IBM

Continued

Table 3.1. Continued

Name	Highlights
	VS FORTRAN, IBM RT PC FORTRAN 77, IBM RT PC VS FORTRAN, and IBM AIX/RT XL FORTRAN • Implements the FORTRAN interface of the SAA CPI in the AIX RISC System/6000 environment • Conforms to ANSI X3.9-1978, ISO 1539-1980(E), and FIPS PUB 69 FORTRAN industry standards • National Language Support, including single- and double-byte character sets
AIX XL FORTRAN Run Time Environment/6000	• For XL FORTRAN applications that use dynamic binding • Contains the AIX XL FORTRAN Compiler Run Time Environment/6000 library of routines called at run-time • Provides run-time error messages • National Language Support, including single- and double-byte character sets
AIX APL2/6000	• Interactive interpretive language rather than a compiled language • Compatible with APL2 programs from PS/1 through ES/9000 with Vector Facilities • Includes AP144 interface to X Windows • Supported on all RISC System/6000 Models and Xstations • National Language Support, including single- and double-byte character sets
AIX Ada/6000	• Modern, higher-order language from a development sponsored by the US Department of Defense • Features modularization, separate compilation and data abstraction • A key application area is embedded systems programming • Important in application development for defence contractors and firms in the aerospace industry • Expanding into scientific and engineering applications and expected to be a significant factor in commercial applications • Scheduled for validation at Level 1.11 of the Ada Compiler Validation Capability (ACVC) test suite • Productivity enhanced by on-line hypertext documentation • Binding to the GL Graphics Support Library of AIX is provided
AIX XL Pascal Compiler/6000	• Produces optimized object code • Source code compatible, with some exceptions, with System/370 VS Pascal • Conforms to ANSI/IEEE-770X3.97-1983, ISO 7185-1983(0), and FIPS PUB 109—Pascal industry standards • National Language Support, including single- and double-byte character sets
AIX XL Pascal Run Time Environment/ 6000	• For XL Pascal applications that use dynamic binding • Contains the AIX XL Pascal Run Time Environment/6000 library of routines called at run-time • Provides run-time error messages

Continued

Table 3.1. Continued

Name	Highlights
AIX VS COBOL Compiler/6000	• National Language Support, including single- and double-byte character sets • Package includes a compiler, data screen entry utility, and debugger • Produces both native and intermediate code • Implements the COBOL interface of the SAA CPI in the AIX RISC System/6000 environment • Conforms to the following standards: 　– ANSI X3.23-1985, ISO 1989–1985 (High Level) 　– ANSI X3.23-1974 (High Level) 　– FIPS PUB 21-2—COBOL • National Language Support, including single- and double-byte character sets
AIX VS COBOL Run Time Environment/6000	• For systems running COBOL applications • Contains the IBM AIX VS COBOL Run Time Environment/6000 library of routines called at run-time • Contains run-time error message file • National Language Support, including single- and double-byte character sets
AIX Personal graPHIGS Programming Interface/6000 Version 2	• PHIGS PLUS functions 　– PHIGS PLUS extended graphics primitives 　– Extended graphics primitives 　– Image display 　– Advanced rendering capabilities 　– Direct colour specification 　– Graphical Kernel System (GKS)–compatibility option • RISC System/6000 Support 　– Support for RISC System/6000 Graphics Adapters 　– Complemented by IBM AIXwindows Environment/6000
Base Application Development Toolkit	• Included in operating system • Collection of common development tools consisting of XDE, AIX Assembler, source code control system (SCCS), system build facility, EMACS Editor, ADF tools, and symbolic debugger (DBX)
AIX Computer Graphics Interface Toolkit/6000	• Supports Computer Graphics Interface (CGI) • Provides ability to direct screen output to hard copy devices and capture the image in a revisable format data file (metafile) • AIXwindows support via Xlib • National Language Support, including single- and double-byte character sets
AIXwindows Environment/6000	• AIXwindows Graphical User Interface based on OSF/Motif • Desktop function for end users • Enhanced X Windows with Display PostScript support • Graphics Library support

3.2.5   Real-time capability

Real-time extensions

A real-time system is essentially one that can respond very quickly to specific events. Let me give an analogy that explains a real-time system. Imagine that I am in my garage washing the car and my wife runs out to me and tells me that the house is on fire. One option I have is to say, 'Fine—I'll just finish washing the car and then I'll come and get a hose to put out the fire'. Perhaps not the best option. Better of course if I just dropped what I was doing and rushed into the house to deal with the fire. This ability to 'drop what you are currently doing' and do something else is what a real-time system provides. This is provided in AIX by a kernel that can be interrupted by other processes —this is a pre-emptible kernel. This makes the RS/6000 capable of controlling other systems in real time of course. But in addition, this kind of function can be used to provide excellent response times when using normal commercial applications. Response times are an important part of a real-time system. Many of the improvements incorporated into AIX Version 3 also improve interactive response.

- *Pre-emptible scheduler*: AIX V3's scheduler interrupts the executing process if a higher priority process needs the CPU.
- *Pre-emptible kernel*: The UNIX kernel was originally designed to be simple and small. It has gradually become more sophisticated and larger. Most operating systems based on UNIX will not respond to a real-time requirement while executing kernel code—AIX V3 will. Its kernel is pre-emptible. This ability to interrupt kernel routines also allows longer running routines to be placed in the AIX V3's kernel to improve efficiency. In more primitive implementations that require the entire kernel to be resident in real memory, this could be expensive. But the AIX V3 kernel is pageable so this problem does not exist.
- *Memory pinning*: If a real-time process is infrequently used, the operating system might page it out to disk. Subsequent use would then require waiting for the code to be paged back in. AIX V3 allows pages to be pinned (sometimes called locked) in real memory in order to control the inconsistent response time that might otherwise occur.
- *Optional fixed priorities*: AIX V3 and most other UNIX systems automatically modify process priorities in order to increase overall system responsiveness. This can pose a problem for some real-time processes. AIX V3 provides some priorities that are immune from scheduler modification. This allows a real-time process that requires substantial CPU time to run

at a predictable fixed priority.

- *Multiple interrupt priorities*: AIX V3 provides a large number of priorities for interrupts. Higher priority interrupt handlers can pre-empt lower priority ones. This allows very time-critical processes to be serviced more quickly.

- *Off-level interrupt handling*: Many interrupt handling functions contain some code which must respond as quickly as possible and other code segments which are less critical. AIX V3 provides a facility to schedule the less critical code at an off-level (i.e. lower priority). This can improve responsiveness for high priority events.

3.2.6   DOS PCs and programs

DOS Affinity

The PC DOS affinity in the AIX operating system provides users with a productive, functional environment in using existing DOS applications, sharing data between AIX and DOS programs, letting DOS programs use the high disk capacity and printer selection of the RS/6000, and letting multiple DOS users access the same data. These functions are delivered in three products: the DOS Server (which works in conjunction with the AIX Access for DOS Users), X Windows for DOS, and the PC Simulator.

DOS Server

DOS Server (a standard feature of AIX Version 3) provides AIX and DOS affinity. DOS Server allows DOS Version 3.3 users and applications running on an attached IBM PC or PS/2 to access an AIX file system. DOS users can also utilize AIX supported printers. Users on the attached PC or PS/2 can execute AIX programs and applications on the AIX host. Emulation of an asynchronous terminal from the DOS-based machine is also supported. DOS Server supports the use of Ethernet, Token Ring, or asynchronous connections. DOS Server runs on the RS/6000 and this works in conjunction with a product running on the DOS machine—this is called AADU (AIX Access for DOS Users).

AIX Access for DOS Users (AADU)

AADU runs on a PC or PS/2 that is attached to the RS/6000. This connection can be a LAN connection or an asynchronous connection. AADU works in conjunction with the DOS Server software on the RS/6000 and gives the DOS user functions such as:

- Ability to log in to the RS/6000 and run AIX applications
- Utilize RS/6000 printers
- Virtual DOS drives on the RS/6000
- File transfer between the systems
- DOS to AIX file conversion and vice versa

X Windows for IBM DOS

Also available for the DOS user is a high function windowing tool. X Windows for DOS allows the DOS user to view multiple X Window applications anywhere on a Local Area Network from a single display via multiple windows. A user who primarily runs DOS programs on a PC, but periodically needs to get to RS/6000 applications will use X Windows for DOS to accomplish this connectivity. This runs over TCP/IP on the LAN. The TCP/IP software is included as part of the X Windows product. This is very similar in principle to the way in which an X station works—the application runs on the RS/6000 but the windowing is performed locally.

PC Simulator

DOS programs can also be run on the RS/6000. AIX Personal Computer Simulator/6000 is designed to support many IBM Disk Operating System (DOS) Version 3.3 applications running without modification on the RS/6000. Multiple, concurrent DOS applications may run either in multiple AIXwindows or multiple shells for a single user or on multiple terminals for multiple users.

The real-mode Intel 80286 processor is simulated along with the standard IBM Personal Computer AT devices including controller chips, disk, diskette, printer and keyboard. The Video Graphics Adapter (VGA) is simulated on AIXwindows. The Monochrome Display Adapter is simulated on virtual terminals (HFT/High Function Terminal), on AIXwindows (xterm), and ASCII terminals.

Mouse support is provided on AIXwindows through the Microsoft Mouse Application Interface (API) only. Microsoft Mouse API calls are intercepted and mapped to the appropriate AIXwindows mouse calls.

Extended memory (i.e. memory above the 1 MB range) will be supported through the architected BIOS INT 15H extended memory interface only.

Direct access to extended memory (switching to protect mode) is not supported.

The PC Simulator product will run on all RS/6000s and was designed to support all the RS/6000 displays.

NetWare

IBM announced a NetWare product for the RS/6000 in January 1992. NetWare for AIX/6000 v3.11 allows RS/6000 workstations to act as servers for NetWare LANs. Based on Novell's NetWare for UNIX v3.11 (formerly known as Portable NetWare), NetWare for AIX/6000 brings the resources and applications of the full function, multi-purpose AIX operating system to PC LAN users. It provides file and print sharing among DOS, Windows 3.x, and OS/2 NetWare clients, and AIX users, as well as network connectivity. NetWare for AIX/6000 combines the function of NetWare LAN server with the RISC System/6000 hardware and UNIX operating system.

Highlights
- Integrates RS/6000 into existing NetWare personal computer LANs.
- Transparent to existing NetWare clients.
- Preserves existing PC desktop environment while adding access to AIX/6000.
- Common file and print resources shared by personal computer and AIX/6000 environments.
- Open AIX/6000 server.
- Support for IPX/SPX protocols in AIX/6000.
- Personal Computer access to AIX/6000 applications via Novell Virtual Terminal.
- DOS or OS/2 are supported as personal computer NetWare clients.

NetWare for AIX/6000 brings the most commonly installed PC network operating system (NOS) to the RS/6000. The result is that the user will see familiar services but with the power and capability of the RS/6000 with its wide variety of extensive processing power, large memory capacity, and wide range of peripherals. These features will bring growth to PC networks which was previously not possible.

Third party products

There are a number of other products available that will provide further integration between PCs or PS/2s and the RS/6000. For example, there is a product that will provide windowed access to the RS/6000 from a PC running Microsoft Windows (Windows/3). This enables Microsoft windows and X Windows applications to be shown on the PC screen concurrently.

Most communications with the RS/6000 involve TCP/IP. One of a number of TCP/IP products available for the PC will often need to be used.

There are products available on the PC to support Network File System (NFS). This is standard on the RS/6000. This allows data to be shared between machines. NFS allows filesystems or directories to be exported or imported for specified users. NFS runs over TCP/IP communications.

3.2.7   Security

Computer system security addresses privacy, integrity and availability issues. A range of functions that address data integrity and controlled access have been incorporated into the RISC System/6000 and its AIX Version 3 operating system.

AIX security features

AIX Version 3 Trusted Computing Base (TCB) security features have been designed to meet the National Computer Security Center (NCSC) Trusted Computer System Evaluation Criteria (TCSEC) Class C2 requirement.

AIX Version 3 incorporates the common security features found in most UNIX systems today. These include login passwords at the user and group level. It also provides file security for read, write, and execute authority at the user and group level, and limits certain system management functions to specific system group level authority.

Within the AIX operating system, security emphasizes a complete system architecture, rather than a broad view of isolated components. The TCSEC guidelines implemented address four major sets of criteria: security policy, accountability, assurance and documentation. In addition, conformance and compliance is provided for certain trusted and secure system standards and specifications, including IEEE POSIX and the X/Open Portability Guide.

Three security policies are defined within AIX: access control, accountability, and administration. Access control policies look at how information resources are created and distributed. Accountability policies address how users are identified on the system and for what actions they are accountable. Administration policies address issues pertaining to administrative users on the system. The following paragraphs further describe these policies.

Access control

Access control policies describe how information flow may be controlled. Many UNIX operating systems use a discretionary access control (DAC) mechanism based on three subjects (user, group, and others) with three possible access rights (read, write, and execute). Access control within AIX uses an abstract data type, to provide extended granularity and to insulate the user from the discretionary access control mechanism.

IBM provides Access Control Lists (ACLs) that extend the normal security of files through permissions. The usual file permissions in UNIX can be restrictive under some circumstances. The limitations of these permissions are extended using ACLs.

Accountability

The goal of an accountability policy is to establish individual responsibility for actions performed in the system.

IDENTIFICATION AND AUTHENTICATION

The AIX identification and authentification component provides configurable authentication modes and methods in order to ensure proper identification of the users of the system. The security of the authentication information storage has been enhanced to provide for greater trust.

USER AUDITING

The auditing subsystem allows the system administrator to specify the security related events to be recorded for each user in the system audit trail. The audit trail can be analysed to detect potential and actual security violations in the system.

TRUSTED COMMUNICATION PATH

The Trusted Communication Path allows a local user to communicate securely with the Trusted Computing Base, to help ensure the integrity and confidentiality of exchanges of security information.

Administration

The AIX administration mechanism allows for separation of different administrative roles.

TRUSTED SYSTEM ADMINISTRATION

Trusted System Administration includes the ability to define and verify the secure system status.

TRUSTED SYSTEM CONFIGURATION AND AUDITING
Procedures are defined to install and configure the system securely. Functions are provided to define the secure status of the system and periodically audit the system according to this status.

STATEMENT OF DIRECTION
IBM intends to provide functions designed to meet the mandatory access control policies defined by the current criteria for B1 level systems, and submit these to the National Computer Security Center for B level evaluation.

RS/6000 HARDWARE SECURITY FUNCTIONS
Hardware functions include a keylock to the RISC System/6000 hardware and removable disk files for additional security, where required.

3.3   AIX communications capabilities

The RS/6000 has a combination of hardware features and software offerings available for communications. These offerings provide methods for connecting to the following systems and devices:

- Other IBM and non-IBM systems
- Other IBM RISC System/6000 systems
- IBM RT System
- IBM Personal System/2
- IBM Personal Computers (IBM Personal Computer, PC XT, and PC AT)
- IBM Application System/400
- IBM System/370 and System/390
- IBM Xstation 120 and 130
- ASCII devices

Any kind of communication involves various aspects. Typically layers define different parts of the communications. Figure 3.3 shows these layers and some of the options available at each level. Simplifying matters, there are two questions that need to be asked when communicating between two systems:

- How do the two systems physically attach (e.g. Token Ring, Ethernet, X.25, coaxial connection)?
- What protocols (software) will be used to communicate (e.g. TCP/IP, SNA, DECNET)?

3.3.1   Communication methods

The RISC System/6000 series can communicate as a workstation, as a peer system, or as a host system, depending on the requirements of the connecting

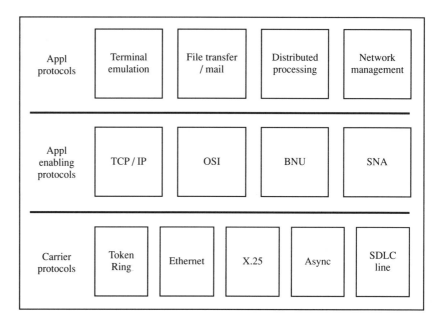

Figure 3.3. Layers of communication protocols.

system and the chosen communication method. The RS/6000 can use the following types of connections to communicate with other systems:

- Ethernet Version 2 Local Area Network (LAN)
- IEEE 802.3 LAN
- IBM Token-Ring LAN (IEEE 802.5)
- X.25 Wide Area Network (WAN)
- Synchronous data link control (SDLC) WAN
- Control unit terminal (CUT) coaxial connection
- Distributed function terminal (DFT) coaxial connection
- 5088 control unit coaxial connection
- Asynchronous connection

The types of connections can be grouped into four categories:

- *Local Area Network (LAN)*
- *Wide Area Network (WAN)*
- *Direct Attach Coaxial*
- *Asynchronous Connection*

Each of these will be discussed separately. There are many options for communications, both using IBM products and non-IBM products. Clearly not all of them can be discussed in this book. Communications is a wide-ranging subject, but it is hoped that you will get an understanding of the kinds of things that are possible. Figure 3.4 shows in outline a demonstration network that was set up in the UK for customers to see. Again, it shows the wide range of communications options available.

3.3.2 Local Area Network

Hardware support for LANs

- Ethernet and IEEE 802.3 connections allow the RS/6000 to participate in a 10 M bps CSMA/CD network. The Ethernet High-Performance LAN Adapter is a high performance adapter, supporting attachment to the standard 50-ohm (thick) coaxial cable or the standard RG-58A/U (thin) coaxial cable.
- IBM Token-Ring connections allow the RS/6000 to participate in a LAN adhering to the IEEE 802.5 Token-Passing Ring standard or the ECMA standard 89 for token-ring baseband local area networks. The Token-Ring High-Performance Network Adapter is a high performance adapter, supporting communication on a token-ring LAN at data rates of 4 M bps or 16 M bps. All adapters on the LAN must be running at the same speed.

Software support for LANs

- The Transmission Control Protocol/Internet Protocol (TCP/IP) communications protocols support several end-user communication programs. Through these programs, users can perform such communications tasks as sending, receiving, and processing mail, logging in to connected systems, transferring files to and from connected systems, and running commands on connected systems. Programs which are included with AIX Version 3 that use TCP/IP protocols to communicate on a LAN are:
  – Network File System (NFS)
  – Standard TCP/IP application functions
  – Basic Network Utilities (BNU)
  – Mail facilities
  – Network Computing System (NCS)
- AIXwindows Environment/6000 interface allows users to interact with connected systems through the familiar windowing environment of OSF/ Motif.
- The SNA Services/6000 licensed program supports communication on a LAN through the Advanced Program-to-Program Communication

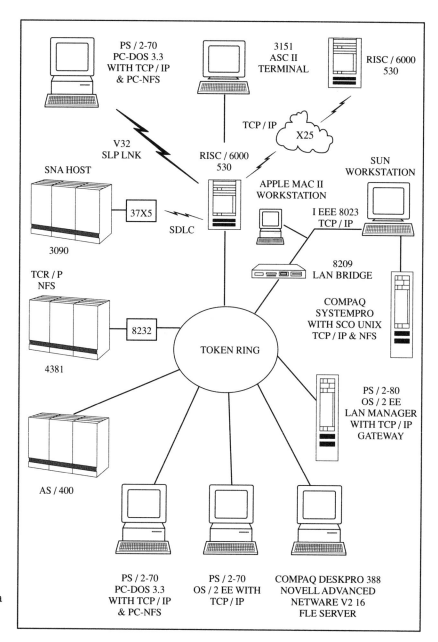

Figure 3.4. Example of a
network recently
demonstrated by IBM.

(APPC) interface for LU6.2. Application developers can write programs that use SNA LU6.2 to communicate with other systems. When the RS/6000 communicates with other systems through SNA LU6.2, the RS/6000 functions as a peer SNA node.

- The AIX Personal Computer Simulator/6000 is designed to support many IBM DOS Version 3.3 applications running without modification on the RS/6000. Multiple, concurrent DOS applications may run either in multiple AIXwindows or multiple shells for a single user or on multiple terminals for multiple users.

3.3.3 Wide Area Network (WAN)

X.25 hardware and software

- The X.25 Interface Co-Processor/2 supports communication on the X.25 WAN through any of the following selectable interfaces: X.21, EIA-232/ V.24, or V.35. The maximum supported line speed for data interchange depends on the type of physical connection: 19.2 K bps for EIA-232D/ V.24 or 64 K bps for X.21 connection or V.35 connection.
- The TCP/IP communications protocols support several end-user communication programs. Through these programs, users can perform such communications tasks as sending, receiving, and processing mail, logging in to connected systems, transferring files to and from connected systems, and running commands on connected systems. Programs which are a part of the AIX operating system on the RS/6000 that use TCP/IP protocols to communicate on an X.25 WAN are:
  – Standard TCP/IP application functions
  – Basic Network Utilities (BNU)
  – Mail facilities
- The AIXwindows Environment/6000 interface allows users to interact with connected systems through a familiar windowing environment.
- The SNA Services/6000 product supports communication on an X.25 WAN through the Advanced Program-to-Program Communication (APPC) interface for LU6.2.
- The X.25 API (part of AIX Version 3) can be used by the X.25 application programs in the AIX operating system.

SDLC WAN

The SDLC WAN connection allows the RS/6000 to participate in a wide area network for managing synchronous half-duplex, code-transparent, serial-by-bit information transfer over a link connection.

• The IBM SNA Services licensed program and various AIX Version 3 APls provide the software base for IBM's SDLC support on the RS/6000. Through the APPC interface, applications can be written that use LU6.2 to communicate with other systems.
• The IBM Multiprotocol Adapter supports communication on an SDLC WAN through any of the following selectable interfaces: X.21, EIA-232/ V.24, EIA-422A, or V.35. Telephone auto-dial functions are also supported for Hayes Smartmodem operation over the EIA-232D and CCITT V.25 bis interfaces.

3.3.4   Direct attach (coaxial)

Hardware support for direct connection

• The IBM 3270 Connection Adapter supports communication through a CUT coaxial connection to the following devices:
  – IBM 3174 Establishment Controller
  – IBM 3274 Control Unit
  – IBM 4361 Display/Printer Adapter or Work Station Adapter
• The IBM 3270 Connection Adapter supports communication through an SNA or non-SNA DFT coaxial connection to the following devices:
  – IBM 3174 Establishment Controller
  – IBM 3274 Control Unit
  – IBM 9370 Work Station Subsystem Controller
• The IBM System/370 and System/390 Host Interface Adapter supports the connection of the RS/6000 to a System/370 and System/390 by way of the IBM 5088 Control Unit.

Software support for direct connection

• The IBM AIX 3278/79 Emulation/6000 licensed program provides the software base for IBM's CUT connection support on the RS/6000.
• The AIX Host Connection Program/6000 licensed program provides the software base for SNA and non-SNA DFT connection support on the RS/6000. The Host Connection Program supports file transfer, multiple

3278 and 3279 emulation sessions, and 3287 printer emulation.

• AIX Network Management/6000 supports remote login from a System/
370 or System/390 host via the Host Command Facility (HCF). In
addition, files can be received from the host and relayed to other LAN
attached nodes. These tasks are accomplished through the interaction of
AIX Network Management/6000 on the RS/6000 and NetView Distribution Manager on the S/370 or S/390 host. AIX Network Management/
6000 also provides an alert agent for sending Network Management
Vector Transport (NMVT) alerts to NetView via an SSCP to PU session
under System Network Architecture.

3.3.5 *Asynchronous connection*

The asynchronous connection allows the RS/6000 to connect to other
systems through three types of physical connections. The maximum
supported line speed for data interchange from the RS/6000 over an asynchronous connection is 38.4 K bps.

Hardware support for asynchronous connection

• The following ports and adapters support asynchronous communication:
  – Two standard EIA-232D ports in each RS/6000.
  – Three IBM 8-Port Adapters, available in either EIA-232D/V.24, EIA-
    422A, or MIL-STD 188 configurations. Used with the IBM 8-Port RS-
    232/RS-422/MIL-STD 188 Cable Assembly.
  – Two IBM 16-Port Adapters, available in EIA-232 or EIA-422A con-
    figurations. Used with the IBM 8-Port RS-232/RS-422/MIL-STD 188
    Cable Assembly.
  – IBM 64-Port RS-232 Asynchronous Controller with the IBM 16-Port
    RS-232 Asynchronous Concentrator.

Software support for asynchronous connection

The following RS/6000 software (included with the AIX operating system)
provides the software base for IBM's asynchronous support on the RS/6000.

• TCP/IP suite of communications protocols
• BNU
• Asynchronous Terminal Emulation (ATE)
• DOS Server program
• Various AIX/6000 V3 APIs

- BNU can also be used independently of TCP/IP to allow users to log in to connected systems, transfer files between systems, and execute commands and queue jobs at remote systems.
- ATE provides an alternative application program for asynchronous communications. ATE allows users to log in to connected systems. The user's display emulates an ASCII terminal.
- The DOS Server program allows a user at an IBM Personal System/2 or an IBM Personal Computer to use the RS/6000 as a file or print server, and to execute AIX commands on the RS/6000 server.

3.4   Communications software products

There is a wide variety of software products from IBM to support communications. Some of these products are described here.

AIX System Network Architecture Services/6000

AIX System Network Architecture Services/6000 communication software supports IBM System Network Architecture (SNA). The product is designed to provide end-user configuration functions and an application program interface that permits user-provided applications to communicate with other applications residing on other IBM systems using IBM's SNA as the communication protocol. The following support is provided:

- Logical Unit (LU) types:
  - LU0 for FM and TS profiles 3 and 4 over SDLC networks for customer defined session support
  - LU 1, 2, and 3 over SDLC networks and X.25 networks and Token-Ring LANs for IBM System/370 and System/390 host communications support
  - LU6.2 over SDLC networks, Ethernet Version 2, IEEE 802.3, and Token-Ring LANs, and X.25 networks for peer to peer communications support
- Application Program Interfaces (APIs) for above LU types
- User interfaces to aid in network configuration and security
- API to provide SSCP-PU sessions for transmission of network management alerts
- Physical Unit type 2.1
- Incorporates an LU0 API that supports operation of an RS/6000 system as an intermediate controller between an IBM System/370 or System/390

host executing the Advanced Data Communication for Stores (ADCS) Licensed Program and an IBM 4680 point-of-sale controller

AIX Network File System/6000 (NFS)

The NFS facilities of AIX Version 3 provide support for ONC/NFS Version 4.0 developed by Sun Microsystems, Inc. NFS allows data to be accessed from attached systems running NFS over either an Ethernet Version 2 and IEEE 802.3, or IBM Token-Ring Internet Protocol LANs. NFS support allows the sharing of data between IBM RS/6000 systems, IBM AIX RT systems, IBM AIX PS/2 systems, IBM AIX/370 systems, IBM VM, MVS and OS/2EE systems, as well as many other vendors' systems supporting NFS. NFS support provides the following functions:

- NFS server and client functions allow access to remote files. As a server, other systems can access RS/6000 system files; as a client, the RS/6000 system uses the files of other systems.
- Network Information Services (NIS) (formerly referred to as Yellow Pages), provides a distributed database look-up facility that assists in the administration of large NFS networks. NIS support simplifies the administration task by providing a central database for user id, host id, and other network resource information.
- Network Lock Manager provides advisory file and record level locking for files accessed using NFS.
- Automounter support allows the automatic mounting and unmounting of NFS file systems.
- Diskless support allows Sun 3 and Sun 4 diskless workstations running SunOS 4.0 to boot from IBM RS/6000 servers over Ethernet.
- Network services provides remote execution and remote statistics support.
- User authentication for NFS is provided via secure RPC's use of functions utilizing Data Encryption Standard (DES) authentication. The AIX NFS Encryption Feature/6000, which provides a general purpose encryption capability, implements the DES standard and requires a special export licence for shipment outside of the US. In the US it is available for general use.
- RPC API (Remote Procedure Call Application Programming Interface) provides a set of program accessible library routines that provide for transparent execution of procedures on remote systems. Application programmers can use this interface to write programs employing RPC technology.

- XDR (External Data Representation) library routines provide a portable definition of data items that can flow between systems on the LAN. XDR defines the size, byte order, and alignment of the data types. The XDR data definitions are presented to the application programmer as an API that can be used for designing LAN based application that can communicate across systems of various hardware and software architectures.
- RPCGEN (RPC Generator) protocol compiler aids programmers with the development of RPC based applications.
- Support for systems running PC-NFS allowing the PC user to obtain NFS identification from RS/6000 servers. This provides the PC user with file access permission to NFS mounted files.

The following additional functions have been included with the NFS support provided for the RS/6000:

- Granular access and privilege controls as supported in the security enhancements to AIX Version 3.
- Remote Mapped file support which allows the RS/6000 NFS client to take advantage of the enhanced virtual memory management function of AIX Version 3. This support allows the remote file to be mapped into virtual memory, thereby presenting the end-user or application with high performance access to the remote programs and data.
- Kernel extension support allows users to install and uninstall NFS without rebuilding the base AIX kernel.
- SMIT (System Management Interface Tool) support designed to provide an easy to use menu/dialogue user interface for NFS configuration and management.
- SRC (System Resource Control) support designed to provide an easy to use and consistent way to start and stop the NFS demons.

AIX 3270 Host Connection Program/6000

The IBM AIX 3270 Host Connection Program/6000 emulates a subset of the IBM 3270 functions and features. It allows an end-user on an RS/6000 to connect to an IBM System/370 or System/390 host and appear to the host as an attached IBM 3270 Display or Printer. It also provides file transfer between the workstation and the IBM System/370 or System/390 host, printer emulation, and an application programming interface permitting a user provided workstation application to communicate with a host application or with the IBM 3270 session. This support is provided through both

System Network Architecture (SNA) and non-SNA connections. Features included in the AIX 3270 Host Connection Program/6000 are:

- IBM 3278/79 display emulation support on the high function terminal (HFT) and ASCII terminals including the IBM 3151, IBM 3161, IBM 3162, IBM 3163, DEC VT100, DEC VT220, WYSE WY-50 and WYSE WY-60. Multiple host sessions are supported within a single AIX terminal or across multiple virtual terminals on the HFT.
- Support for IBM 3278/79 Models 2, 3, 4 and 5. Models, 3, 4 and 5 are only available on HFT displays. Model 5 is available on some ASCII and all HFT displays.
- IBM 3286/87 printer emulation support on most of the printers that are supported by RS/6000.
- Distributed function terminal (DFT) connection support via the RS/6000 3270 Connection Adapter. Each model of the RS/6000 can support up to four adapters, and each adapter can have up to five active sessions for the following interfaces:
  - IBM 3174 or 3274 control unit
  - IBM 4361 Workstation Adapter
  - IBM 9370 Workstation Subsystem Controller
- Support for up to 16 sessions by connecting to the IBM 5088 Graphic Channel Control Unit unit via the System/370 Host Interface Adapter.
- A single user can have more than one active session (up to a maximum of 26 per user). The total number of user sessions cannot exceed the number of sessions available through the hardware interface connections.
- Extended data stream includes support for seven colours plus either reverse video, underlining, or blink. The actual attributes displayed depend on the capabilities of the display.
- File transfer:
  - Supports queued or immediate file transfer requests
  - C, FORTRAN and Pascal programming interface to file transfer
- Application Program Interface:
  - Workstation application to host application communication
  - Workstation application control of emulation session
  - C, FORTRAN and Pascal
- Automatic logon and logoff function for file transfer or for a properly written user API application.
- Supports multiple IBM Hosts concurrently.
- A user can interact with the AIX 3270 Host Connection Program/6000 on either a local or remote X-server or remotely via TCP/IP, telnet or remote

login. When running remotely, the user must be aware that Host Connection functions are executed on the 'connected to' system. The display emulation functions will still be viewed where the user is running, but other Host Connection functions will run and affect files (via file transfer) and facilities (e.g. printers) on the 'connected to' system rather than the local system where the user is viewing the emulation.

- Support for Type 2.1 Node connections via AIX SNA Services/6000 using any of the following adapters:
  - IBM 4-port Multiprotocol Communications Controller
  - IBM Token-Ring High-Performance Network Adapter
  - IBM X.25 Interface Coprocessor/2 Adapter
- Utility session support where all the frequently used supported utilities are centralized. It includes:
  - colour redefinition
  - keyboard redefinition
  - session logon and logoff support
  - file transfer support
  - generation of session logon/logoff scripts.

AIX 3278/79 Emulation/6000

This emulation package provides the RS/6000 with an alternative direct attachment to an IBM host as an IBM 3270 terminal connected to a host control unit. This emulates a subset of IBM 3270 functions and features and provides file transfer to and from System/370 and System/390 host environments. Support is provided for the IBM 3278 Model 2 and 3279 Models 2A and S2A. The IBM RISC System/6000 3270 Connection Adapter (CUT mode) is required.

- Standard 3270 emulation functions:
  - View/edit/update host files
  - Query host data base
  - Invoke host applications
- Screen print and save functions.
- Keyboard layout definition, display colour and mode customization.
- The ability to switch back and forth from the emulator to an AIX virtual terminal.
- EBCDIC to/from RS/6000 ASCII conversion during file transfer. Part of the conversion is done in the control unit interface.
- Supports a single System/370 or System/390 host session.

A user at an HFT display can interact with AIX 3278/79 Emulation/6000 on either a local or remote X-server. When running remotely, some functions are executed on the system that is connected to the System/370 or System/390 host. The display emulation functions will be viewed where the user is running, but other functions (e.g. file transfer) will run and affect system facilities on the host connected system. The host connected system will only support a single System/370 or System/390 host session; that is, a single X-server user.

AIX OSI Messaging and Filing/6000

AIX Open Systems Interconnection Messaging and Filing/6000 (AIX OSIMF/6000) is a program offering which provides electronic mail (MHS) and file transfer (FTAM) services for RS/6000 users. These services support the Open System Interconnection (OSI) standards specified by the International Organization for Standardization (ISO). AIX OSIMF/6000 allows AIX Version 3 to communicate with other OSI systems through OSI connections over ISO 8802/3 CSMA/CD, ISO 8802/5 Token Ring or X.25 networks. AIX OSIMF/6000 operating with AIX, also provides bidirectional application gateways to the mail (SMTP) and filing (FTP) services of the Transmission Control Protocol/Internet Protocol (TCP/IP) program which may coexist on the same RS/6000. AIX OSIMF/6000 and TCP/IP applications may operate concurrently and share the RS/6000 communication adapters. AIX OSIMF/6000 meets the requirements of US GOSIP Version 1 which became mandatory for US federal government procurements in August 1990.

AIX Version 3 TCP/IP

TCP/IP is provided as a standard part of the AIX Version 3 operating system. TCP/IP allows the RS/6000 to communicate with many other computer systems. TCP/IP is supported by most major computer manufacturers and suppliers.

AIX AS/400 Connection Program/6000

AIX AS/400 Connection Program/6000 allows an RS/6000 user to communicate with an AS/400 system. Operating under SNA or TCP/IP, it provides access to applications and data residing on the AS/400 system from the RS/6000. The RS/6000 may be attached to the AS/400 via a Token Ring network, an Ethernet LAN or synchronous data link control (SDLC). Under

SNA, 5250 emulation, file transfer and remote commands are supported. Under TCP/IP, only 5250 emulation is supported. With AS/400 TCP/IP Release 3.0, RS/6000 terminals can emulate 5250 terminals with full functionality.

AIX Viaduct for MVS

The AIX Viaduct for MVS (MVS Viaduct) is an interactive data bridge that enables RS/6000 customers to integrate AIX applications with DATABASE 2 (DB2) data bases. This bridge allows AIX RS/6000 application users to access information resident on the MVS system.

The AIX Viaduct for MVS provides interoperability between AIX and SAA environments. The AIX Viaduct for MVS provides an SQL pathway from AIX to the MVS operating environment. Customers can remain with an IBM mainframe system strategy and incorporate an RS/6000 application into their environment.

AIX Viaduct for MVS communicates via dynamic SQL with DB2, the Systems Application Architecture (SAA) database for MVS. AIX Viaduct for MVS does not conform to nor support the SAA Common Programming Interface–Database (CPD–DB). Therefore, Viaduct should not be viewed as an IBM SAA distributed relational database family product, but as a solution for enabling an AIX workstation to remotely access DB2 data.

Customers or vendors who plan to write AIX applications using the Viaduct application programming interface (API), and have dynamic SQL (or static SQL) SAA or AIX distributed database application requirements, will be able to migrate their Viaduct applications to the IBM SAA and AIX relational database products that support the SAA CPI–DB.

The MVS Viaduct enhances the AIX application programmer's productivity by providing an easy-to-use API. The API accesses the Viaduct's functions through subroutine calls. These subroutine calls are interpreted and use the systems network architecture (SNA) LU6.2 APPC protocol to transfer an SQL request to the MVS DB2 database.

The MVS Viaduct can be customized either to wait for the MVS/DB2 request to complete (synchronous mode) or return to the application immediately, and subsequently notify the application when the request completes (asynchronous mode). The workstation feature provides the necessary link from the RT or the RISC System/6000 to the MVS host. This link will enable the RT or the RISC System/6000 to access the database information via SNA LU6.2 protocol.

The MVS Viaduct consists of two separate components:

- Server software installed on the MVS machine
- Client software installed on the AIX machine

The two components communicate through either an IBM Token-Ring or SDLC network. If the communications link becomes inactive, each of these processes will automatically shut down to avoid leaving any open processes in either system. Error and/or information messages will be written in job logs.

Default data conversion rules are provided to support the different data types of the AIX and MVS systems. A user can change these defaults or prevent the conversions from taking place through an MVS Viaduct subroutine call. The MVS Viaduct utilizes CICS as a window into the DB2 database.

AIX Viaduct for AS/400

There is a Viaduct product to enable the RS/6000 and the AS/400 to communicate in the same way as the MVS Viaduct product described above. See Table 3.2 for a summary of this section.

Table 3.2. Connectivity programs summary

Name	Highlights
AIX Systems Network Architecture Services/6000	<ul><li>Provides various SNA connection services for user-provided applications</li><li>Supports Logical Unit (LU) types: – LU0 for FM and TS profiles 3 and 4 over SDLC networks for customer defined session support – LU 1, 2, and 3 over SDLC networks and Token-Ring LANs for IBM System/370 host communications support – LU6.2 over SDLC networks, Ethernet II, IEEE 802.3, and Token-Ring LANs, and X.25 networks for peer to peer communications support.</li><li>Provides application program interface for above LU types</li><li>Includes user interfaces to aid in network configuration and security</li><li>Supports an API to provide SSCP-PU sessions for transmission of network management alerts</li><li>Supports Physical Unit type 2.1</li></ul>
Network File System	<ul><li>Support for ONC/NFS Version 4.0 is included in AIX Version 3. NFS allows data sharing between IBM and non-IBM systems.</li><li>Remote Procedure Call API provides for transparent execution of procedures on remote systems</li><li>Network Information Services (Yellow Pages) provides a distributed database look-up facility</li><li>Supports record level locking *Continued*</li></ul>

Table 3.2. Continued

Name	Highlights
AIX 3270 Host Connection Program/6000	• Permits an end-user or a user-provided application to establish an SNA or non-SNA Distributed Function Terminal (DFT) connection with an IBM System/370 or System/390 host • IBM 3278/79 display emulation support on the high function terminal (HFT) and ASCII terminals and IBM 3286/3287 printer emulation • File transfer between workstation and System/370 and System/390 hosts • Multiple host session support within a single AIX terminal • API support in C, FORTRAN, and Pascal for file transfer and workstation applications
AIX 3278/79 Emulation/6000	• Provides terminal emulation and file transfer in CUT mode
AIX OSI Messaging and Filing/6000	• Provides OSI electronic mail (MHS) and file transfer services (FTAM) • Allows AIX to communicate with other OSI systems • With AIX Version 3 provides bidirectional gateways to the mail and filing services of TCP/IP
AIX Version 3 TCP/ IP	• Included in AIX operating system • Based on Tahoe version of 4.3 BSD • Provides connectivity to IBM and non-IBM systems over LANs, WANs and asynchronous networks
AIX AS/400 Connection Program/6000	• Provides access to data and applications residing on an AS/400 from an RS/6000 • Under TCP/IP or SNA, 5250 emulation is provided for the RS/6000 • Under SNA, file transfer and remote command function are also supported

3.5   Network management

Network management is a wide-ranging area. It involves a number of different functions including remote login to systems and collecting alerts from systems which are then collected centrally.

In the case of a large network of RS/6000s remote login can be provided as long as the network is configured correctly. This may be achieved by using telnet over a TCP/IP network, or Host Command Facility over an SNA network. In addition, there are third parties that can provide software to support full screen support from a 3270 screen.

In terms of network alerts, again there are a number of options. TCP/IP supports SNMP (Simple Network Management Protocol) and this is supported on the RS/6000. There are also products such as Network Management/6000, AIX Netview Service Point, and Netview/6000. These will provide integration with an SNA network that uses Netview on an IBM mainframe for network management. These products are described below.

AIX Network Management/6000

For an SNA network, AIX Network Management/6000 provides the following support for a S/370 NetView host. AIX can send generic alerts to the host, receive remote login from the host via the Host Command Facility (HCF), and send/receive files to/from the host via the NetView Distribution Manager (NetView DM) or the Distributed Systems Executive (DSX) for VSE environments only.

Generic alert support allows the host NetView program to receive generic alerts from AIX systems as NMVTs (Network Management Vector Transport) through an SNA SSCP-PU session. AIX Network Management/6000 also provides manager support for Simple Network Management Protocol (SNMP) for TCP/IP networks. SNMP is an emerging industry standard for managing TCP/IP networks. SNMP provides the capability of get, set, and trap and a Management Information Base (MIB) for a TCP/IP environment. TCP/IP hosts that support SNMP may provide either or both the functions of an SNMP agent or SNMP manager. The SNMP manager is able to respond to agent generated traps and to send get and limited set requests to the agents.

The following services are provided for SNA networks:

- Generate and send generic alerts to an S/370 NetView host
  - Log and report data link control alerts from communication adapters in generic alert format as defined by the SNA Management Services architecture
  - Alert log for later analysis
  - Dynamic alert reporting
  - Held alert generation
  - Allow an AIX system to send generic alerts to a NetView host in NMVT format through SNA SSCP-PU session
  - Allow an AIX system to send generic alerts to another AIX system via standard AIX communications facilities. The receiving system can then forward this data to a Netview host.
- Allow remote login to an AIX system through an S/370 host HCF
  - Via LU0 session running from the Host to AIX system
  - Execute shell scripts or commands from host HCF.
- Allow an AIX system to send/receive a file to/from a S/370 host via the NetView DM or DSX

- Via LU0 protocol
- File distribution may be intended for the host connected AIX node or for other SNA LU0 (SDLC) connected AIX nodes (via relaying capability). Relaying requires that the AIX Network Management/6000 licensed program be installed on both nodes.

The following services are provided for SNMP management of TCP/IP networks:

- SNMP Manager application
  - Full IBM Enhanced X Windows support for real-time graphical and colour display support including a network topology window, multiple virtual machine windows, and a console (command) window
  - ASCII display and console command/output support available for limited display environments
  - Audible alarm support for network problem notification
  - Network throughput for monitoring incoming/outgoing packet information on an agent system
  - Event logging for get, set, and traps
  - Trap-directed status polling
- SNMP Application Programming Interfaces and Commands
  - Display/save traps
  - Make SNMP request packets
  - Send/receive/parse SNMP packets to and from SNMP Agents
  - Save retrieved SNMP variables
  - SNMP get, next, and set commands

The SNMP manager works in conjunction with SNMP agents on this or other systems. AIX Version 3 includes support for SNMP agents and for the SNMP Management Information Base. The SNMP agent forwards SNMP trap information to the designated SNMP manager. Examples of traps are:

- Start/Restart SNMP Agent demon
- Link up or down because of a network change
- Authentication failure when an agent receives a request from an unknown SNMP manager
- Exterior Gateway Protocol neighbour loss

There is no relationship between SNA generic alerts and SNMP traps.

AIX NetView Service Point

The AIX NetView Service Point program allows the AIX and Unix environments to exchange network management information with NetView running on an IBM mainframe, enabling centralized NetView network management for non-SNA devices. As a gateway to NetView, AIX NetView Service Point operates in a screenless environment on the RS/6000. This product contains the Distributed Application Support Workstation feature that can be downloaded to a remote machine allowing AIX NetView Service Point applications to operate on distributed platforms.

AIX NetView Service Point provides a function-rich gateway to NetView for centralized management of non-SNA network elements. It operates on all models of the RS/6000 running AIX and also selected Sun SPARC stations running SunOS. AIX NetView Service Point enhances system management by:

- Coexisting and interoperating with management applications running on other systems in a heterogeneous network
- Allowing network element management systems (NEMS), being built on an AIX/UNIX workstation, and NEMS already available on this operating system to use AIX NetView Service Point in their native environment
- Assisting in translation of network elements unique alarm and command language to a generic SNA format, and transporting it over an SSCP-PU session to and from NetView
- Providing distributed application support, allowing element-specific applications to run on a remote workstation for administrative (security) or logistical (geography) reasons
- Providing the capability of managing networks through local element managers or centrally, with NetView
- Complementing existing IBM network-management capabilities by providing management capabilities to non-SNA devices in an AIX or UNIX environment

In addition to providing the distributed application support feature for centralized NetView management of remote element-management systems or devices, AIX NetView Service Point provides an automation capability which can increase reliability, provide a programmable interface in the AIX/UNIX native environment, and reduce the number of remote on-site personnel required to manage local systems.

Netview/6000

Netview/6000 was announced in January 1992. AIX NetView/6000 is a licensed program product that facilitates network management in a multivendor Transmission Control Protocol/Internet Protocol (TCP/IP) network. It provides management of TCP/IP devices that include SNMP agents and monitors all IP addressable devices.

Highlights

- Enhances network management and improves network support productivity by providing 'state-of-the-art' SNMP fault, performance, and configuration application functions.
- Includes a graphical user interface based on OSF/Motif that enables SNMP network administrators to view their heterogeneous networks at a glance, thus minimizing network downtime and maximizing their productivity.
- Expands cooperative network management capabilities by interfacing to System/370, System/390 NetView when used with the AIX NetView Service, Point product.
- Provides tailored SNMP support for the IBM 6611 Network Processor including preloaded MIB extensions, customizable traps and MIB query facilities.

The AIX NetView/6000's graphical user interface was designed to reduce the actions needed to identify a failed device and to minimize unnecessary window management. These features help to maintain network availability by rapid recognition of network problems.

In a mixed TCP/IP and SNA environment, the AIX NetView Service Point product and AIX NetView/6000 provide a means for cooperative network management. Cooperative management allows for the quick recognition of network management information from different sources. This results in improved response time to error conditions or performance degradations. NetView automation capabilities, used in conjunction with AIX NetView/6000 SNMP management functions, will also result in faster responses to network situations which would otherwise require the attention of an operator or network administrator. AIX NetView/6000 also provides logging and tracing capabilities to help isolate problems in the network so that they can be resolved quickly.

With AIX NetView/6000's Management Information Base (MIB) loader, standard MIB-II objects as well as enterprise-specific MIB objects can be easily added to AIX NetView/6000 so that they can be managed. Once an MIB is loaded, MIB values can be retrieved or set by a simple point and click method of the AIX NetView/6000's MIB browser. When specific MIB objects need to be monitored on a regular basis, AIX NetView/6000's MIB application builder can be used to build applications easily for standard and enterprise-specific MIB objects without any programming involved. Once an application is built, AIX NetView/6000 automatically adds a menu item to AIX NetView/6000's menu, thus giving the network administrator easy access to the new application.

In addition, using the MIB data collector, MIB information can be easily collected in a file and thresholds can be identified on the collected data so that events are generated once a threshold is exceeded. Performance problems can be detected easily by using this data collection function of AIX NetView/6000. The MIB data collector continually monitors devices in the network based on polling parameters set by the user.

AIX NetView/6000 provides an event configurator function to define what actions to take when AIX NetView/6000 receives a standard or enterprise specific SNMP trap. This provides for automation of fault management such as specifying the text message that is logged or programs/applications to be executed when a SNMP trap arrives. In addition, AIX NetView/6000 provides user-configurable status changes that allow a user to specify the meaning of status events for specific traps. One enterprise specific trap could indicate that a node is down where another trap could indicate that a node is up. The status changes are reflected dynamically in the network topology display as a colour change.

4
RISC System/6000

4.1   RISC v CISC

To explain Reduced Instruction Set Computing (RISC) and Complex Instruction Set Computing (CISC), I will give an analogy. Imagine that we have two computers that are capable of being programmed to make a cup of instant coffee. On the first computer, we write a series of instructions such as:

- Fill the kettle with water.
- Put the kettle on to boil.
- Put instant coffee powder into cup.
- When the kettle has boiled put hot water into cup.
- Add sugar if required.
- Add milk if required.
- Stir coffee.

This is analogous to a RISC computer. All of the instructions are very simple instructions and a lot of them will be executed.

If our computer were a CISC computer, our instructions would look like this:

- Make a cup of coffee.
- Add milk and sugar, if required, then stir.

The instructions on a CISC computer are more complex, but fewer of them need to be executed. Both of these systems are carrying out one operation, but the RISC one runs seven instructions, whereas the CISC one runs only two instructions. They both achieve the same thing.

There is a lot of discussion these days about whether a RISC or a CISC architecture is the way forward. In fact, the difference between the two is becoming less obvious. For example, recent CISC processors, such as the Intel 80486 and the Motorola 68040, have implemented some concepts in a

CISC processor that previously were only associated with a RISC processor. Clearly, since THE RISC processor is carrying out much simpler instructions, the control structure is also greatly simplified. However, second generation RISC processors, such as in the proprietary RS/6000 processor, have a high level of parallelism and use pipelining techniques.

The question as to whether CISC or RISC *should* be used is not as important as the question of how well performance is achieved with a particular implementation by optimizing the definition of the instruction set, machine organization and logic design.

There are a few main architectures of RISC processors that are commonly used in UNIX based systems at the moment. These include:

- MIPS
- SPARC
- Precision Architecture (PA)
- RS/6000

The architectural efficiency of any particular design can be assessed by comparing the performance with the clock speed of the processor. Clearly if two processors produce the same performance, the one with the lower clock speed will be a better design from an architectural point of view and will allow more room for growth within the same design. The RS/6000 compares favourably in this respect with other processor designs. Figure 4.1 shows how the RS/6000 design compares with the architectural efficiency of some other processors.

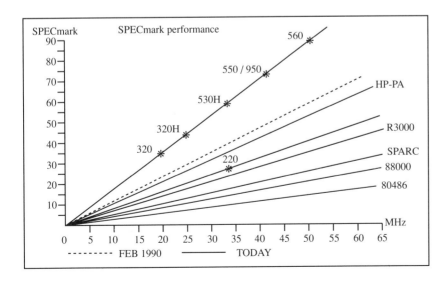

Figure 4.1. Processor design.

4.2   AIX family

The RS/6000 is one of a family of AIX products available from IBM. The RS/6000 and AIX version 3 is the subject of this book, but AIX can run on a Personal System/2 (PS/2), or equally AIX/370 or AIX/ESA can run on an IBM mainframe—e.g. 3090 or ES/9000. There is a different version of AIX that presently runs on each of these platforms, but the AIX Family Definition results in a consistent programming interface.

The AIX Family Definition has been defined for quite some time but the move towards OSF compliant systems is also important in terms of standardization. IBM has already announced a mainframe AIX product—AIX/ESA that is based on OSF/1. AIX Version 3 on the RS/6000 also fully complies with the OSF Application Environment Specification (AES).

In order to support uniformly the different hardware architecture IBM defined the AIX Family Definition, a set of interfaces, conventions and protocols, that can be implemented across the three AIX hardware platforms. This Family embraces popular UNIX and industry standards and includes extensive IBM enhancements. These provide software developers and application users with a consistent operating environment as well as a full range of hardware.

The AIX Family Definition is a framework for building portable, consistent AIX applications for IBM System/370 and System/390, RISC System/6000 Performance Optimization with Enhanced RISC (POWER) architecture, and Personal System/2 386 and 486 computing environments. Current AIX family implementations include AIX/370, AIX Version 3 for RISC System/6000, and AIX PS/2.

The AIX Family Definition describes an open systems architecture providing a complete system environment. This includes operating system calls, high-level languages, programming interfaces, powerful distributed processing/networking capabilities, and user interfaces.

AIX operating system environments on multiple IBM processor architectures provide platforms for consistent application design. Common languages and programming interfaces enhance application portability across the AIX environments. Consistent networking and distribution processing capabilities facilitate transparent sharing of presentation graphics, data and other selected resources.

The six related elements of the AIX Family Definition are:

- AIX Base System
- AIX Programming Interface
- AIX User Interface
- AIX Communications Support
- AXI Distributed Processing
- AIX Applications

4.3   RISC System/6000 hardware architecture

IBM announced and started shipping the RISC System/6000 or RS/6000 in 1990. IBM previously had the 6150 or PC RT which also has a RISC architecture but, as you will see from this chapter, the RS/6000 has a revolutionary architecture. There were a number of specific objectives or design goals that IBM had in mind when designing the RS/6000. These were as follows:

- The system would be designed to give outstanding performance.
- The RS/6000 would have an integrated floating-point processor.
- IBM would ensure that the RS/6000 would be a significant player in the open systems arena.
- IBM would provide a range of systems and allow room for growth.
- The RS/6000 would be designed to be a balanced system for both numeric intensive and commercial multi-user computing.

IBM decided that RISC technology held the key, but that a new era of RISC and a new generation of technology would be required.

4.3.1   RISC System/6000 packaging

There are a number of models in the RS/6000 range. They can broadly be divided into four groups:

- Entry Desktop models—often diskless machines
- Desktop models—looking much like a PC
- Deskside models—that slide underneath or alongside a desk
- Rack mounted models—that utilize an industry standard 19 inch rack.

Figure 4.2 shows some of the models. There is a range in the performance of these systems within the desktop, deskside and rack models. The details of all of the models are discussed later in this chapter.

4.3.2   Advanced second-generation RISC

The RS/6000 is a highly concurrent, superscalar, second-generation RISC computer. The new generation of RISC is known as POWER architecture (Performance Optimization with Enhanced RISC). IBM has learned from its experience in designing powerful mainframes and other mid-range systems, and has used many of these techniques in the design of the RS/6000. The RS/6000 has been specifically designed as described earlier to perform well in numerically-intensive, engineering and scientific applications as well as in a multi-user commercial arena.

Figure 4.2. RS/6000 entry desktop, desktop and deskside models.

The RS/6000 uses a superscalar implementation. Multiple instructions are issued and are executed simultaneously. The RS/6000 has separate branch, floating-point and fixed-point units integrated within the CPU design. There is a high instruction bandwidth that feeds these processors and enables the high levels of parallelism.

Dr John Cocke of IBM Research won the 1987 Turing Award, computer science's most prestigious recognition, for his pioneering work in computer design. Some of his key ideas would later be incorporated in the computer design philosophy which has come to be known as RISC (Reduced Instruction Set Computer). Professor David Patterson, of the University of California at Berkeley, and his students were actually the first to coin the acronym RISC. Professor Patterson published an article entitled 'Reduced Instruction Set Computers' in the January 1985 edition of Communications of the ACM. Working independently, he came up with some design ideas similar to Dr Cocke's. The antithesis of RISC is CISC, or Complex Instruction Set Computer, typified by designs such as Intel 80386, Motorola 68030, VAX, AS/400, and S/370.

Although there is no precise definition for RISC, first generation designs typically implemented a small set of instructions that executed quickly. Reducing the complexity of the instruction set allowed these instructions to be economically implemented in hardware rather than microcode. So most RISC instructions execute in a single cycle (tick of the computer's clock) rather than taking several cycles as is usual for CISC designs. The reduced instruction set complexity of RISC designs also allowed more registers to be implemented. Since data in registers can be accessed much faster than that in memory, more registers could enhance performance.

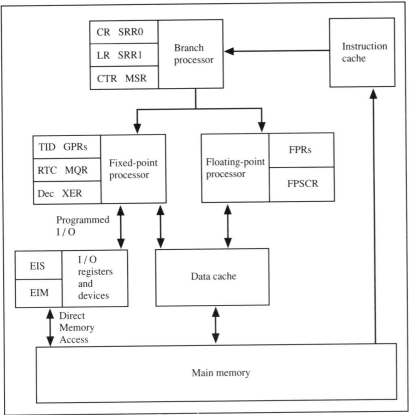

CR	Condition Register	GPRs	General Purpose Registers
LR	Link Register	MQR	Multiplier and Quotient Register
CTR	Count Register	XER	FX Exception Register
SRR0	Save and Restore Register	FPRs	Floating Point Registers
SRR1	Save and Restore Register	FPSCR	Floating Point Status and Control
MSR	Machine State Register		Register
TID	Transaction Identifier	EISR	External Interrupt Summary
RTC	Real Time Clock		Register
Dec	Decrementer	EIMR	External Interrupt Mask Register

Figure 4.3. RS/6000 architecture.

RISC System/6000 series processors are based on RISC principles, but go beyond first generation implementations. Through a technique known as pipelining, results from complex instructions such as floating-point multiply can be achieved every cycle. The RISC System/6000 series also has logically independent processors that operate in parallel on the instruction stream. Multiple instructions can be executed in a single cycle. This has recently been called a superscalar architecture. Figure 4.3 shows the logical architecture of the RS/6000.

Superscalar design: Up to five operations per cycle

In most cases, vector machines are capable of executing multiple floating-point instructions every cycle because they have a vector processor that consists of multiple floating-point engines that operate in parallel. Advances in system architecture have allowed machines which act as if they have a single engine (i.e. they are scalar processors) to execute internally multiple instructions in parallel. The term 'superscalar' has begun to be used to describe these advanced architectures.

The RISC System/6000 series can perform up to four instruction executions per cycle and up to five operations in a single cycle—fixed point, branch, condition code operation, floating-point add/multiply. (This counts as two operations.)

Integrated high-speed floating-point unit

The RISC System/6000 series integrated IEEE-754 conforming floating-point unit contains 32 64-bit dedicated floating-point registers. Hardware instructions include division, which is unusual for RISC-type processors. The multiply–add instruction is believed to be unique. With the multiply–add instruction, a double precision floating-point add and a double precision floating-point multiply can be completed each cycle. This reduces instruction path lengths by combining two instructions into one and enhances floating-point performance significantly. Accuracy is increased over two separate instructions, because the result of the multiply is not rounded before being added to another operand. This allows the RISC System/6000 series to produce accurate approximations in fewer iterations for mathematical functions that are often calculated by series (e.g. sin, cos, etc.).

Multiple condition codes

Condition codes are optically set by selected instructions. The code's value can be used later to decide if a branch is required. Each of the RISC System/6000 series's functionally independent processors is capable of setting a condition code. In order to prevent contention for a single condition code, and the resultant reduction in parallelism, the RISC System/6000 series implements eight independent condition code fields. By using multiple condition codes, interlocks caused by the sharing of a single condition code can be avoided and more instructions can be executed in parallel.

Update forms of loads and stores

These instructions perform a load or store and update an address register in a single cycle. This can significantly reduce processing time for large arrays.

String operations

The architecture specifies five instructions that provide exceptional performance when manipulating strings of characters or data. Movement of long strings may attain a rate of two bytes per cycle, regardless of the storage address alignment, when both storage locations are in the cache.

The Load String Indexed and Load String Immediate instructions cause 0 to 128 sequential bytes from the source storage location to be loaded into sequential general purpose registers. The Store String Indexed and Store String Immediate instructions cause 0 to 128 bytes from the general purpose registers to be stored into sequential bytes at the target storage location. There is no restriction on the alignment of the storage addresses. These instructions allow a string of arbitrary length to be moved from one location of storage to a second location, regardless of the alignment of either location.

The Load String and Compare Byte Indexed instruction is provided to manipulate strings terminated by a unique character, or to locate a particular character in a string. There is no restriction on the alignment of the source storage address. A string of 0 to 127 bytes at a time may be loaded into the general purpose registers. If the target character is detected during the loading of the string, no further bytes are loaded and no further memory locations are accessed. The number of bytes loaded is recorded.

Zero-cycle branches

Branches usually take several cycles to execute, especially on most computers employing pipelining. The RISC System/6000 series branch processor contains all information and resources necessary to execute branch instructions on its own. This allows branches to be processed in parallel with other instructions. So even though most processors require several cycles after a branch to 're-prime' the pipeline, the RISC System/6000 series design allows many branches to be executed in parallel with other work yielding a branch which effectively executes for free (i.e. zero-cycles).

For example, on the Dhrystone 1.1 benchmark, the net effect of this branch processing is that of the 83 branches present, only 20 cause any pipeline delay. The total delay is 41 cycles yielding an average branch cost of less than one half cycle (41/83).

Large set of registers

All models of the RISC System/6000 series implement 32 32-bit general purpose registers and 32 64-bit floating-point registers. Additional specialized registers include 16 segment registers, 6 floating-point rename registers and 2 floating-point divide registers. AIX Version 3 for RISC System/6000's compilers uses an advanced technique called graph colouring to make unusually effective use of the general purpose registers.

4.3.3   Memory subsystem

Since the RISC System/6000 series CPU can execute up to five operations per cycle, it can put tremendous demands on the memory subsystem. A fast CPU will not be fully exploited unless its memory subsystem can keep up with its demand for data and instructions.

Instruction cache

RISC System/6000 series processors contain a dedicated instruction cache. Up to four instructions may be fetched from the instruction cache every cycle. These instructions are fed into a 12-word instruction buffer that allows the branch processor to look ahead for upcoming branches. The instruction cache is two-way set associative with a line size of 64 bytes. When a cache miss occurs, two instructions (64 bits) per cycle can be retrieved from memory. This design allows the RISC System/6000 series's parallel execution units to operate at full speed.

Data cache

The smaller models of RS/6000 have 32 KB four-way associative data caches while all the larger models have 64 KB four-way associative data caches.

The RISC System/6000 64 KB data cache implements a line size of 128 bytes. This unusually large line can be moved to a special store-back buffer or retrieved from a reload buffer in two cycles. By decoupling cache loads and stores from actual memory access, the CPU can continue to operate, using data in registers and the cache, while memory is being accessed. The store-back and reload buffers move data to or from memory in 128 bit blocks requiring only eight cycles for an entire 128 byte line. This translates to a memory bandwidth of 400 MB per second for a 25 Mhz processor model of RS/6000. Cache performance is further improved by ensuring that the data requirement that caused the reload sequence is satisfied in the first 16 byte block (followed by the remaining seven blocks).

Other features of the RISC System/6000 design include four-way set associativity store-back design, and software visibility. Four-way associative cache reduces thrashing and the store-back design reduces memory bandwidth requirements. Store-back means that writes do not automatically updata memory. Only when a changed cache line must be replaced does the write occur. Software visibility of the cache permits software to prevent unnecessary loads or stores, further reducing demands on memory. For example, when programs are first loaded in memory, significant areas are often zeroed out. A software visible cache allows the same effect to be achieved without referencing memory.

RISC System/6000 series processors with 32 KB data caches are similar to those using 64 KB, but line size and memory interface width are cut in half. RISC System/6000 series processors with 64 KB caches also have more internal data paths, further contributing to performance.

Memory interleaving

Memory interleaving is a technique that improves transfer rates to and from main memory. This enables the RISC System/6000 processors to provide higher performance for programs or multi-user requirements that are memory intensive. Four-way interleaving enables RISC System/6000 series to access two words of memory from each of two cards (for a total of four 32-bit words) per cycle. On a 25 MHz machine, this translates into a 400 MB/sec memory bandwidth.

Address translation

RISC System/6000 processors use separate instruction and data Translation Look-aside Buffers (TLBs) for virtual address translation. The 32-entry instruction TLB and 128-entry data TLB are each two-way associative in order to minimize thrashing. The data TLB contains information for page protection and data locking, as well as address translation.

Inverted page table

The RISC System/6000 series implements an unusually large address space (52-bit) broken into over 16 million 256 MB segments. Traditional virtual memory implementations map virtual to real addresses through a number of page tables. The amount of memory taken by these tables is proportional to the size of the virtual address space. Because the RISC System/6000 series's address space is so large, an inverted page table approach was chosen. This approach only requires one entry per real page frame, significantly reducing the demands on real memory for storing page tables.

Mapped files

Mapped files are a type of single level storage. That is, programmers do not have to be concerned about whether data is on disk or in memory once a file is opened. It appears that opening a file preloads all of it into memory. AIX Version 3 for RISC System/6000 treats local and remote files as mapped. This facility can improve performance, make better use of memory and ease some kinds of programming.

With AIX Version 3 for RISC System/6000, files are treated like any other pageable object so the paging supervisor has control of which portions reside in real memory. As workload characteristics change according to requirements, the system can adapt, allocating memory in a way that reduces overall system I/O thereby potentially improving responsiveness and throughput. And because paging supervisors are among the most carefully tuned sections of any operating system, I/O path lengths are very short, further contributing to performance.

Programmers can access AIX Version 3 for RISC System/6000's memory mapped files using standard (and portable) UNIX operating system I/O routines. For performance critical code, files can be directly accessed as if they were a preloaded array in memory. This can improve programming productivity and improve performance even more because some of the checking and buffering in normal I/O is no longer required. The paging supervisor and hardware assists take over these functions.

Pageable kernel

AIX Version 3 for RISC System/6000's kernel (which is the core or nucleus of the operating system) is pageable. Other operating systems (e.g. UNIX System V, XENIX and BSD) fix the kernel in memory. On single user workstations, large portions of the kernel may be tying up memory without being used. The AIX Version 3 for RISC System/6000 implementation can provide better performance in a memory constrained environment by dynamically adapting to usage patterns rather than pre-allocating the entire kernel in memory.

4.3.4   I/O subsystem

The high speed of RISC System/6000 CPUs and memory subsystems would be constrained were it not for RISC System/6000's high performance I/O subsystem.

Micro Channel bus

The RISC System/6000 series Micro Channel bus is compatible with the PS/2 Micro Channel bus. But the power of the RISC System/6000 CPU and memory subsystem demanded an increase in performance of the I/O system over that of the PS/2. The Micro Channel architecture has been used to enable balanced, reliable performance for the RISC System/6000 series.

The RISC System/6000 has implemented the Streaming Data Transfer Mode that transfers blocks of data rather than individual words. This type of technique is sometimes called 'burst mode'. The reduced handshaking overhead of block transfers increases the maximum I/O capacity of the 32-bit Micro Channel bus from 20 MB per second to 40 MB per second. This technique allows individual adapter transfers to be quicker. More importantly, the bus is freed more quickly, providing increased capacity for concurrent I/O. RISC System/6000 micro Channel cards such as SCSI, Token-Ring and Ethernet exploit this new capability.

The RISC System/6000 has also implemented data and address parity. This precaution was taken because increased I/O rates increase the chance for undetected errors. It also helps protect against errors caused by electromagnetic radiation or an improperly seated card.

Another function of the Micro Channel architecture is the provision for synchronous exception handling. Previous implementations of the Micro Channel architecture only supported signalling of catastrophic errors after they had been detected. With the new feature, exceptions can be raised during the same bus cycle that caused the exception and can be used to signal synchronous events such as page faults in addition to error signalling.

Many high-speed Micro Channel cards can also act as bus masters. This means that they can off-load the CPU by acting as a type of internal distributed processor. A bus master card can move a block of data to or from main memory and a device or adapter buffer without using any CPU cycles. Examples of RISC System/6000 series bus master cards are SCSI, Token Ring, Ethernet and the 4-Port Multi-Protocol Communications Adapter (64 K bits per second per port).

Multiple distributed I/O processors

Distributed I/O processors are used on many of the high performance I/O adapters to enhance overall system performance. These on-board processors manage I/O functions without per character intervention of the POWER processor. Some examples include the SCSI adapter, Multiprotocol adapter, the 64-Port adapter, and the X.25 Interface Co-Processor/2.

SCSI read ahead buffers

All RISC System/6000 SCSI disk devices implement a pre-read buffer. This provides for increased sequential read performance and lower bus demands.

High performance token-ring LAN

Sixteen megabit per second token ring adapters are supported. This clock speed is 60 per cent faster than standard Ethernet, and token ring protocols can provide better throughput on a heavily used LAN. This allows a greater number of processors to be connected to a LAN or better response time for the same number of processors.

4.3.5   Large capacity

Memory

High-speed memory is supported via eight memory card slots (two in the desktop unit) on the CPU planar board for the deskside and rack mounted models, allowing RISC System/6000 series processors to support up to 512 MB of memory (128 MB for the desktop unit). The RISC System/6000 series uses IBM's new 4 megabit memory chips and is able to support up to 256 MB of memory on the CPU planar board. The memory bus is separate from the I/O bus enabling better performance for each.

Virtual address space

All models of the RISC System/6000 series support 48 bit virtual addresses. This very large address space (256 Terabytes) enables all local and remote files to be automatically mapped to virtual storage. Over 16 million 256 MB segments are available. By treating files as in-storage objects, memory utilization is improved and higher performance can be obtained. See 'Mapped files' on page 132 for additional information.

CD ROM

The CD ROM drive for read-only optical disks holds approximately 600 MB of data on a durable 5.25 inch disk. Optical disks are available for RISC System/6000 series and AIX Version 3 for RISC System/6000 publications as well as the InfoExplorer hypertext help system. The effective access time of the drive is improved with a built-in buffer.

2.3 GB 8 mm tape drive

The 8 mm tape drive provides highly convenient, cost-effective media for backup, recovery and archiving. The streaming tape transfers at 246 KB per second. The 5.25 inch form factor contains helical scan video technology to achieve its high capacity. Each IBM 8 mm data cartridge is capable of storing a maximum of 2.3 GB. This large capacity makes unattended back-up or archiving very convenient and the small size of the cartridge minimizes storage space requirements.

4.3.6   Reliability

Although the RISC System/6000 series includes workstations and mid-range systems, their internal data speeds are more typical of mainframes. These high performance characteristics demand error detection and correction capabilities which are atypical for systems in the RISC System/6000 series price range.

   Although RISC System/6000 systems are no more likely to experience errors than other systems with similar performance characteristics, unusually rich error detection/correction facilities have been incorporated into the RISC System/6000 design in order to provide an extra margin of safety.

Extensive parity checking

All chip-to-chip buses are parity checked. Most chip data paths, registers, caches and translation look-aside buffers are also protected by parity. RISC System/6000 series Micro Channel cards can also implement parity checks (using previously reserved pins) for address and data lines.

ECC memory

RISC System/6000 memory is of the Error Correcting Code (ECC) type. This enables single bit error correction and double bit detection for each word of memory.

Memory scrubbing

Main memory consists of DRAMs which are susceptible to 'soft' or temporary single-bit errors. Since RISC System/6000 systems may be operated continuously, single bit errors may accumulate into uncorrectable double bit errors over a long period. To reduce the changes of soft single bit errors accumulating into a double bit error, memory is periodically checked and corrected by a low priority background task. This process is known as memory scrubbing.

Bit scattering

In the design of the RISC System/6000 series reliability, availability, and serviceability are main considerations. Extensive use of parity and memory ECC are found throughout the system.

A built-in self test is performed at power-on. It tests the processor complex by generating test patterns which are used by the POWER processor VLSI chips to verify correct chip operation. All processor chips have data parity in their data paths. Internal arrays and processor chip to chip data buses have parity.

The memory subsystem is tested extensively during power-up. It implements ECC with detection of double bit errors and detection and correction of single bit errors. Bit steering is provided to substitute a spare bit of memory automatically for a faulty data bit or ECC bit. Bit scattering ensures a given memory chip contains no more than one bit of any word. Memory Control also provides hardware assisted memory scrubbing which is a memory test to detect and correct single bit memory errors.

Spare bit

Each word of memory in RISC System/6000 series includes a spare bit. If a solid failure (hard error) develops in one of the bits in a word, the RISC System/6000 series can substitute the spare bit for the failed one. Full ECC protection remains in effect after the bit substitution for continued protection against another failed bit.

Built-in self checks

Each of the chips in the RISC System/6000 series central processor complex contains on-chip logic to perform self-diagnosis. At power-up, the built-in self-check sequence is performed. Any errors detected are recorded as an aid to service. This feature reduces the likelihood of failures during normal operations.

Mirrored files

When very high data availability is required, file mirroring, sometimes called disk shadowing, can be used. This technique simultaneously updates more than one disk so that even if there is a disk failure, data is still available. See the section on 'Logical Volumes' for implementation information.

4.3.7   RISC System/6000 future directions

Processor directions

IBM is much more open these days about the future of its products. IBM often speaks openly to customers and the press about product plans and is quite happy to share this kind of information with customers, usually under a 'non-disclosure' agreement. The views in this section however, are my own personal views on the future of the RS/6000 product family. Some of these views have been expressed in press articles discussing the RS/6000.

The design goal for the RS/6000 is to double performance every 12 to 16 months. To achieve this, IBM has put together a technology plan, a set of advanced VLSI design tools, and an implementation road-map. The products announted in February 1990 were the beginning of the road and demonstrated technology leadership in both hardware and software.

Since that announcement, IBM has continued to maintain technology leadership and has met its design goals. Over time, IBM will continue to announce performance improvements, as well as introduce more function. There will be a major focus on extending the RS/6000 range in both directions—at the top and at the bottom. There is now a low entry diskless workstation with high function graphics and the ability to configure with disk technology if appropriate. The machine has exceptional floating-point price/performance. This product exploits the same 'next generation' silicon that enabled IBM to deliver the industry-leading performance of the RS/6000 model 550.

In addition to delivering low end solutions, IBM will extend the high end of the range. There are three factors that are critically important to performance: compiler efficiency, clock rate, and number of instructions per cycle.

IBM has already boosted the performance of the RS/6000 in two stages, simply through making available even more efficient compilers. These are not

minor improvements. The FORTRAN compilers show on average a 25–40
per cent improvement on numeric-intensive applications. IBM will continue
to harness the expertise of the compiler technology group based in Toronto
to deliver even more efficient compilers.

Clock rate and hence performance may be improved in a variety of ways.
Faster circuit technology, superpipelining and tuning techniques may be
used. The current products are running at relatively low clock speeds. IBM
knows that this technology can run at 60–70 MHz and beyond that IBM will
use MultiChip module packaging of the kind used in the ES/9000 to achieve
80–90 MHz and beyond. IBM will also incorporate superpipelined
capabilities.

Finally, the superscalar architecture of the RS/6000 provides for multiple
execution units. In the current implementation, we have one branch
execution unit, one fixed-point and one floating-point unit, providing
execution of up to five instructions per cycle. Future designs can have two or
three execution units for fixed and floating point, providing an equivalent
factor of performance improvement by executing perhaps ten instructions
per cycle.

In summary, IBM has many options to improve performance. The architecture is in its infancy, yet already leading the field. A reasonable and widely
quoted metric for assessing architectural efficiency and future extensibility of
first generation and superscalar RISC designs consists of taking the ratio of
overall SPECmark performance divided by the clock speed in megahertz. The
model 320H, the smallest of the desktop machines, delivers a ratio of 1.74
SPECmarks per MHz. Other RISC architectures rarely achieve a ratio in
excess of 1.0 and indeed many are much lower. By extrapolation, it can be
seen that the architectural advantage of an RS/6000 will in theory support an
absolute performance of over 80 SPECmarks simply by boosting the clock
rate to 50 MHz.

Where the differential is even greater, though, is in the floating-point
performance. The Model 550 provides a floating-point SPECmark today of
just under 120, and leads the field by a significant margin.

Bus and I/O directions

Because of the performance of the CPU, it is essential to have an appropriate
bus architecture. The requirement to move data very quickly from memory
to the CPU to keep it busy led to the need for a separate high-speed memory
bus and a separate I/O bus. Many workstations today with slower CPUs use
a single bus for memory and I/O, but as CPU speed increases a balanced

system requires more than one bus. The memory bus today has a capacity of from 160 to over 650 MB per second. This provides sufficient bandwidth for the CPU without clogging the I/O bus.

The I/O bus is based upon the Micro Channel Architecture. Employing a physically separate I/O bus means that IBM can move to faster implementations of the Micro Channel in the future as CPU speeds increase. There are four implementation levels defined for the Micro Channel. The IBM PS/2 implements level 1 at 20 MB per second the RISC System/6000 implements level 2 at 40 MB per second, and levels 3 and 4 are defined but as yet not implemented at 80 MB per second and 160 MB per second. IBM has publicly stated its intention to introduce the first implementations of the higher level bandwidth in the near future, in order to keep a balanced system for the new faster processors. IBM will also introduce faster adapters to exploit the increased bandwidth available.

In addition to extending the Micro Channel, IBM has recently introduced new, even faster, disk technology. This serial disk technology builds on the success of the industry leading disks designed and manufactured at the Havant plant in the UK. These disks will extend further the technology lead in this market segment.

The RS/6000 can also provide shared access to this new disk subsystem from two processors. This facility will enable the delivery of low cost, high availability Unix servers. This, together with the disk mirroring technology available today, will be the key to the success of many customer implementations.

Memory directions

IBM is one of the world's largest semiconductor makers. The investment has allowed IBM to lead the field consistently in memory chip densities. When the RS/6000 was announced in February 1990, it was to be delivered with 1 Mbit memory chips. IBM stated its intention then to deliver 4 Mbit chips and the 4 Mbit technology has now been incorporated into the whole RS/6000 range. Desktop machines initially limited to 32 MB can now go to 128 MB, and floor-standing models can contain 512 MB. The performance and price of the memory is comparable to the 1 Mbit chip. If history is anything to go by, memory densities should continue to quadruple every two to three years and the price per bit should decline. With advanced applications such as voice, image and multi-media, this memory capacity will be critical.

RS/6000 road-map

As I have already stated, IBM talks much more openly these days about the future directions of the RS/6000. The following predictions are my own thoughts on what we might see happening to the RS/6000 product over the coming months and years. Some of these predictions may come true, others clearly may not happen.

> The RS/6000 range will be expanded in both directions. In the next year or two we will see the UNIX laptop from IBM, and at the top end a very powerful multi-processing machine with up to 16 CPUs. A 64 bit RS/6000 will be announced mid-decade. In the near future, clock speeds (which are currently quite low) will be increased to 60 MHz and then to 100 MHz—this can happen within the same RS/6000 architecture. I think competition will find it difficult to follow without re-redesigning their chip architecture.
>
> IBM aims to be the number one or number two position in the UNIX marketplace by 1993/94. This will mean continued big investment and technology leadership.
>
> By 1993, a 5–8 fold increase in RS/6000 performance is likely. This will be achieved by implementing more integer and floating-point processors within the CPU, as well as increasing clock speed. In addition, better and faster compilers will increase performance as they have already done during the life of the RS/6000. Optimized compilers could improve performance by 50 per cent.
>
> Clustering of RS/6000s using fibre-optic channels can give a 100-fold increase in performance so that 10 000 times today's performance will be possible.

4.4   Current RISC System/6000 models

The RS/6000 used the POWER (Performance Optimization with Enhanced RISC) architecture and the models can either be POWERstations or POWERservers. This is just a reflection of how the system is configured with disk, memory and adapters. The RS/6000 can be used in a number of different situations as already discussed. However, for simplicity I will consider the two markets:

- *Technical workstations*
  This is the engineering/scientific market-place where systems typically need high function graphical capabilities and the system is often used by one person at a time. High rates of computation are also often a feature of this kind of work. The RS/6000 can be used as a POWERstation for a user or alternatively the RS/6000 can be configured as a POWERserver

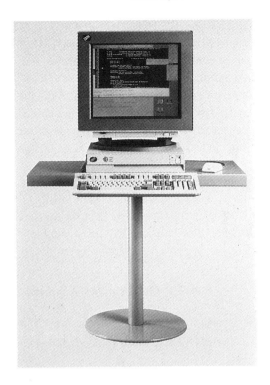

Figure 4.4. RS/6000 model 220.

where its disk or processor capabilities are accessed by other POWER-stations over a network.

● *Commercial data processing*
This will typically be a system with a large number of users accessing a multi-user application from ASCII screens or PCs which are either locally attached or communicate over a Wide Area Network (WAN).

These models are correct at the time of writing, but I expect many announcements on new models in the RS/6000 range over a period of time. Indeed, already, there are models of RS/6000 that are no longer current—they have been replaced with faster and cheaper models. Clearly there are many of these systems installed at customer sites so I will still discuss some of them here for completeness.

Entry desktop models

The RS/6000 model 220 shown in Fig. 4.4 was announced in January 1992. It is binary compatible with the rest of the RS/6000 family. It features a single chip RISC processor. The standard system comes as a diskless machine, although disk can be added. The model 220 has integrated SCSI and Ethernet controllers. It can have up to 64 MB of memory and up to 400 MB of internal disk. External disks can also be configured. The model 220 can be used either in diskless mode or dataless mode.

As the name implies, a diskless system has no disk at all. When the system is powered on, it gets all of its software from a server machine. All disk activity will take place across the network in conjunction with the server. This type of environment can be much easier to manage and has advantages in terms of security.

In a dataless situation, a model 220 will have a small disk, where the AIX operating system and probably paging space will be kept locally. The application being used and any associated data will be kept on the server.

Preconfigured models of the RS/6000 model 220 are available.

- Model 22W
  - 160 MB disk   – Mouse
  - Keyboard/speaker   – POWER Gt1 Graphics Adapter
- Model 22G
  - 400 MB Disk   – Mouse
  - Keyboard/speaker   – POWER Gt3 Graphics Adapter

Desktop models

At present there are three desktop models (see Fig. 4.5) The desktop model numbers start with a '3'. The RS/6000 desktop models are 320H, 340, and 350.

The model 320H has a SPECmark rating of 43.4 and the models 340 and 350 have SPECmark ratings of 56.6 and 71.4. The desktop models have four Micro Channel slots available for adapters.

A model 320H comes with 16 MB of main memory and this can be upgraded to 128 MB. It has a 400 MB disk as standard, but a second internal 400 MB drive can be added. With both of the disk bays filled with a 400 MB drive, the maximum internal disk is 800 MB. External disk can be attached. The total maximum disk storage theoretically could be as large as 12 GB, but IBM would advise configurations to have less than this.

A model 340 also comes with 16 MB of main memory and this can be upgraded to 128 MB. It has a 160 MB disk as standard, but this can be changed at the time of ordering for a 400 MB disk. With both of the disk bays filled with a 400 MB drive, the maximum internal disk is 800 MB. External disk can be attached as with the model 320H.

The model 350 is similar to the model 340 but with increased CPU power.

Figure 4.5. Desktop model.

Both the 340 and 350 have an integrated SCSI adapter and Ethernet adapter. These are integrated with the mother board and leave more Micro Channel slots available for other uses. The model 340 can be upgraded to utilize the model 350 processor. Table 4.1 overleaf shows the details for the desktop and entry-desktop systems.

Table 4.2 on page 145 shows the details for memory and disk in the desktop RS/6000 models.

Deskside models

There are currently four deskside models of RS/6000: 520H, 530H, 550 and 560 (see Fig. 4.6).

Note that the models 520, 530, and 540 are no longer marketed. Upgrades from these models to current models are available at the time of writing.

The deskside model numbers all start with a '5'. The last two digits in the model number indicate the processor power. An 'H' means that this replaces a previous model but now has faster performance. In other words, the model 520H processor is the same power as the model 320H processor. The most powerful in the range at the moment is the model 560 which will be described soon.

The deskside models have eight Micro Channel slots. Typically, one of these will be used for a SCSI adapter to attach disks and tapes. The latest

Table 4.1. RS/6000 desktop and entry desktop details

Desktop Machines

	RISC System/6000 Model					
	220	22W	22G	320H	340	350
Clock (MHz)	33	33	33	25	33	42
Standard Features						
3.5″ Diskette				√	√	√
Parallel Port	√	√	√	√	√	√
2 Serial Ports	√	√	√	√	√	√
Keyboard Port	√	+ kbd	+ kbd	√	√	√
Mouse Port	√	+ mouse	+ mouse	√	√	√
Tablet Port	√	√	√	√	√	√
SCSI Adapter	√	√	√	√	√	√
Ethernet Adapter	√	√	√		√	√
Optical Card Slot						
Gt1 Slot	√	+ Gt1	√			
Graphics Proc'r			Gt3			
8 mm Tape Drive						
CD-ROM Drive						
Free Adapter Slots	2	2	1	3	4	4

Removable Media Configurations

		220	22W	22G	320H	340	350
3.5″ Diskette	Int	1 Max	1 Max	1 Max	Std	Std	Std
	Ext						
5.25″ Diskette	Int						
	Ext				1 Max		
1/4″ Tape	Int						
	Ext	√	√	√	√	√	√
1/2″ Tape	Int						
	Ext	√	√	√	√	√	√
8 mm Tape	Int						
	Ext	√	√	√	√	√	√
CD-ROM	Int						
	Ext	√	√	√	√	√	√

models have an integrated SCSI and Ethernet adapter leaving Micro Channel adapter slots free for other purposes.

Table 4.3 on page 147 shows the memory and DASD and other characteristics of the deskside and rack models.

Table 4.4 (page 148) shows the details for memory and disk in the deskside RS/6000 models. All of the deskside models can be configured as POWERstations or POWERservers by using standard components.

Table 4.2. RS/6000 desktop models—memory and disk

Memory and DASD — Desktop

		RISC System/6000 Model					
		220	220W	220G	320H	340	350
Memory (MB)	Standard	16	16	16	16	16	32
	Maximum	64	64	64	128	128	128
	Increments	8	8	8	8	8	8
Internal Disks	Standard DASD (MB)	0	160	400	400	160	160
	Maximum DASD (MB)	400	400	400	800	800	800
	DASD Increments (MB)	160 400	400	–	160 320 400	160 400	160 400
Ext Disks	DASD Increments (MB)	320 355 670	320 355 670	320 355 670	320 355 670	320 355 670	320 355 670
	Maximum Ext DASD (MB)	4020	4020	4020	12730	12730	12730
9334 Unit	DASD Increments (MB)				670 857	670 857	670 857
	Maximum 9334 DASD (MB)	0	0	0	3428	3428	3428
9333 Syst	DASD Increments (MB) Maximum 9333 DASD (MB)	0	0	0	0	0	0
	Maximum Total DASD (MB)	4420	4420	4420	8840	8840	8840
	Max # of SCSI Adapters	1	1	1	3	3	3
	Max # of 9333 Adapters	0	0	0	0	0	0

Rack mounted models

There are two rack models (see Fig. 4.7) of RS/6000: 930 and 950.

The rack mounted models utilize an industry standard 19 inch rack. They have the largest internal disk capacity and can be used as POWERservers or for multi-user commercial systems.

The model 930 has 32 MB and the model 950 has 64 MB of memory as standard. This can be expanded to 512 MB. The total maximum DASD for

Figure 4.6. Deskside
model.

both of the rack-mounted models when the 9333 Subsystem is used amounts
to 53 134 MB. The total maximum advised SCSI DASD is 20 568 MB.

Model upgrades

The upgrades are shown in Fig. 4.8.

Note that upgraded models are labelled with an 'E', 'F' or 'S' to show that
they have been upgraded. For example, a model 320 when upgraded to a
model 320H is actually called a 320E. Upgrades for older models that are no
longer marketed by IBM are shown here.

Micro Channel Architecture

Any computer system consists of a number of subsystems. These subsystems
are things like the processor, memory, DASD, and others. All these

Table 4.3. Details of RS/6000 deskside and rack models

Deskside and Rack Machines

	RISC System/6000 Model					
	520H	530H	930	550	950	560
Clock (MHz)	25	33.3	25	41.6	41.6	50
Standard Features						
3.5″ Diskette	√	√	√	√	√	√
Parallel Port	√	√		√		√
2 Serial Ports	√	√	√	√	√	√
Keyboard Port	√	√		√		√
Mouse Port	√	√		√		√
Tablet Port	√	√		√		√
SCSI Adapter	√	√	√	√	√	√
Ethernet Adapter						
Optical Card Slot	√	√	√	√	√	√
Gt1 Slot						
Graphics Proc'r						
8 mm Tape Drive			√		√	
CD-ROM Drive			√		√	
Free Adapter Slots	7	7	7	7	7	7

Removable Media Configurations

		520H	530H	930	550	950	560
3.5″ Diskette	Int	Std	Std	Std	Std	Std	Std
	Ext						
5.25″ Diskette	Int			1 Max		1 Max	
	Ext	1 Max	1 Max		1 Max		1 Max
1/4″ Tape	Int			2 Max		2 Max	
	Ext	√	√		√		√
1/2″ Tape	Int			1 Max		1 Max	
	Ext	√	√		√		√
8 mm Tape	Int	1 Max	1 Max	1 Std 3 Max	1 Max	1 Std 3 Max	1 Max
	Ext	√	√		√		√
CD-ROM	Int	1 Max	1 Max	1 Std 5 Max	1 Max	1 Std 5 Max	1 Max
	Ext	√	√		√		√

subsystems need to be able to communicate with each other. This communications path is called a channel. The Micro Channel Architecture (MCA) defines how this channel works. It was originally designed for the Personal System/2 (PS/2) and is now used in the RS/6000.

The MCA is an architecture and is not dependent on any specific IBM machine. The designers of the PS/2 and the RS/6000 have implemented some (but not all) of the MCA rules in these machines. Having an architecture means compatibility with future products. The RS/6000 can use PS/2 MCA

Table 4.4. RS/6000 deskside models—memory and disk

Memory and DASD—Deskside/Rack

		RISC System/6000 Model					
		520H	530H	930	550	950	560
Memory (MB)	Standard	16	32	32	64	64	64
	Maximum	512	512	512	512	512	512
	Increments	8	16	16	16	16	16
Internal Disks	Standard DASD (MB)	400	400	670	800	1714	800
	Maximum DASD (MB)	2571	2571	11998	2571	11998	2571
	DASD Increments (MB)	400	400	670	800	670	800
		857	800	857	857	857	857
			857				
Ext Disks	DASD Increments (MB)	320	320		320		320
		355	355		355		355
		670	670		670		670
	Maximum Ext DASD (MB)[4]	21440	21440	0	21440	0	21440
9334 Unit	DASD Increments (MB)	670	670	670	670	670	670
		857	857	857	857	857	857
	Maximum 9334 DASD (MB)[4]	10284	10284	20568	10284	20568	10284
9333 Syst	DASD Increments (MB)	857	857	857	857	857	857
	Maximum 9333 DASD (MB)	13712	13712	51420	13712	51420	13712
	Maximum Total DASD (MB)	26567	26567	53134	26567	53134	26567
	Max # of SCSI Adapters[3]	5	5	7	5	7	5
	Max # of 9333 Adapters[3]	4	4	4	4	4	4

adapters for example. The use of MCA in the RS/6000 ensures that the system will be a balanced system providing good performance for a wide variety of workloads.

As the RS/6000 is a super-scalar implementation (executing multiple instructions per cycle), it is necessary to have a separate I/O bus and a separate memory bus. This will provide for a balanced system without bottlenecks

Figure 4.7. Rack model.

which could otherwise occur in attempting to keep such a fast processor busy by getting data from the main memory at very fast speeds.

The I/O bus is physically separate in the RS/6000 allowing for the possibility of moving to faster levels of the MCA as CPU speeds increase. There are four implementation levels defined for the Micro Channel. Level 2 is currently used in the RS/6000. The various levels that are defined are shown in Table 4.5.

Features of the Micro Channel Architecture include:

● Auto configuration
   The RS/6000 will recognize at boot-up time any MCA adapters that are in the machine and will register these within the system. If they can be

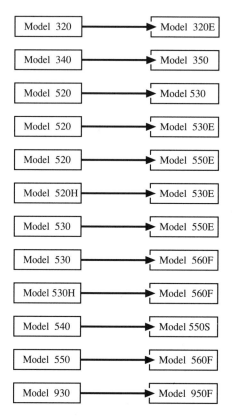

Figure 4.8. RS/6000 upgrades.

utilized straight away they will be. Other adapters may need to be configured. For example, the Token Ring adapter would need a network address of some kind before it can be used.

- Interrupt handling
- Data transfer
- Bus masters

This allows an adapter or a device to gain control of the system's I/O bus and transfer information to or from either system memory or other adapters. The CPU can therefore off-load tasks to bus master adapters

Table 4.5. Micro channel implementation levels

Level	Product	Speed
1	PS/2	20 MB/sec
2	RS/6000 and PS/2	40 MB/sec
3	None yet	80 MB/sec
4	None yet	160 MB/sec

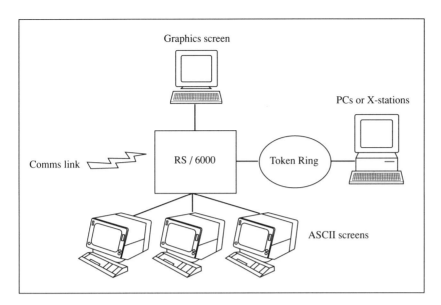

Figure 4.9. Attaching
displays to the RS/6000.

and then leave that adapter, which is dedicated to performing that specific job, to carry out the task. This leaves the CPU to do other more important tasks. The bus master adapter reports back to the CPU when the task is completed.

● Arbitration

4.5   Displays and graphics

There are a number of ways in which displays of various kinds can be used with an RS/6000. I will discuss some of the more common ones in more detail. Figure 4.9 shows ways in which displays can be attached to an RS/6000.

ASCII displays

The simplest way to attach a display is to use a directly attached ASCII screen. This is a fixed function or 'dumb' terminal that is attached over an RS232 or RS442 connection to an RS/6000 adapter.

Two asynchronous ports are standard on the RS/6000 along with one parallel port. These two serial ports can be used for terminals, printers or modem connections. In a system with no graphics screen, an ASCII terminal will probably be used as a console and will be attached via one of these serial ports.

In a system with many ASCII screens, some kind of adapter must be used to provide extra asynch connections. There are a number of different adapters that can be used. ASCII displays can be directly attached to the RS/6000 as discussed above, or they can be attached remotely in a number of different ways. These will be explained in more detail in the section on communications.

Native graphics screen

There are a range of high function graphic displays that can be used with the RS/6000. These range from lower priced, smaller displays, up to very high quality 23 inch displays that are suitable for CAD applications. These displays are discussed later in this book. A screen of this kind will attach to one of the range of graphics adapters that can be slotted into a Micro Channel adapter slot. These range from low entry monochrome graphics adapters (suitable for example for image based applications) right up to very fast 3D colour graphics adapters. These are discussed in Sec. 4.5.2.

Personal computers

Personal computers can also run a variety of ASCII emulation software packages. PCs can also run software of various kinds to provide a more intelligent method of accessing the RS/6000. Some of the common ways in which an IBM PS/2 can be connected to the RS/6000 are as follows:

- *ASCII emulation* There are a variety of software packages that will allow a PC to emulate an ASCII screen. The PC can be attached to the RS/6000 in a number of different ways. For example, it can be directly attached to the RS/6000 using an RS232D connection, or it can access the RS/6000 over a Local Area Network (LAN) or even come into the RS/6000 over a remote link of some kind. The function provided by this software is very similar to a normal ASCII screen—i.e. fairly limited. If additional function is required, a more intelligent method of connection would be better.
- *AIX Access for DOS Users* In this case, the RS/6000 runs some DOS Server software and some software called AIX Access for DOS Users (AADU) is also located onto the PC. As the name suggests, this is for use with a DOS PC. This provides a number of different functions.

  Firstly, the PC can have terminal emulation to log into RS/6000 applications. In addition, the PC can use RS/6000 printers for output. The RS/6000 will also give the PC user virtual disks on the RS/6000 itself.

This, of course, will be transparent to the user. For example, the C drive may actually be a hard disk drive which is physically in the PC, whereas the F drive might be a virtual drive actually located on the RS/6000. The user will see the data and programs on the F drive in the usual way, and need not be aware that this drive is located elsewhere.

Copying or moving data between the C and F drives will actually result in a 'file transfer' and any translation of data to the correct format will be automatically taken care of by the RS/6000.

The physical connection can either be direct, across a LAN—Ethernet or Token Ring—or remote across an asynchronous connection.

- *TCP/IP*   There are a number of different software packages to give a PC TCP/IP networking capability. The section on communications discusses TCP/IP in more detail. Typically not all TCP/IP functions will be available but the common software packages at least include support for:
  - telnet—which allows terminal emulation and the ability to log onto other systems.
  - ftp—to allow file transfer between systems.

  TCP/IP is the basis for a number of other functions such as Network File System (NFS) and X Windows which will provide the ability to share information across a network and the ability to use windows on a graphics screen.

- *X Windows for DOS*   There is a software product from IBM that will provide a windowed access into the RS/6000 using X Windows. There are also products from third parties that provide similar functions in a Windows/3 environment.

Xstations

Section 4.6 explains how an Xstation functions. An Xstation may be used to provide windowing capability or graphics to a user that does not require a PC.

Communications links

Users can also get access to an RS/6000 and its applications over a communications link of some kind—Token Ring, Ethernet, SDLC or Asynchronous using any one of a number of communications protocols such as SNA, TCP/IP, DECNET, OSI, etc.

4.5.1   ASCII displays

Each of the IBM ASCII displays are described here. There are also a number of non-IBM displays that are supported on the RS/6000, including the following DEC and Wyse displays along with other compatible displays:

- DEC VT100
- DEC VT220
- DEC VT320
- DEC VT330
- WYSE 30
- WYSE 50
- WYSE 60
- WYSE 3500

3151 ASCII Display Station

The 3151 ASCII Display Station is a stand-alone, 14-inch monochrome display station used for displaying up to 3300 characters and for entering data into and retrieving data from a host processor. The 3151 Display Stations provide an asynchronous communication interface with a 7-bit or 8-bit word length, using EIA-232 (CCITT V.24/28) interface or EIA-422 (CCITT V.11) interface. The RISC System/6000 computers support Models 11X, 31X, 41X, 51X, and 61X. The 3151 Display Stations are supported in 3161 mode. The 3151 Display Stations support transmission speeds from 50 to 38.4 K bps on EIA-232 and EIA-422 interfaces. The displays are 80/132 column format with 24 or 25 lines. A multi-function attachment cable, an accessory, is used to attach a 3151 to RISC System/6000 computers using the IBM Cabling System.

Characteristics

Size	14 inch
Characters	Up to 3300
Type	Monochrome/green or amber-gold

3163 ASCII Display Station

The 3163 ASCII Display Station is a stand-alone, 12-inch monochrome display station used for displaying up to 1920 characters and for entering data into and retrieving data from a host processor. The 3163 Display Stations provide an asynchronous communication interface with a 7-bit or 8-bit word length, using EIA-232 (CCITT V.24/28) interface or EIA-422 (CCITT V.11) interface. The 3163 Display Stations are supported in 3161 mode.

The 3163 Models 11X/12X/2XX can communicate to the host processor without a modem, up to 1219 m (4000 ft) at 50 to 19 200 bps depending on the type of cable used when using the EIA-422 (CCITT V.11) interface. For EIA-422, a shielded communication cable is recommended. A multi-function attachment cable, an accessory, is used to attach a 3163 to RISC System/6000 computers using the IBM Cabling System.

Characteristics

Size   12 inch
Characters Up to 1920
Type   Monochrome/green or amber-gold
Other   Advanced editing functions

3164 ASCII Display Station

The 3164 ASCII Display Station is a stand-alone, 14-inch colour display station used for displaying up to 1920 characters and for entering data into and retrieving data from a host processor. The 3164 Display Stations provide an asynchronous communication interface with a 7-bit or 8-bit word length, using EIA-232 (CCITT V.24/28) interface or EIA-422 (CCITT V.11) interface. The 3164 Display Stations are supported in 3161 mode.

The 3164 Models 11X/12X can communicate to the host processor without a modem, up to 1219 m (4000 ft) at 50 to 19 200 bps depending on the type of cable used when using the EIA-422 (CCITT V.11) interface. For EIA-422, a shielded communication cable is recommended. A multi-function attachment cable, an accessory, is used to attach a 3164 to the RISC System/6000 computers using the IBM cabling system. See Table 4.6 for a summary of ASCII Display Stations.

Characteristics
Size   14 inch
Characters Up to 1920
Type   Colour
Other   Advanced editing functions

4.5.2   Graphics adapters

There is a range of graphics adapters for the RS/6000 from greyscale adapters through to the very fast 3D adapters. These adapters will operate in all

Table 4.6. ASCII Display Stations—summary

Display	Type	Size	Characters	Advanced editing functions
3151	Monochrome/ green/amber-gold	14 in.	Up to 330	Via RPQs
3163	Monochrome/ green/amber-gold	12 in.	Up to 1920	Yes
3164	Colour	14 in.	Up to 1920	Yes

Note: 3163 Display is no longer being marketed.

RS/6000 models as long as enough slots are available. Suitable graphics screens can then be attached directly to the adapter. These adapters are discussed in more detail here.

Grayscale Graphics Display Adapter

The Grayscale Graphics Display Adapter provides support for a 19-inch monochrome, analog non-interlaced, 1280 × 1024, 67 Hz graphic display. Sixteen current shades of grey may be displayed from a palette of 256 shades of grey. This feature requires one card slot in the RS/6000. The Grayscale Graphics Display Adapter is an entry-function monochrome graphics adapter that can attach to the 8508 Monochrome Display. This adapter fits into any Micro Channel adapter slot.

Characteristics

Resolution   1280 × 1024   4-bit pixels
Palette   Up to 256 shades of grey, 16 at a time
2D Rate   72 000 lines/sec Raw 2D
Features   Programmable 2-plane 64 × 64 pixel hardware cursor

Colour Graphics Display Adapter

The Colour Graphics Display Adapter provides support for 16-inch, 19-inch, and 23-inch, analog non-interlaced, 1280 × 1024, 60 Hz colour graphic displays. Up to 256 concurrent colours from a palette of 16.7 million colours may be displayed. This feature requires one Micro Channel card slot in the IBM RISC System/6000 processor. The cable from the adapter to the display is included.

Characteristics

Resolution	1280 × 1024 8-bit pixels
2D Rate	Up to 125 000 lines per second
Palette	Up to 256 colours out of 16.7 million colours
Features	Programmable 2-plane 64 × 64 pixel hardware cursor

High-Performance 8-bit 3D Colour Graphics Processor

The High-Performance 8-bit 3D Colour Graphics Processor provides support for 16-inch, 19-inch, and 23-inch, analog non-interlaced, 1280 × 1024, 60 Hz colour graphic displays. Up to 256 concurrent colours may be displayed from a palette of 16.7 million colours. This adapter provides higher function that the Colour Graphics Display Adapter and a modular approach to graphics. The cable from the adapter to display is included. This base feature provides an 8-bit, 256 colour, 2D and 3D adapter. The modular design of this card allows upgradability to the High-Performance 24-bit 3D Colour Graphics Processor, with or without the Z-buffer option. This adapter fits into any two adjacent Micro Channel adapter slots.

Characteristics

Resolution	1280 × 1024 8-bit pixels
Palette	Up to 256 colours out of 16.7 million colours
Vector rate	90 000 2D and 3D Vectors/sec 10 000 Shaded Triangles
Planes	2 overlay planes 2 window control planes
Features	Programmable cursor—3 colour sprite
	Arbitrarily shaped windows
Lighting	Multiple, coloured, local and infinite lights
	Diffuse, ambient, and specular (Phong) lighting models
	Flat and smooth (Gouraud) shading
	Dithered RGB shading
	Anti-aliased lines
	Plan and zoom of images

High-Performance 24-bit 3D Colour Graphics Processor

The High-Performance 24-bit 3D Colour Graphics Processor is the same as the High-Performance 8-bit 3D Colour Graphics Processor with the addition of the 24-bit 3D Colour Graphics Frame Buffer as a standard feature. The High-Performance 24-bit 3D Colour Graphics Processor provides support for 16-inch, 19-inch, and 23-inch, analog non-interlaced, 1280 × 1024, 60 Hz colour graphic displays. 24-bit 'true colour' with appropriate APIs can be displayed from a palette of 16.7 million colours. This adapter provides higher function than the High-Performance 8-bit 3D Colour Graphics Processor and a modular approach to graphics. The cable from the adapter to display is included. This upgraded adapter provides 8 or 12-bit double buffered pixels or 24-bit pixels.

The 16 sets of 256 concurrent colours provide for defining colours in separate windows to keep the colours consistent when the cursor is moved from window to window. The modular design of this card allows upgradability with the Z-Buffer option. This adapter fits into any two adjacent Micro Channel adapter slots.

Characteristics

Resolution	1280 × 1024 8- or 12-bit double buffered pixels or 24-bit pixels
Palette	256, 1024, or 24-bit 'true colour'
Vector rate	90 000 2D and 3D Vectors/sec 10 000 Shaded Triangles
Planes	4 overlay planes 4 window control planes
Features	Programmable cursor—3 colour sprite
	Arbitrarily shaped windows
Lighting	Multiple, coloured, local, and infinite lights
	Diffuse, ambient, and specular (Phong) lighting models
	Flat and smooth (Gouraud) shading
	8- or 12-bit dithered RGB shading
	Anti-aliased lines
	6 axis clipping
	Pan and zoom of images

Z-Buffer Option

The Z-Buffer Option is an optional feature of both the 8-bit and the 24-bit 3D Colour Graphics Processors. The Z-Buffer Option provides a 24-bit Z buffer Solid Rendering Option. This option provides for hidden line and hidden surface removal.

6094 Graphics Device Input Adapter

The 6094 Graphics Device Input Adapter provides attachment of the IBM 6094 Model 010 Dials and the IBM 6094 Model 020 Lighted Program Function Keys. This two port card provides control lines as well as DC power to the attached devices. This adapter can fit into any Micro Channel Adapter slot. Only one 6094 Graphics Device Input Adapter can be allowed per system.

Characteristics
Features   Provides attachment of dials and lighted program function keys
            Provides control lines as well as DC power to devices

RS/6000 7235 POWERgraphics GTO

The RS/6000 7235 POWERgraphics GTO is an externally attached powerful graphics subsystem that provides high-function high-performance graphics capability via a single Micro Channel adapter slot. The POWERgraphics GTO is available in two models, an 8-bit Model 001 with dual frame buffers, area fill, 256 colours, and a 24-bit Model 002 with shading, 24-bit Z-Buffer, anti-aliasing, and 16.7 million direct colours. Both models require the POWERgraphics GTO Accelerator feature if they are to be installed on the RS/6000.

The POWERgraphics GTO provides excellent performance for PHIGS based applications. It also supports IRIS GL based applications, however, previously written GL applications may not port directly to the 7235 POWERgraphics GTO. The POWERgraphics GTO is the functional equivalent of the graphics subsystem of the RS/6000 POWERstation 730 reconfigured to provide increased attachment flexibility.

The POWERgraphics GTO provides high-function, high-performance graphics for all of the RS/6000 models except 730. Only one high-function high-performance graphics subsystem is supported for each RS/6000. The GTO is packaged separately from the RS/6000 and is connected via one Micro Channel adapter (POWERgraphics GTO Accelerator). The POWER-graphics GTO supports AIXwindows Environment/6000, IBM Personal graPHIGS, and GL.

Applications requiring the level of function and performance that the POWERgraphics GTO offers are typically users in the scientific and technical community, including high-end mechanical CAD, molecular modelling, scientific visualization, and entertainment graphics.

RS/6000 POWER Gt4X, Gt4, and Gt3

IBM announced the POWER Gt4x, Gt4, and Gt3 graphics subsystems for RS/6000 in 1991. These products offer a variety of function and configurability at three distinct performance levels. Of these three graphics subsystems, the POWER Gt4x offers the highest performance level. The POWER Gt4x features 3D solid surface modelling and rendering, as well as 2D applications. The POWER Gt4x addresses a diverse set of applications such as design automation, architectural design, geophysical analysis, molecular modelling, high energy physics, image rendering, visualization, and animation.

The POWER Gt4 addresses similar applications, but with a more modest performance level. The POWER Gt3 addresses 2D graphics applications. The POWER Gt4x and Gt4 support the following application program interfaces: GL, graPHIGS, X Window System Version 11 Release 4, Display Postscript, and OSF/Motif. The POWER Gt3 supports X Window System Version 11 Release 4, OSF/Motif, graPHIGS through the Enhanced X Windows driver interface and Display Postscript.

- POWER Gt4x
  - Wireframe and 3D solid surface modelling
  - True Colour, up to 16.7 million colours per pixel
  - Frame Buffers—8-bit double-buffered and 24-bit double-buffered
  - Up to 800 000 Hardware Rated 2D Vectors per second
  - Up to 800 000 Hardware Rated 3D Vectors per second
  - Up to 80 000 Hardware Rated Gouraud Shaded Triangles per second
  - Display resolution of 1280 × 1024
- POWER Gt4
  - Wireframe and 3D solid surface modelling
  - True Colour, up to 16.7 million colours per pixel
  - Frame Buffers—8-bit double-buffered and 24-bit double-buffered
  - Up to 650 000 Hardware Rated 2D Vectors per second
  - Up to 400 000 Hardware Rated 3D Vectors per second
  - Up to 20 000 Hardware Rated Gouraud Shaded Triangles per second
  - Display Resolution of 1280 × 1024
- POWER Gt3
  - 256 colours per pixel from a palette of 16.7 million colours
  - Up to 600 000 Hardware Rated 2D Vectors per second
  - Display Resolution of 1280 × 1024

The POWER Gt4x, Gt4, and Gt3, along with the RS/6000, enable users to develop and execute graphics-based business solutions. The POWER Gt4x and Gt4 help facilitate solutions to complex graphics-oriented problems in the areas of scientific visualization, fluid mechanics, molecular modelling, design automation, design animation, product modelling, architectural design, geophysical analysis, and entertainment graphics. The POWER Gt3 helps facilitate solutions to problems where fast 2D graphics capacity is important.

The POWER Gt4x and Gt4 are designed to provide significant performance improvements over the IBM High-Performance 8-bit/24-bit 3D Colour Graphics Processors. These performance gains should allow you to execute applications with complex objects in less time. The POWER Gt3 is designed to provide significant performance improvements over the IBM Colour Graphics Display Adapter. Performance gains in the execution of 2D graphics functions should help increase productivity.

Programs written to the application program interfaces GL, graPHIGS, AIXwindows, Enhanced X Windows, GKS-CO, Display Postscript and OSF/Motif are supported on the Gt4x and Gt4, subject to the appropriate adapter resources being available. Note that GL applications requiring 12-bit colour index mode are *not* supported on the Gt4x and Gt4. Programs written to Enhanced X Windows, GKS-CO, Display Postscript, graPHIGS (when using Enhanced X Windows driver) and OSF/Motif are supported on the Gt3, subject to the appropriate adapter resources being available.

The 7325 POWERgraphics GTO is the functional equivalent of the graphics subsystem of the IBM RS/6000 model 730, reconfigured to attach to other RS/6000 models.

4.5.3 Graphics displays

There is a range of graphics displays for the RS/6000. These may be required to run a graphics application of some kind, or simply to run a windowing environment such as X Windows. These displays attach directly to a suitable graphics adapter as discussed in the previous section. The various graphics displays are discussed in this section.

5081 Display Model 16

The 5081 Model 16 is a high-resolution colour raster display especially well suited for applications that create detailed or large images, such as graphics applications. The display includes a tilt and swivel pedestal. The 5081 Model 16 screen, which measures 16 inches diagonally, has a resolution of 1024×1024 pixel array and a 60 Hz non-interlaced refresh rate. The actual

Table 4.7. Graphics adapter summary

Name	Resolution	Palette	2D performance
Grayscale	1280 × 1024	16 concurrent, 256 maximum	72 000 lines per second
Colour Graphics Adapter	1280 × 1024	256 out of 16.7 million	125 000 lines per second
8-bit 3D Colour Graphics Processor	1280 × 1024	256 out of 16.7 million	90 000 vectors per second
24-bit 3D Colour Graphics Processor	1280 × 1024	256 out of 16.7 million	90 000 vectors per second
POWER Gt3 Colour Graphics Processor	1280 × 1024	256 out of 16.7 million	600 000 vectors per second
POWER Gt4 8-bit Colour Graphics Processor	1280 × 1024	256 out of 16.7 million	800 000 vectors per second
POWER Gt4 24-bit Colour Graphics Processor	1280 × 1024	16.7 million	800 000 vectors per second
POWER Gt4x 8-bit Colour Graphics Processor	1280 × 1024	256 out of 16.7 million	800 000 vectors per second
POWER Gt4x 24-bit Colour Graphics Processor	1280 × 1024	16.7 million	800 000 vectors per second

viewing area is 9.3 inches (236 mm) square. User controls are provided for coarse convergence adjustment, picture centring, contrast and brightness. These controls are located at the front of the display and behind a flip-down cover.

The 5081 Display provides EIA-343 outputs for the cable connection of additional 5081s. All 5081s connected in this way will display the same image. An anti-reflective treatment and a tilt and swivel mechanism for viewing positions provide clear, comfortable operator viewing. The IBM 5081 Model 16 attaches to the RS/6000 by using the Display Adapter Cable plugged into one of the various graphics adapters.

Characteristics

Display type   Colour
Input signal   RGB Analog Interface
Display size   16 inches (diagonal measurement)
Addressability   1280 × 1024
Palette   Graphics Card dependent
Highlights   Tilt and swivel stand   Anti-reflective screen

Size   Height 16.38 inches (with stand), width 16.0 inches,
                depth 17.57 inches, weight 68.2 lb
Speed   60 Hz non-interlaced refresh rate

6091 Display Model 19

The 6091 Model 19 is a high-resolution colour raster analog display that
provides powerful capabilities and outstanding image quality. The display
features a built-in tilt and swivel pedestal. The screen measures 19 inches
diagonally, with customer selectable screen resolutions:

- 1024 × 1024 at 60 Hz, non-interlaced
- 1280 × 1024 at 60 Hz, non-interlaced

User controls are provided for horizontal and vertical static convergence,
vertical centring, brightness, contrast, and selectable screen sizes. These
controls are located at the front of the display and behind a flip-down cover.

The 6091 Display provides EIA-343 outputs for the cable connection of
additional 6091s. All 6091s connected in this way will display the same image.
The 6091 Display provides a video and sync redrive capability for attachment
of additional video devices, a wide-band video amplifier, a universal power
supply, a bright aperture grill CRT. An anti-reflective treatment and a tilt
and swivel mechanism for viewing positions provide clear, comfortable
operator viewing.

The 6091 Colour Display Model 19 attaches to the RISC System/6000
computer using a Display Adapter Cable and a graphics adapter. The IBM
6091 Model 19 Display also attaches to the Xstation 120 or Xstation 130.

Characteristics

Display type   Colour
Input signal   RGB Analog Interface
Display size   19 inches (diagonal measurement)
Addressability   1024 × 1024 or 1280 × 1024
Palette   Graphics Card dependent
Highlights   Tilt and swivel stand
                    Front accessible operator controls
                    Anti-reflective screen
                    Video and sync redrive capability
Size   Height 19.1 inches (with stand), width 18.9 inches, depth
                    19.2 inches, weight 74.9 lb
Speed   60 Hz non-interlaced refresh rate

6091 Display Model 23

The 6091 Model 23 is a high-resolution colour raster analog display that provides powerful capabilities and outstanding image quality. The screen, which measures 23 inches diagonally, offers a large viewing area that provides greater image magnification than smaller screen sizes. The display features a built-in tilt and swivel pedestal. This display is similar in function to the model 19 but is larger in size.

Characteristics

Display type	Colour
Input signal	RGB Analog Interface
Display size	23 inches (diagonal measurement)
Addressability	1024×1024 or 1280×1024
Palette	Graphics Card dependent
Highlights	Tilt and swivel stand
	Front accessible operator controls
	Anti-reflective screen
	Video and sync redrive capability
Size	Height 21.4 inches (with stand), width 23.9 inches, depth 23.5 inches, weight 123 lb
Speed	60 Hz non-interlaced refresh rate

8503 Monochrome Display

The Monochrome Display 8503 is an analog multimode, paper-white phosphor, monochrome display featuring advanced text, graphics and imaging capabilities. Up to 64 shades of grey can be shown when attached to the IBM Xstation 120 or the IBM Xstation 130. It can also provide addressability of 640×480 for graphics and 720×400 for text. The integrated tilt and swivel base is standard. The 8503 attaches to the IBM Xstation 120 or the IBM Xstation 130 display port.

Characteristics

Display type	Monochrome
	White-on-black or black-on-white
Input signal	Analog
	Display size 12 inches (diagonal measurement)
Addressability	720×400 text 640×480 graphics
Palette	Up to 64 shades of grey
Highlights	Tilt and swivel stand

Size   6 foot signal cable
                 Reduced glare
                 Height 12.3 inches (with stand), width 12.6 inches, depth
                 12.2 inches, weight 18.8 lb
Speed   31.5 KHz horizontal scan frequency non-interlaced up to
                 70 Hz vertical refresh rate

8507 Monochrome Display

The 8507 Monochrome Display is a low cost 19-inch analog, multimode, white phosphor, monochrome raster display capable of displaying up to 1024 × 768 pixels at 73 pels per inch in a viewable area of 14.0 inches × 10.5 inches (356 mm × 267 mm).

The 8507 display is capable of displaying advanced text, graphics, and images in up to 64 shades of grey when attached to the IBM Xstation 120 or IBM Xstation 130. The unit contains a universal power supply and an anti-reflective screen to reduce glare. The display includes a tilt and swivel pedestal to accommodate operator comfort and convenience. The 8507 monochrome display attaches to the IBM Xstation 120 or IBM Xstation 130 display port.

Characteristics

Display type   Monochrome
                   White-on-black or black-on-white
Input signal   Analog
Display size   19 inches (diagonal measurement)
Addressability   1024 × 768 graphics
Palette   Up to 64 shades of grey
Highlights   Anti-reflective screen
                   Tilt-and-swivel stand standard
                   External brightness and contrast controls
Base   Adjustable tilt and swivel pedestal
Size   Height 17.75 inches (with stand), width 18.75 inches,
                   depth 17 inches, weight 51.7 lb
Speed   31.5 KHz horizontal scan frequency non-interlaced up to
                   70 Hz vertical refresh rate

8508 Monochrome Display

The 8508 Monochrome Display is a horizontally oriented 19-inch analog, multimode, white phosphor raster display capable of displaying up to

1200 × 1600 pixels in a viewable area of 14.0 inches × 10.5 inches (356 mm × 267 mm). The analog technology provides increased capability for selection of grey shades. Up to 16 of 256 shades of grey, dependent on selected screen mode, are available to allow the user to highlight, detail, and accentuate complex graphics and images.

An anti-reflective screen to reduce glare, front accessible operator controls, and a tilt-swivel pedestal to accommodate operator comfort and convenience is standard. The 8508 Monochrome Display attaches to the RS/6000 Grayscale Graphics Adapter using a built-in cable. The 8508 attaches to the IBM Xstation 120 and IBM Xstation 130 display port.

Characteristics

Display type	Monochrome
	White-on-black or black-on-white
Input signal	Analog
Addressability	Up to 1200 × 1600
Palette	Up to 16 of 256 shades of grey
Highlights	Tilt-and-swivel stand
	Reduced glare
Size	Height 17.75 inches (with stand), width 18.75 inches, depth 17.00 inches, weight 51.7 lb
Speed	Up to 70.7 KHz horizontal scan frequency
	Up to 93.5 KHz vertical scan frequency

8512 Colour Display

The 8512 Colour Display is a low cost analog colour display. It offers excellent colour graphics capabilities (up to 256 colours) and provides addressability up to 640 by 480 in graphics mode. It can also be used with the current line of IBM Personal System/2 systems.

The 8512 Colour Display has been designed as a balance between the need for addressability and the ability to blend colours for near image quality application output. An optional colour display stand is available, which enhances flexibility in installing the IBM 8512 Display. This option snaps onto the bottom of the 8512 Colour Display and allows the user to adjust the display both horizontally and vertically for maximum comfort. It is easily removable should requirements change. The 8512 Colour Display attaches to the IBM Xstation 120 or the IBM Xstation 130 using the display port.

Characteristics

Display type	Colour
Input signal	Analog
Display size	14 inches (diagonal measurement)
Addressability	320, 640, and 720 dot lines of horizontal addressability
	350, 400, and 480 lines of vertical addressability
Palette	Up to 256 colours on screen out of 256 000 colours
Highlights	Tilt and swivel stand
	6 foot signal cable
	Reduced glare
	0.41 mm stripe format
Size	Height 14.6 inches (with stand), width 14 inches,
	depth 15.5 inches, weight 33 lb
Speed	31.5 KHz horizontal scan frequency
	Non-interlaced with up to 70 Hz vertical refresh rate

8513 Colour Display

The 8513 Colour Display is an analog, multimode colour display featuring advanced text, graphics, and imaging capabilities. The 8513 Colour Display provides addressability of 640 × 480 pixels for graphics and 720 × 400 pixels for text. The 0.28 mm dot pitch produces sharp characters that are easy on the eyes during extended use.

Etched glass screen cuts glare from surrounding light source, important in reducing fatigue and eyestrain. Previously displayed text and graphics disappear quickly when screen content changes. There are external contrast and brightness controls to vary screen intensity and a tilt and swivel base to adjust the display to the most comfortable viewing position. The 8513 Colour Display attaches to the IBM Xstation 120 or the IBM Xstation 130 using the display port.

Characteristics

Display type	Colour
Input signal	Analog
Display size	12 inches (diagonal measurement)
Addressability	7204 × 400 text 640 × 480 graphics
Palette	Up to 256 colours on screen out of 250 000
Highlights	Tilt-and-swivel stand
	6 foot signal cable
	Reduced glare
	0.28 mm dot pitch

Size   Height 12.3 inches (with stand), width 12.6 inches,
                depth 12.2 inches, weight 23 lb
Speed   31.5 KHz horizontal scan frequency non-interlaced with up
                to 70 Hz vertical refresh rate

8514 Colour Display

The 8514 Colour Display is a high quality, high content, analog multimode colour display featuring advanced text, graphics, and imaging capabilities. The 8514 Colour Display provides addressability of 1024 × 768 pixels for graphics applications. The 0.31 mm dot pitch produces sharp characters that are easy on the eyes during extended use.

Phosphors and high screen refresh rates combine to reduce 'ghosts' and 'smearing'. Previously displayed text and graphics disappear quickly when screen content changes. The etched glass screen cuts glare from surrounding light sources, important in reducing fatigue and eyestrain.

There are external contrast and brightness controls to vary screen intensity and a tilt and swivel base to adjust the display to the most comfortable viewing position. The 8514 Colour Display attaches to the IBM Xstation 120 using the display port.

Characteristics

Display type   Colour
Input signal   Analog
Display size   16 inches (diagonal measurement)
Addressability Up to 1024 × 768 graphics
Palette   Up to 256 colours on screen out of 256 K
Highlights   Tilt-and-swivel stand
                6 foot signal cable
                Reduced glare
                0.31 mm dot pitch
Size   Height 14.2 inches (with stand), width 15.8 inches,
                depth 16.3 inches, weight 41.9 lb
Speed   31.5 KHz horizontal scan frequency non-interlaced up to
                70 Hz vertical refresh rate

Table 4.8 summarizes the range of graphic displays for the RS/6000.

4.6   Xstations

There are two models of Xstation—the model 120 and the model 130. These allow the user to run an application (using X Windows) across a LAN. The

Table 4.8. Display summary

Name	Display type	Display size	Attachment
5081-016	Colour	16 in.	RISC System/6000 and Xstation 120 Xstation 130
6091-019	Colour	19 in.	RISC System/6000 and Xstation 120 Xstation 130
6091-023	Colour	23 in.	RISC System/6000
8503	Monochrome	12 in.	Xstation 120 Xstation 130
8507	Monochrome	19 in.	Xstation 120 Xstation 130
8508	Monochrome	19 in.	RISC System/6000 and Xstation 120 Xstation 130
8512	Colour	14 in.	Xstation 120 Xstation 130
8513	Colour	12 in.	Xstation 120 Xstation 130
8514	Colour	16 in.	Xstation 120 Xstation 130

user uses the Xstation, which provides the windowing support, but the application runs on the RS/6000 itself. A PC or PS/2 with suitable software can perform similar functions, as well as run PC applications. An Xstation would be used when a user does not require a PC, or PC applications. An Xstation will typically work out cheaper than a PC. In addition, a network of Xstations is easy to manage as all software is held on the host RS/6000. The two models of Xstation are discussed here. Figure 4.10 shows an Xstation with a graphics screen attached.

4.6.1   IBM Xstation 120

The IBM Xstation 120 is an advanced function LAN (Local Area Network) attached Xstation supporting the Massachusetts Institute of Technology X Window System. It uses the processing power of an AIX host and the graphics capabilities of the Xstation 120. For X Window System applications, it provides an attractive, lower-cost alternative to dedicated workstations on a LAN.

In a LAN-based X Window System environment, the X Window System protocol allows the separation of the computing function (at the host) from user interaction (at the Xstation). From the Xstation 120, the user can control and view multiple executing applications concurrently. The Xstation

Figure 4.10. IBM Xstation.

120 can support multiple graphical applications and interfaces, as well as character based ones. Attachment of a local printer allows the Xstation 120 to be used as a print server or to provide convenience printing to remote users. The Xstation 120 requires the AIX Xstation Manager/6000 and AIXwindows Environment/6000 licensed programs to be installed on the RS/6000 host.

Highlights

- Quiet, compact lower-cost alternative to a workstation in an X Window System environment
- Simultaneous dual LAN support (Ethernet and optional Token-Ring)
- Wide range of greyscale and colour display support—up to 256 colours from a palette of 16.7 million
- Local printer support
- Performance features
  - Separate processors for graphics and I/O functions
  - Expandable to 9.0 MB of system and I/O memory
  - Local caching
- Advanced functions
  - Save under (pop-up windows)
  - Backing store (local storage of images hidden by overlapping windows)
  - Multiple host attachment capability
  - Colour and greyscale graphics support on multiple windows
- Downloaded X server software

Hardware description

Within a LAN-attached X Window System environment, the IBM Xstation 120 offers a lower-cost alternative to a dependent workstation on a LAN. Its quiet and compact packaging makes it attractive in many environments. With the Ethernet and optional Token Ring adapter, the IBM Xstation 120 can be attached to two LANs concurrently, fitting into most customer environments and providing high availability to host resources. Its built-in serial and parallel ports allow local attachment of IBM supported printers and other serial I/O devices.

The Xstation 120 supports windowing on a wide range of all-points addressable displays, including those supported by the IBM PS/2 family and the IBM RISC System/6000 family. No feature cards are needed; however, additional video memory is required to accommodate more colours and shades on the higher resolution displays. With both colour and greyscale support standard, the Xstation 120 has a colour palette of 16.7 million colours, from which up to 256 can be displayed at one time.

The IBM Xstation 120 includes two processors. The TMS 34010 Graphics Processor controls the graphics and windowing functions. The Intel 80186 Processor controls I/O functions. This dual processor approach improves system performance, reduces LAN overheads, and provides rapid keyboard response and mouse tracking.

The Xstation 120 implements local caching, save under, and backing store to reduce LAN traffic and provide quick access to windows and fonts stored in local memory. Its 8 MB system memory expansion capability to 8.5 MB maximum (9 MB maximum system and I/O memory) is designed to enhance productivity and provide the capability for a large number of windows to be utilized.

The Xstation 120 can be used with multiple hosts on one LAN. If one host fails, the Xstation 120 can continue to function using other hosts. Since host resources are shared by multiple users, resources not needed by one user are available to other users on the LAN.

Software description

The X-server software is downloaded at initial program load from an RS/6000 host, running the AIX Xstation Manager/6000 licensed program. This centralized location simplifies maintenance and upgrading of the software and enables functional growth, protecting the customer's hardware investment.

AIX Xstation Manager/6000 provides X Window System 11.4 server capability, and compatibility with X 11.3 and 11.4 client applications. It provides host printer support, transparent font access from multiple hosts, video memory panning, user selection of initial login host, primary and secondary boot hosts, access to other networks through bridges and gateways, System Management Interface Tool (SMIT) support for Xstation configuring, and X Display Manager Control Program (XDMCP).

AIX Xstation Manager/6000 has two configuration options for the Xstation 120. Function based on X Window System Version 11 Release 3 operates with the base Xstation 120 system memory (512 KB). Function based on X Window System Version 11 Release 4 requires a minimum of 1.5 MB system memory.

Standard features

The following features come standard with the IBM Xstation 120.

- TMS 34010 Graphics Processor with 512 KB system memory and 512 KB video memory
- Intel 80186 I/O Processor with 512 KB DRAM
- Ethernet port (compatible with Ethernet Version 2 and IEEE 802.3, 10Base2 or 10Base5)
- Integrated video display adapter
- Serial port (19 2000 baud maximum, 25 pin D-shell connector)
- Parallel printer port
- Keyboard
- Three button mouse

Optional features

The following features are optional with the IBM Xstation 120.

- Up to 8.5 MB system memory
- Up to 2 MB video memory
- Token Ring Network 16/4 Adapter/A and Riser Card
- Cables for device attachment
- Maintenance package

System memory features

System memory may be expanded to provide increased X-server efficiency and LAN throughput. Up to a maximum of four memory features (in either

1 MB or 2 MB increments) may be added to the base Model 120 for a total of 8.5 MB.

Video memory

Video memory may be expanded by 512 KB or 1.5 MB to provide support for additional colours or increased resolution. Video memory provides support for the following modes:

- The base 512 KB video memory configuration supports:
  - 640 × 480 × 256 Grey/colour
  - 1024 × 768 × 18 Grey/colour
  - 1280 × 1024 × 4 Grey/colour
- The expanded 1 MB video memory configuration supports:
  - 1024 × 768 × 256 Grey/colour
  - 1280 × 1024 × 16 Grey/colour
  - 1600 × 1200 × 4 Grey
- The expanded 2 MB video memory configuration supports:
  - 1280 × 1024 × 256 Grey/colour
  - 1600 × 1200 × 16 Grey

Supported displays

There are a number of displays available to attach to the Xstation 120 ranging from grayscale to 19 inch colour displays.

Supported printers

A range of IBM and non-IBM printers are supported.

4.6.2   IBM Xstation 130

The IBM Xstation 130 is a higher-performance, advanced function LAN attached Xstation supporting the Massachusetts Institute of Technology X Window System. It uses the processing power of an AIX host and the graphics capabilities of the Xstation 130. For X Window System applications, it provides a powerful, lower-cost alternative to dedicated workstations on a LAN.

Standard features

The following features come standard with the IBM Xstation 130.

- TMS 34020 Graphics Processor with 2 MB system memory and 1 MB video memory

Table 4.9. IBM Xstation 120 summary

Feature	Highlights
Processors	TMS 34010 Graphics Processor, Intel 80186 I/O Processor
Standard memory	512 KB System and I/O, 512 KB Video
Max memory	9 MB System and I/O, 2 MB Video
Input/output	Ethernet (thick and thin), serial, parallel printer, video display, mouse, keyboard, optional Token Ring
Supported displays	8503, 8507, 8508, 8512, 8513, 8514, 8515, 5081-16 with RPQ 8K1700, 6091-19
Other	• Local caching • Save under (pop-up windows) • Backing store (local storage of images hidden by overlapping windows) • Multiple host attachment capability • Colour and greyscale graphics support with multiple windows • Downloaded X-server for easier system maintenance • Support for X 11.3 and 11.4 client applications • Simultaneous dual LAN support

- Intel 80C186 I/O Processor with 512 KB DRAM
- Ethernet port (compatible with Ethernet Version 2 and IEEE 802.3, 10Base2 or 10Base5)
- Integrated video display adapter
- Two serial ports (19 2000 baud maximum, 25 pin D-shell connector)
- Parallel printer port
- Riser Card
- Keyboard
- Three button mouse

Optional features

The following features are optional with the IBM Xstation 130.

- Up to 16 MB system memory
- Up to 2 MB video memory
- 30 MB direct attached disk drive
- Token-Ring Network 16/4 Adapter/A
- Second Ethernet adapter
- PS/2 Dual SYNC Adapter/A
- Cables for device attachment
- Maintenance package

System memory features

System memory may be expanded to provide increased X-server efficiency and LAN throughput. Up to a maximum of four memory features (in either

1 MB, 2 MB, or 4 MB increments) may be added to the base Model 130 for a total of 16 MB, providing a total of 16.5 MB system and I/O memory.

Video memory

Video memory may be expanded by 1 MB (for a maximum of 2 MB) to provide support for additional colours or increased resolution. Video memory provides support for the following modes:

- The base 1 MB video memory configuration supports:
  - 640 × 480 × 256 Grey/colour   – 1280 × 1024 × 16 Grey/colour
  - 1024 × 768 × 256 Grey/colour   – 1600 × 1200 × 2 Grey
- The expanded 2 MB video memory configuration supports:
  - 1280 × 1024 × 256 Grey/colour
  - 1600 × 1200 ×   4 Grey

30 MB direct attached disk drive option

The fixed disk option is intended for those users whose applications require significant offscreen pixel resources, such as multiple imaging applications or panning images larger than the viewed image. Images can be stored in server memory on the Xstation for local screen refresh (rather than over the network) or smoother panning of large images. The disk drive offers an alternative to addition of system memory.

An Xstation 130 with a fixed-disk drive can automatically utilize backing store on all windows, reducing or eliminating LAN traffic for many user window manipulation actions. The disk drive can also serve as a local font cache for all fonts received from the network.

With the disk drive installed, the Xstation 130 can locally IPL from the resident fixed disk, resulting in minimal network traffic at IPL time for the server.

Supported displays

There are a number of displays available to attach to the Xstation 120 ranging from greyscale to 19 inch colour displays.

Supported printers

A range of IBM and non-IBM printers are supported.
See Table 4.10 for a summary of Xstation features and highlights.

Table 4.10. IBM Xstation 130 summary

Feature	Highlights
Processors	TMS 34020 Graphics Processor, Intel 80C186 I/O Processor
Standard memory	2.5 MB System and I/O, 1 MB Video
Max memory	16.5 MB System and I/O, 2 MB Video
Standard input/output	Ethernet (thick and thin), 2 serial ports, parallel printer port, video display adapter, mouse, keyboard
Optional input/output	Token-Ring, 30 MB hardfile, second Ethernet
Supported displays	8503, 8507, 8508, 8512, 8513, 8514, 8515, 5081-16 with RPQ 8K1700, 6091-19
Other	• Local caching • Save under (pop-up windows) • Backing store (local storage of images hidden by overlapping windows) • Multiple host attachment capability • Colour and greyscale graphics support with multiple windows • Downloaded X-server for easier system maintenance • Support for X 11.3 and 11.4 client applications • Simultaneous dual LAN support • Extensive I/O support (tables, plotters, modems) • Host printer support • Flexible login and boot management • Disk drive option for local boot, font caching, and offscreen pixmaps

4.7   I/O adapters

I/O adapters for the RS/6000 are Micro Channel adapters. There is compatibility with PS/2 adapters and in many cases PS/2 adapters can be used in the RS/6000. There are adapters to perform communications, to attach SCSI tapes and disks, to attach graphics screens and many other functions.

Separate slots are used for memory cards. Micro Channel adapters and memory cards can be added completely independently. The larger sizes of RS/6000 can hold more adapters. All the different Micro Channel adapters are discussed in other sections of this book depending on the functions that they perform.

4.8   Printers and plotters

There are a number of printers and plotters that will operate with the RS/6000. The IBM printers and plotters are discussed here. The RS/6000 will also support non-IBM printers, including the following, and other compatible printers:

• DATAPRODUCTS LZR 2665   • PRINTRONIX P9012

- DATAPRODUCTS BP2000
- HP LaserJet Series II

- Texas Instruments Omnilaser Model 2115

3812-2 page printer

The 3812 Model 2 is a non-impact page printer that can be used for departmental letter-quality printing applications. It can print up to 12 pages per minute.

The printer attaches to the RS/6000 using an Async Cable EIA-232/V.24 (with a Printer/Terminal Interposer EIA-232) to an 8-, 16- or 64-Port Asynchronous Controller port. The printer can also attach to an 8- or 16-Port Asynchronous Adapter-EIA-422A port.

Characteristics

Technology	LED/electrophotographic
Speed	Up to 12 pages per minute
Quality	240 × 240
Pitches/typestyles	Up to 62 fonts (Courier, Prestige, Elite, Gothic, OCR-A, OCR-B, Essay, Serif, Sonoran Serif, bar codes and much more)
Graphics resolution	240 × 240
Paper sizes (inches)	8.5 × 11, 8.5 × 14, 7 × 10.5, 7.25 × 10.5, 7.5 × 10.5, A4, B4
Forms handling	Cut sheet—2 input bins (550 and 250), optional 1200
Modes of operation	PMP
Capacity	18 000 pages per month
Attachment	Serial

3816 Model 01S Printer

The 3816 is a letter-quality non-impact printer that can print up to 24 pages per minute. It is a heavy-duty printer designed for average usage of 40 000 pages per month of letter-quality printing. The printer offers 1.5 MB of memory for printer operations and resident font storage and 2 MB for page map storage.

The printer attaches to the RS/6000 using an Async Cable EIA-232/V.24 (with a Printer/Terminal Interposer EIA-232) to an 8-, 16- or 64-Port Asynchronous Controller port. The printer can also attach to an 8- or 16-Port Asynchronous Adapter-EIA-422A port.

Characteristics

Technology	LED/electrophotographic
Speed	Up to 24 pages per minute
Quality	240 × 240
Pitches/typestyles	Up to 62 fonts (Courier, Prestige Elite, Gothic, OCR-A, OCR-B, Essay, Serif, Sonoran Serif, bar codes and many more)
Graphic resolution	240 × 240
Paper sizes (inches)	8.5 × 11, 8.5 × 14, 7 × 10.5, 7.25 × 10.5, 7.5 × 10.5, 8.27 × 12.5, A4, B4
Forms handling	Cut sheet—2 input bins (550 and 250), optional 1200
Modes of operation	5202 Emulation, PMP
Capacity	40 000 impressions per month
Attachment	Serial

4019 Laserprinter 001 and E01

The 4019 LaserPrinter is a desktop laser printer that has a single-element operator-replaceable print cartridge. Its speed, function, and extensive font and paper-handling features make the IBM 4019 laserPrinter an excellent workstation page printer. The printer can print up to ten pages per minute (001) or five pages per minute (E01).

The 4019 LaserPrinter attaches to the RS/6000 using a PC Parallel Printer Cable to the standard parallel port. Serially, the printer can attach to the RS/6000 using an Async Cable EIA-232/V.24 (with a Printer/Terminal Interposer EIA-232) to an 8-, 16- or 64-Port Asynchronous Controller port. For high graphics applications in a multi-user environment, serial connection is recommended.

Characteristics

Technology	Electrophotographic
Speed	Up to 10 pages per minute (001), up to 5 pages per minute (E01)
Resolution	300 × 300 dpi
Pitches/typestyles	6.5, 8.1, 10, 12, 15, 16.7, 17.1, 20, 25 cpi, Proportional/ 6–60 pt Times New Roman, 6–60 pt Helvetica, Palatino, Century Schoolbook, Baskerville and many more
Paper sizes	Manual feed (3.875 in. to 8.5 in.) Auto feed (7.2 in. to 8.5 in.)

Forms handling	Cut sheet—2 input bins (200 standard, and 500 optional), 75 envelope feed (optional), transparencies, labels, sequenced and unsequenced output trays
Modes of operation	PPDS, HP Laserjet Series II (PCL4) Plotters (IBM 7372, HP 7475A), Post Script
Capacity	20 000 pages per month (001), 12 000 pages per month (E01)
Attachment	Serial, parallel

4201 Proprinter II

The 4201 Proprinter II provides low-cost dot-matrix printer operation.

The 4201 Proprinter II attaches to the RS/6000 using a PC Parallel Printer Cable to the standard parallel port. With the Serial Interface option installed, the printer can attach using an Async Cable EIA-232/V.24 (with a Printer/ Terminal interposer EIA-232) to a standard serial port or to an 8-, 16- or 64-Port Asynchronous Controller port.

Characteristics

Technology	9 wire matrix
Speed	200–240 cps (draft), 40 cps (near letter quality)
Pitches/typestyles	5, 6, 8.5, 10, 12, 17.1, Proportional NLQ II
Graphics resolution	60×144, 120×144, 240×144 dpi
Paper sizes	Cut sheet – 3 to 11 in., continuous forms – 3 to 10 in., print line – 8 in.
Forms handling	Cut sheet, envelopes, continuous forms (up to 4-part), Document on Demand, Paper Tear Assist, Forms Load
Attachment	Serial, parallel

4201 Proprinter III

The 4201 Proprinter III provides low-cost dot-matrix printer operation.

The 4201 Proprinter III attaches to the RS/6000 using a PC Parallel Printer Cable to the standard parallel port. With the Serial Interface option installed, the printer can attach using an Async Cable EIA-232/V.24 (with a Printer/ Terminal interposer EIA-232) to a standard serial port or to an 8-, 16- or 64-Port Asynchronous Controller port. The printer can also attach to an 8- or 16-Port Asynchronous Adapter-EIA-422A port. The printer can also be attached to the Xstation 120 via a serial or parallel port.

Characteristics

Technology	9 wire matrix
Speed	270–320 cps (draft), 65 cps (near letter quality)
Pitches/typestyles	5, 6, 8.5, 10, 17.1, 20, Proportional, Sans Serif NLQ, Serif NLQ II, Italics NLQ II
Graphics resolution	144 × 240, 144 × 120, 144 × 240 dpi
Paper sizes	Cut sheet—3 to 11 in., continuous forms—3 to 10 in., print line—8 in.
Forms handling	Cut sheet, envelopes, continuous forms (up to 4-part), Document on Demand, Propark, Paper Tear Assist, Forms Load Assist, Sheet Feed Option
Attachment	Serial, parallel

4202 Proprinter II XL

The 4202 Proprinter II XL provides low-cost dot-matrix printer operation.

The 4202 Proprinter II XL attaches to the RS/6000 using a PC Parallel Printer Cable to the standard parallel port. With the Serial Interface option installed, the printer can attach using an Async Cable EIA-232/V.24 (with a Printer/Terminal interposer EIA-232) to a standard serial port or to an 8-, 16- or 64-Port Asynchronous Controller port.

Characteristics

Technology	9 wire matrix
Speed	200–240 cps (draft), 40 cps (near letter quality)
Pitches/typestyles	5, 6, 8.5, 10, 12, 17.1, Proportional, Sans Serif NLQ, Serif NLQ II
Graphics resolution	60 × 144, 120 × 144, 240 × 144 dpi
Paper sizes	Cut sheet—3 to 16.5 in., continuous forms—3 to 15 in., print line—13.6 in.
Forms handling	Cut sheet, envelopes, continuous forms (up to 4-part), Document on Demand, Paper Tear Assist, Forms Load
Attachment	Serial, parallel

4202 Proprinter III XL

The 4202 Proprinter III XL provides low-cost dot-matrix printer operation.

The 4202 Proprinter III XL attaches to the RS/6000 using a PC Parallel Printer Cable to the standard parallel port. With the Serial Interface option installed, the printer can attach using an Async Cable EIA-232/V.24 (with a Printer/Terminal interposer EIA-232) to a standard serial port or to an 8-, 16- or 64-Port Asynchronous Controller port. The printer can also attach to an 8- or 16-Port Asynchronous Adapter-EIA-422A port.

Characteristics

Technology	9 wire matrix
Speed	270–320 cps (draft), 65 cps (near letter quality)
Pitches/typestyles	5, 6, 8.5, 10, 12, 17.1, 20, Proportional, Sans Serif NLQ, Serif NLQ II, Italics NLQ II
Graphics resolution	144 × 240, 144 × 120, 144 × 240 dpi
Paper sizes	Cut sheet—3 to 16.5 in., continuous form—3 to 15 in., print line—13.6 in.
Forms handling	Cut sheet, envelopes, continuous forms (up to 4-part), Document on Demand, Propark, Paper Tear Assist, Forms Load Assist, Sheet Feed Option
Attachment	Serial, parallel

4207 Proprinter X24E

The 4207 Proprinter X24E is a high-speed, letter-quality impact printer.

The 4207 Proprinter X24E attaches to the RS/6000 using a PC Parallel Printer Cable to the standard parallel port. With the Serial Interface option installed, the printer can attach using an Async Cable EIA-232/V.24 (with a Printer/Terminal interposer EIA-232) to a standard serial port or to an 8-, 16- or 64-Port Asynchronous Controller port. The printer can also attach to an 8- or 16-Port Asynchronous Adapter-EIA-422A port. The printer can also be attached to the Xstation 120 via a serial or parallel port.

Characteristics

Technology	24 wire matrix
Speed	240–288 cps (draft), 80–96 cps (letter quality)
Pitches/typestyles	5, 6, 8.55, 10, 12, 17.1, Proportional/Courier, Prestige Elite
Graphics resolution	180 × 360 dpi
Paper sizes	Cut sheet—11 in., continuous form—10 in., print line —8 in.
Forms handling	Cut sheet, envelopes, continuous forms (up to 4-part), Document on Demand, Propark, Paper Tear Assist, Forms Load Assist
Attachment	Serial, parallel

4208 Proprinter XL24E

The 4208 Proprinter XL24E is a wide carriage, high-speed, letter-quality printer.

The 4208 Proprinter XL24E attaches to the RS/6000 using a PC Parallel Printer Cable to the standard parallel port. With the Serial Interface option installed, the printer can attach using an Async Cable EIA-232/V.24 (with a Printer/Terminal interposer EIA-232) to a standard serial port or to an 8-, 16- or 64-Port Asynchronous Controller port. The printer can also attach to an 8- or 16-Port Asynchronous Adapter-EIA-422A port.

Characteristics

Technology	24 wire matrix
Speed	240–288 cps (draft) 80–96 cps (letter quality)
Pitches/typestyles	5, 6, 8.55, 10, 17.1, Proportional, Courier, Prestige Elite
Graphics resolution	180 × 360 dpi
Paper sizes	Cut sheet—16.5 in, continuous forms—15 in., print line—13.6 in.
Forms handling	Cut sheet, envelopes, continuous forms (up to 4-part), Document on Demand, Propark, Paper Tear Assist, Forms Load Assist
Attachment	Serial, parallel

4224 Model 301

The 4224 Model 301 is a serial dot-matrix impact printer. This is an ideal desktop printer in a multi-user environment for various data processing and word processing applications.

The 4224 Model 301 attaches to the RS/6000 using an Async Cable EIA-232/V.24 (with a Printer/Terminal Interposer EIA-232) to a standard serial port or to an 8-, 16- or 64-Port Asynchronous Controller port. The printer can also attach to an 8- or 16-Port Asynchronous Adapter-EIA-422A port.

Characteristics

Technology	9 wire matrix
Speed	200 cps (DP), 100 cps (text), 50 cps (near letter quality)
Pitches/typestyles	10, 12, 15, Proportional, OCR-A, OCR-B, numerous bar codes
Graphics resolution	144 × 144, 144 × 72 dpi

Paper sizes	3 in. to 15 in.
Forms handling	Document on Demand, continuous forms (up to 6-part), Document Insertion, heavy duty
Attachment	Serial

4224 Model 302

The 4224 Model 302 is a serial dot-matrix impact printer. This is an ideal desktop printer in a multi-user environment for various data processing and word processing applications.

The 4224 Model 302 attaches to the RS/6000 using an Async Cable EIA-232/V.24 (with a Printer/Terminal Interposer EIA-232) to a standard serial port or to an 8-, 16- or 64-Port Asynchronous Controller port. The printer can also attach to an 8- or 16-Port Asynchronous Adapter-EIA-422A port.

Characteristics

Technology	18 wire matrix
Speed	400/200/100 cps
Quality	DP/text/near letter quality
Pitches/typestyles	10, 12, 15, Proportional, OCR-A, OCR-B, numerous bar codes
Graphics resolution	$144 \times 144, 144 \times 72$
Paper sizes	3 in. to 15 in.
Forms handling	Document on Demand, continuous forms (up to 6-part), Document Insertion, heavy duty
Attachment	Serial

4224 Model 3C2

The 4224 Model 3C2 is a serial dot-matrix impact printer. This is an ideal desktop printer in a multi-user environment for various data processing, graphics and word processing applications.

The 4224 Model 3C2 attaches to the RS/6000 using an Async Cable EIA-232/V.24 (with a Printer/Terminal interposer EIA-232) to a standard serial port or to an 8-, 16- or 64-Port Asynchronous Controller port. The printer can also attach to an 8- or 16-Port Asynchronous Adapter-EIA-422A port.

Characteristics

Technology	18 wire matrix
Colour printing	Four or eight colours
Speed	400/200/100 cps
Quality	DP/text/near letter quality
Pitches/typestyles	10, 12, 15, Proportional, OCR-A, OCR-B, numerous bar codes
Graphics resolution	144 × 144, 144 × 72 dpi
Paper sizes	3 in. to 15 in.
Forms handling	Document on Demand, continuous forms (up to 6-part), Document Insertion, heavy duty
Attachment	Serial

4224 Model 3E3

The 4224 Model 3E3 is a heavy-duty serial dot-matrix impact printer. This is an ideal desktop printer in a multi-user environment for various data processing and word processing applications.

The 4224 Model 3E3 attaches to the RS/6000 using an Async Cable EIA-232/V.24 (with a Printer/Terminal interposer EIA-232) to a standard serial port or to an 8-, 16- or 64-Port Asynchronous Controller port. The printer can also attach to an 8- or 16-Port Asynchronous Adapter-EIA-422A port.

Characteristics

Technology	18 wire matrix
Speed	600/300/150 cps
Quality	DP/Text/Near letter quality
Pitches/typestyles	10, 12, 15, 16.7, Proportional, OCR-A, OCR-B, numerous bar codes
Graphics resolution	144 × 144, 144 × 72 dpi
Paper sizes	3 in. to 15 in.
Forms handling	Document on Demand, continuous forms (up to 6-part), Document Insertion, Heavy Duty
Attachment	Serial

4234 Dot Band Printer Model 013

The 4234 is a Dot Band line-matrix impact printer suitable for heavy-duty line dot-matrix printing applications in a shared environment.

The 4234 Model 013 attaches to the RS/6000 using an Async Cable

EIA-232/V.24 (with a Printer/Terminal interposer EIA-232) to a standard serial port or to an 8-, 16- or 64-Port Asynchronous Controller port. The printer can also attach to an 8- or 16-Port Asynchronous Adapter-EIA-422A port.

Characteristics

Technology	Dot Band
Speed	800/600/200 lpm
Quality	Draft/DP/near letter quality
Pitches/typestyles	10, 12, 13.3, 15, 16.7, 18, Essay, Gothic
Graphics resolution	180 × 72, 120 × 72, 60 × 72 dpi
Paper sizes	3.5 in. to 16 in.
Forms handling	Continuous forms (up to 6-part), power assisted loading
Modes of operation	4202 Emulation
Attachment	Serial, parallel

5202 Quietwriter III

The Quietwriter III Printer is a high-speed, executive letter-quality, non-impact printer designed for the executive office environment.

The printer attaches to the RS/6000 using a PC Parallel Printer Cable to a standard parallel port.

Characteristics

Technology	Resistive Ribbon Thermal Transfer
Speed	160–274 cps/100–171 cps/80–136 cps
Quality	Draft/quality/enhanced quality
Pitches/typestyles	10, 12, 15, 17.1, Proportional, Artisan, Courier, Boldface and others
Graphics resolution	240 × 240, 120 × 120, 72 × 240, 72 × 120, 72 × 60, 60 × 60 dpi
Paper sizes	Continuous (pin to pin)—2.5 in. to 14.5 in., Manual cut sheet—3 in. to 16.54 in., Single drawer—8.5 in. Dual drawer—5.8 in. to 14 in.
Forms handling	Cut sheet, continuous forms, envelopes, dual drawer, some transparencies
Attachment	Parallel

Table 4.11. Printer summary

Printer	Speed	Quality	Forms handling/remarks
3812 2	Up to 12 pages per minute	240 × 250 dpi	Cut sheet—2 input bins (550 and 250), optional 1200
3816 01S	Up to 24 pages per minute	240 × 240 dpi	Cut sheet—2 input bins (550 and 250), optional 1200
4019 001 4019 E01	Up to 10 pages per minute – 001. Up to 5 pages per minute – E01	300 × 300 dpi	Cut sheet—2 input bins (500 and 200), envelope feed, transparencies, labels, sequenced and unsequenced output trays
4201 II	240 cps/ 200 cps/40 cps	Fastfont/draft/ near letter quality	Cut sheet, envelopes, continuous forms (up to 4-part), Document on Demand, Paper Tear Assist, Forms Load
4201 III	320 cps/ 270 cps/65 cps	Fastfont/draft/ near letter quality	Cut sheet, envelopes, continuous forms (up to 4-part), Document on Demand, Propark, Paper Tear Assist, Forms Load
4202 II XL	240 cps/ 200 cps/40 cps	Fastfont/draft/ near letter quality	Cut sheet, envelopes, continuous forms (up to 4-part), Document on Demand, Paper Tear Assist, Forms Load
4202 III XL	320 cps/ 270 cps/65 cps	Fastfont/draft/ near letter quality	Cut sheet, envelopes, continuous forms (up to 4-part), Document on Demand, Propark, Paper Tear Assist, Forms Load
4207 X24E	240–288 cps/ 80–96 cps	Draft/letter	Cut sheet, envelopes, continuous forms (up to 4-part), Document on Demand, Propark, Paper Tear Assist, Forms Load
4208 XL24E	240–288 cps/ 80–96 cps	Draft/letter	Cut sheet, envelopes, continuous forms (up to 4-part), Document on Demand, Propark, Paper Tear Assist, Forms Load
4224 301	200 cps/ 100 cps/50 cps	DP/text/near letter quality	Document on Demand, continuous forms (up to 6-part), Document Insertion, heavy duty

Continued

Table 4.11. Continued

Printer	Speed	Quality	Forms handling/remarks
4224 302	400 cps/ 200 cps/100 cps	DP/text/near letter quality	Document on Demand, continuous forms (up to 6-part), Document Insertion, heavy duty
4224 3C2	400 cps/ 200 cps/100 cps	Colour-DP/text/ near letter quality	Document on Demand, continuous forms (up to 6-part), Document Insertion, heavy duty
4224 3E3	600 cps/ 300 cps/150 cps	DP/text/near letter quality	Document on Demand, continuous forms (up to 6-part), Document Insertion, heavy duty
4234 013	800 lpm/ 600 lpm/ 200 lpm	Draft/DP/near letter quality	Continuous forms (up to 6-part), power assisted loading
5202 2	160–274 cps/ 100–171 cps/ 80–136 cps	Draft/quality/ enhanced quality	Cut sheet, continuous forms, envelopes, dual drawer, some transparencies
5204 1	330 cps/ 110 cps/55 cps	DP/Letter quality/executive letter quality	Document on Demand, continuous forms (up to 5-part), envelopes, dual drawer option

5204 Quickwriter

The 5204 Quickwriter is a multimode 24-wire dot-matrix impact printer. This is an ideal desktop printer in a multi-user environment for various data processing and word processing applications. Equipped with the 5204 Film Ribbon and optional Selectric Font, the 5204 provides print quality as acceptable as that produced by an IBM Selectric III Typewriter.

The 5204 Quickwriter attaches to the RS/6000 using a PC Parallel Printer Cable to the standard parallel port. Serially, the printer can attach to the RISC System/6000 computer using an Async Cable EIA-232/V.24 (with a Printer/Terminal interposer EIA-232) to a standard serial port or to an 8-, 16- or 64-Port Asynchronous Controller port. The printer can also attach to an 8- or 16-Port Asynchronous Adapter-EIA-422A port.

Characteristics

Technology	24 wire matrix
Speed	330/110/55 cps
Quality	DP/Letter quality/Executive letter quality

Pitches/typestyles	10, 12, Selectric, Scientific, Engineering, Multilingual
Graphics resolution	180 × 360, 240 × 240 dpi emulation
Paper sizes	3 in. to 15 in.
Forms handling	Document on Demand, continuous forms (up to 5-part), envelopes, dual drawer option
Attachment	Serial, parallel

The above printers are summarized in Table 4.11.

6180 Colour Plotter Model 1

The 6180 Colour Plotter is an 8-pen desktop, high resolution vector plotter capable of producing quality graphics on paper or transparency film with accurate registration and repeatability.

The optional Graphics Enhancement Cartridge provides compatibility for the 7372 Colour Plotter, and greatly increases the number of commands and character sets.

The 6180 Colour Plotter Model 1 attaches to the RS/6000 using an Async Cable EIA-232/V.24 (with a Printer/Interposer EIA-232C) to a standard asynchronous port or to an 8-, 16- or 64-Port Asynchronous Adapter port. The plotter can also attach to the 5086 Graphics Processor using a standard EIA-232 port.

Characteristics

Plotter type	Pen
Pen type	Fibre-tip pen for paper or transparency film
Media types	Paper or transparency film
Media size	A and A4 drawing sizes
Features	8 pen carousel Automatic pen capping
	Excellent line quality

6182 Auto-Feed Colour Plotter

The 6182 Auto-Feed Colour Plotter is a high performance 8-pen desktop plotter with automatic sheet feed. It can plot A or B sized plots on paper, transparency, vellum or polyester film. The plotter has a maximum pen speed of 80 cm/sec (31.5 inch/sec).

The 6182 Auto-Feed Colour Plotter attaches to the RS/6000 using an Async Cable EIA-232/V.24 (with a Printer/Interposer EIA-232C) to a standard asynchronous port or to an 8-, 16- or 64-Port Asynchronous Adapter port. The plotter can also attach to the 5086 Graphics Processor using a standard EIA-232 port.

Characteristics

Plotter type	Pen
Pen type	Fibre-tip
Pen speed	80 cm/sec (31.5 inch/sec) maximum
Media types	Paper or vellum, transparency or polyester film
Media size	A and B drawing sizes
Features	8 pen carousel

6184 Colour Plotter Model 1

The 6184 Colour Plotter is an 8-pen drafting plotter that produces large format, C/A2 and D/A1 size engineering drawings. It can produce plots on chart paper, vellum and double-matte polyester film. The 6184 Colour Plotter Model 1 has high line quality which provides smooth circles, consistent line widths, and crisp characters.

The 6184 Colour Plotter Model 1 attaches to the RS/6000 using an Async Cable EIA-232/V.24 (with a Printer/Interposer EIA-232C) to a standard asynchronous port or to an 8-, 16- or 64-Port Asynchronous Adapter port. The plotter can also attach to the 5086 Graphics Processor using a standard EIA-232 port.

Characteristics

Plotter type	Pen
Pen type	Fibre-tip pen for chart paper and vellum, or polyester film
Media types	Chart paper, vellum or polyester film
Media size	A1, A2, C, and D drawing sizes
Features	8 pen carousel Excellent line quality Smooth circles Consistent line widths Crisp characters

6185 Colour Plotter Models 1 and 2

The 6185 Colour Plotters are high quality, 8-pen, large format devices that produce A through D or A through E size engineering drawings on a variety of media. For increased productivity, the 6185 Colour Plotters provide optional expandable buffer options to enable plotting while making the workstation available for other tasks. The 6185 Colour Plotter Model 1 has high line quality which provides smooth circles, consistent line widths, and crisp characters.

The 6185 Colour Plotters can attach to the RS/6000 using an Async Cable EIA-232/V.24 (with a Printer/Interposer EIA-232C) to a standard asynchronous port or to an 8-, 16- or 64-Port Asynchronous Adapter port. The plotter can also attach to the 5086 Graphics Processor using a standard EIA-232 port.

Characteristics

Plotter type	Pen
Pen acceleration	2 g axial, 2 g diagonal
Pen speed	80 cm/sec (32 inch/sec) axial
Resolution	Addressable 0.025 mm (0.001 inch)
Media types	Chart paper, vellum, tracing bond, translucent bond, polyester film, glossy presentation paper, overhead film
Media size Mod. 1	A/A4, B/A3, C/A2, D/A1, Architectural C and D
Media size Mod. 2	A/A4, B/A3, C/A2, D/A1, E/A0, Architectural C, D, and E
Features	8 pen carousel Expandable buffer Excellent line quality Smooth circles Consistent line widths Crisp characters

6186 Colour Plotter Models 1 and 2

The 6186 Colour Plotter is a high performance, 8-pen colour plotter capable of producing A/A4 through E/A0 size engineering drawings. The 6186 is software compatible with IBM's 7374/7375 line of plotters which it replaces.

The 6186 Colour Plotter was designed to provide superior line quality and plot resolution. Its plotting mechanism incorporates high-performance, digitally controlled servo-motors mounted in a precision chassis. This design reduces the number of parts required and results in a more economical plotter with increased reliability. The 6186 supports up to six different media types and has a maximum pen speed of 60 cm/sec (24 inch/sec).

The 6186 Model 1 Colour Plotter supports cut sheet media and the 6186 Model 2 supports continuous roll 26 KB buffer. The continuous roll capability permits plotting multiple drawings without reloading media for each plot.

The 6186 Colour Plotters attach to the RS/6000 using an Async Cable EIA-232/V.24 (with a Printer/Interposer EIA-232C) to a standard asynchronous port or to an 8-, 16- or 64-Port Asynchronous Adapter port. The plotter can also attach to the 5086 Graphics Processor using a standard EIA-232 port.

Characteristics

Plotter type	Pen
Pen speed	60 cm/sec (24 inch/sec)
Acceleration	5.7 g
Resolution	0.025 mm (0.00098 inch)
Repeatability	0.10 mm (0.004 inch)
Pen type	Fibre-tip, roller ball, re-usable ink, disposable ink, overhead transparency
Media types	Chart paper, vellum, tracing bond, polyester film, glossy paper, overhead film
Media size	A/A4, B/A3, C/A2, D/A1, E/A0
Features	8 pen carousel Cut sheet and continuous roll media 7374/ 7375 software compatible Superior design Excellent line quality Smooth circles Consistent line widths Crisp characters

7372 Colour Plotter

The 7372 Colour Plotter is a 6-pen desktop, high resolution vector plotter. It provides the capability to produce A/A4 or B/A3 size drawings on paper or transparency film.

The 7372 Colour Plotter Model 1 attaches to the RS/6000 using an Async Cable EIA-232/V.24 (with a Printer/Interposer EIA-232C) to a standard asynchronous port or to an 8-, 16- or 64-Port Asynchronous Adapter port. The plotter can also attach to the 5086 Graphics Processor using a standard EIA-232 port.

Characteristics

Plotter type	Pen
Pen type	Fibre-tip pen for paper
	Fibre-tip pen for transparency film
Media types	Paper or transparency film
Media size	A/A4 and B/A3 sizes
Features	6 pen carousel Automatic pen capping Excellent line quality Simple and convenient pushbutton controls

4.9   Direct access storage devices (DASD)

There are a number of disks that can be used in the various RS/6000 models. These are discussed in this section. IBM often announces new disk units with higher performance. This information was correct at the time of writing. Up-to-date information can be obtained from IBM.

4.9.1   Removable DASD

3.5 Inch Diskette Drive

The 3.5 Inch Diskette Drive, standard on all RS/6000 systems, is identical to the 3.5-inch drive in the PS/2 Family. The drive has a 1.44 MB capacity and can be used with all RS/6000 models. RS/6000 computers support only one internal 3.5 Inch Diskette Drive. The drive attaches to the RS/6000 using an appropriate cable to the diskette controller on the standard I/O board.

5.25 Inch Diskette Drive (1.2 MB)

The 1.2 MB 5.25 Inch Diskette Drive provides data interchange capability between the RS/6000 and other systems. The RS/6000 supports only one 5.25 Inch Diskette Drive; the drive can be either internal on models 930 and 950, or external on all RS/6000 models.

355 MB Portable Disk Drive

The 355 MB Portable Disk Drive is a portable disk drive power unit with a standard 355 MB Portable Disk Drive Module. The portable disk drive power unit is a self-powered, enclosed unit. The 355 MB disk drive module can be plugged into the power unit. The 355 MB Portable Disk Drive Module, a 5.25 inch device, features an average access time of 16 milliseconds and a rotational speed of 3600 rpm. The 355 Portable Disk Drive Power Unit connects to the RS/6000 model using an appropriate cable to a SCSI Device Adapter.

Characteristics

Formatted capacity	355 MB
Form factor	5.25 inch
Average seek time	16 ms
Average latency	8.33 ms
Rotational speed	3600 rpm
Data transfer rate	1.875 MB/sec
Interface	SCSI (single ended)

670 MB Portable Disk Drive

The 670 MB Portable Disk Drive is a portable disk drive power unit with an optional 670 MB portable disk drive module. The portable disk drive power unit is a self-powered, enclosed unit. The 670 MB disk drive module can be plugged into the power unit. The 670 MB Portable Disk Drive Module, a 5.25 inch device features an average access time of 18 milliseconds and a rotational speed of 3600 rpm. The 670 MB Portable Disk Drive connects to the RS/6000 using an appropriate cable to a SCSI Device Adapter.

Characteristics

Formatted capacity	670 MB
Form factor	5.25 inch
Average seek time	18 ms
Average latency	8.33 ms
Rotational speed	3600 rpm
Data transfer rate	1.875 MB/sec
Interface	SCSI (single ended)

CD-ROM Drive

The CD-ROM Drive is an optional, read-only, optical compact disk drive that supports distribution and use of on-line databases (e.g. soft copy publications on-line reference). The compact disk resides in a caddy that is inserted into the drive. The drive features a 150 KB per second data transfer rate and an average access time of 380 milliseconds.

The internal CD-ROM Drive can be used with RS/6000 floor-standing models and in the POWERserver 930 and POWERserver 950 SCSI Device Drawer. The desktop systems do not support internal drives.

The external CD-ROM Drive attaches to the RS/6000 using an appropriate cable to a SCSI Device Adapter port. A jack for audio output is provided on the CD-ROM bezel.

Characteristics

Formatted capacity	600 MB
Form factor	5.25 inch
Average seek time	380 ms
Buffer	64 KB
Data transfer rate	150 KB/sec
Interface	SCSI (single ended)

4.9.2 Fixed disks

160 MB Fixed Disk Drive

The 160 MB Direct Attached Fixed Disk Drive is a 3.5-inch drive standard in the desktop RS/6000 model—320 and 320H system units. The drive features an average access time of 16 milliseconds, a disk-to-buffer data transfer rate of 1.50 MB per second, and a rotational speed of 3600 rpm. The RS/6000 model 320 and model 320H can house up to two 160 MB drives. The 160 MB Direct Attached Fixed Disk Drive connects directly to a unique connector in the unit.

Characteristics

Formatted capacity	160 MB
Form factor	3.5 inch
Average seek time	16.0 ms
Average latency	8.33 ms
Rotational speed	3600 rpm
Data transfer rate	1.50 MB/sec
Interface	Directly into unique RISC System/6000 Model 320 connector

320/640 MB Fixed Disk Drive

This Fixed Disk Drive is a high-performance 3.5-inch drive that features an average access rate of 12.5 milliseconds, a disk-to-buffer data transfer rate of 2.0 MB per second, and a rotational speed of 4318 rpm. When doubled up, it becomes a 640 MB drive. Separate 320 drives can be used in the desktop models. The 640 MB drive can be used in the deskside models. The 320 MB Fixed Disk Drive attaches to the RS/6000 using an appropriate cable to a SCSI Device Adapter.

Characteristics

Formatted capacity	320 MB (or 640 MB)
Form factor	3.5 inch
Average seek time	12.5 ms
Average latency	7 ms
Rotational speed	4318 rpm
Data transfer rate	2.0 MB/sec
Interface	SCSI (single ended)

355 MB Fixed Disk Drive

The 355 MB Fixed Disk Drive is a 5.25-inch drive that features an average access time of 16 milliseconds and a rotational speed of 3600 rpm. Internally the storage device can be used on certain desktop models. The 355 MB Fixed Disk Drive connects to the RS/6000 using an appropriate cable to a SCSI Device Adapter.

Characteristics

Formatted capacity	355 MB
Form factor	5.25-inch
Average seek time	16 ms
Average latency	8.33 ms
Rotational speed	3600 rpm
Data transfer rate	1.875 MB/sec
Interface	SCSI (singe ended)

400 MB Fixed Disk Drive

The 400 MB Direct Attached Fixed Disk Drive is a 3.5-inch drive optional in the desktop models of RS/6000. The drive features an average access of 11.5 milliseconds, a disk-to-buffer data transfer rate of 2 MB per second, and a rotational speed of 4316 rpm. The 400 MB Fixed Disk Drive connects to the system unit via an appropriate SCSI connector.

Characteristics

Formatted capacity	400 MB
Form factor	3.5 inch
Average seek time	11.5 ms
Average latency	6.95 ms
Rotational speed	4316 rpm
Data transfer rate	2.0 MB/sec
Interface	SCSI

670 MB Fixed Disk Drive

The 670 MB Fixed Disk Drive is a 5.25-inch drive that features an average access time of 18 milliseconds and a rotational speed of 3600 rpm. The floor-standing or tower models can house up to three 670 MB drives, and the POWERserver models 930 and 950 can house up to four per SCSI fixed disk drawer. The 670 MB Fixed Disk Drive connects to the RS/6000 using an appropriate cable to a SCSI Device Adapter.

Characteristics

Formatted capacity   670 MB
Form factor   5.25 inch
Average seek time   18 ms
Average latency   8.33 ms
Rotational speed   3600 rpm
Data transfer rate   1.875 MB/sec
Interface   SCSI (single ended)

800 MB Fixed Disk Drive

The 800 MB Fixed Disk Drive is composed of two 400 MB Fixed Disk Drives. It is only supported on the RS/6000 model 550 and is the standard drive for that unit. The drive has an average seek time of 11.5 ms, average latency of 6.95 ms, a data transfer rate of 2 MB per second, and a rotational speed of 4318 rpm. The 800 MB Fixed-Disk Drive connects to RS/6000 using an appropriate cable to a SCSI Device Adapter.

Characteristics

Formatted capacity   800 MB
Form factor   3.5 inch
Average seek time   11.5 ms
Average latency   6.95 ms
Rotational speed   4318 rpm
Data transfer rate   2 MB/sec
Interface   SCSI (single ended)

857 MB Fixed Disk Drive

The 857 MB Fixed Disk Drive is a 5.25-inch high-performance drive that features an average access time of 11.2 milliseconds, a disk-to-buffer data transfer rate of 3 MB per second, and a rotational speed of 4986 rpm. The storage device can be used in the deskside RS/6000 models and rack models. The 857 MB Fixed Disk Drive is standard in the POWERserver model 950. These disks are also used in the IBM 9333 disk subsystem. The floor-standing models can support a configuration of up to three 857 MB drives. The 857 MB Fixed-Disk Drive connects to RS/6000 computers using an appropriate cable to a SCSI Device Adapter.

Characteristics

Formatted capacity	857 MB
Form factor	5.25 inch
Average seek time	11.2 ms
Average latency	6.02 ms
Rotational speed	4986 rpm
Data transfer rate	3 MB/sec
Interface	SCSI (single ended)

IBM 9333 High-Performance Disk Drive Subsystem

The two models of the IBM 9333 High-Performance Disk Drive Subsystem. Model 010 Drawer, and Model 500 Deskside, bring new levels of disk storage performance to the RS/6000 range of systems. They also significantly increase the maximum supported disk storage configurations on all deskside and rack-mounted systems. Both models include a standard 857 MB Serial-Link Disk Drive, and capacity within the subsystem can be expanded to 3428 MB using four Serial-Link Disk Drives.

The IBM 9333 High-Performance Disk Drive Subsystem requires a port on a High-Performance Disk Drive Subsystem Adapter in the attaching system. The adapter has four ports, and each port supports the attachment of a single subsystem. The adapter is designed to support the attachment of four subsystems without performance degradation.

The IBM 9333 Model 010 Drawer High-Performance Subsystem is for integration into the POWERserver 900 series system racks, or attached IBM 7202 Model 900 Expansion Racks. Up to 15 drawers may be attached, provided that the required four Micro Channel slots are available.

The IBM 9333 Model 500 Deskside High-Performance Subsystem is for attachment to deskside systems. Up to four subsystems may be attached via a single High-Performance Disk Drive Subsystem Adapter.

Highlights

- Improved performance when compared with SCSI disk subsystems
  - Significantly reduced controller/adapter command processing time
  - High speed, 8 MB per second, full duplex, point-to-point, Serial-Link connection to the system
  - Improved disk drive performance for configurations up to 16 drives per Micro Channel adapter
- Enables high availability system configurations by providing independent links to two RS/6000 systems.

The IBM 9333 Model 500 Deskside High-Performance Subsystem increases the maximum supported disk storage configuration for the POWERstation/POWERserver 500 series systems to 16.3 GB, with four IBM 9333 Model 500 Deskside High-Performance Subsystems being supported from a single High-Performance Disk Drive Subsystem Adapter.

The IBM 9333 Model 010 Drawer High-Performance Subsystem increases the maximum supported disk storage configuration for POWERserver 900 series systems to 53.1 GB. This capacity is supported with the use of only four Micro Channel slots, leaving three Micro Channel slots available for use with other adapters.

The interactive performance characteristics of the IBM 9333 High-Performance Disk Drive Subsystem allow more users to be supported, at the same response time, than could be supported by the same number of IBM SCSI disk drives. The sequential performance characteristics of the IBM 9333 High-Performance Disk Drive Subsystem enable growth by providing more throughput than can be achieved with IBM SCSI disk drives, and therefore can increase the workload throughput of compute intensive applications running on an RS/6000.

Model 010: Drawer High-Performance Subsystem

This rack-mounted product includes a single Serial-Link Disk Drive, expandable to a total of four Serial-Link Disk Drives giving a maximum capacity of 3428 MB of storage. It may be installed in the POWERserver 900 series system rack, or in an IBM 7202 Model 900 Expansion Rack. Up to four Model 010 subsystems may be supported, with no performance degradation, from a single High-Performance Disk Drive Subsystem Adapter in the attaching POWERserver 900 series system.

Model 500: Deskside High-Performance Subsystem

This free-standing product includes a single Serial-Link Disk Drive, expandable to a total of four Serial-Link Disk Drives giving a maximum capacity of 3428 MB of storage. It may be attached to any deskside RS/6000 system. Up to four Model 500 subsystems may be supported, with no performance degradation, from a single High-Performance Disk Drive Subsystem Adapter in the attaching system.

7202 Expansion Rack

The IBM 7202 Expansion Rack provides mounting space and power distribution for the IBM 9333 Model 010 High-Performance Disk Drive Subsystem, IBM 9334 Model 010 Drawer Expansion Unit and the IBM 1/2-inch 9-Track Tape Drive Drawer. It provides I/O expansion capability beyond the base system enclosure. Two RS/6000 Expansion Racks, in conjunction with the IBM 9333 Model 010 High Performance Disk Drive Subsystem, extend the maximum disk storage capacity of the Rack mounted RS/6000 models to 53.1 GB provided enough Micro Channel slots are available in the system. The RS/6000 Expansion Rack is 1.6 m (62.1 inches) high and contains space for up to six optional device drawers. The Expansion Rack conforms to the 19-inch mounting dimension and universal spacing hole pattern in Electronic Industries Association (EIA) RS-310-C standard for racks, panels, and associated equipment.

Maximum disk capacity of the RS/6000 rack models may be expanded by attachment of up to two Expansion Racks. Capacity expansion capability is provided with either standard SCSI disk subsystems like the IBM 9334 Model 010 Drawer Expansion Unit, or the high performance IBM 9333 Model 010 High-Performance Disk Drive Subsystem mounted in the Expansion Rack. Capacity expansion provided by the Expansion Rack helps enable applications with large storage requirements to take advantage of the extended fixed disk capacity. In multi-user environments the extended capacity may allow more users to be supported by disk I/O limited applications.

The dual processor attachment capability of the IBM 9333 Model 010 High-Performance Disk Drive Subsystem enables new higher availability configurations of POWERserver systems. These features allow you to configure two POWERserver systems which can both access the disk drives of the IBM 9333 Subsystem, eliminating single points of failure in the configuration.

Also available on the Expansion Rack is a Battery Backup Option which provides emergency DC power for up to three IBM 9333 Model 010 Subsystems or IBM 9334 Model 010 Drawers for a minimum of 10 minutes with a fully charged set of batteries. With the Battery Backup Extender Cable, emergency power can be extended to an additional three drawers for a minimum of 10 minutes.

A Dual Power Control Feature is available for the Expansion Rack which allows the power to the IBM devices installed in the rack to be controlled from either of two CPUs for high availability configurations with dual systems. The Expansion Rack is mounted on casters to make it easy to move. Once in place the casters can be secured for increased stability.

Battery Backup option
The Battery Backup (BBU) option, plant or field installable, is designed to provide emergency DC power for up to three IBM 9333 Model 010 Subsystems or IBM 9334 Model 010 drawers for a minimum of 10 minutes with a fully charged set of batteries. The purpose of the BBU is to allow I/O devices mounted in the Expansion Rack enclosure to perform normally through short power outages without an IPL of the system. Space is reserved for this option in the portion of the rack occupied by the power distribution unit.

Dual power control feature
This feature consists of an optional set of power control cables for the rack. It permits power to the IBM devices installed in the RS/6000 Expansion Rack to be controlled from either of two CPUs for high availability configurations with dual systems.

9334 IBM SCSI, Drawer and Deskside Expansion Unit

The IBM 9334 SCSI Expansion Unit provides additional SCSI fixed disk capacity for all members of the RS/6000 family.

With the IBM 9334 Model 010, in conjunction with the IBM 7202 Model 900 Expansion Rack, the POWERserver 900 series systems will be able to increase their fixed disk capacity from 11.9 GB to 22.2 GB provided there are available Micro Channel slots.

Using the IBM 9334 Model 500, the RS/6000 desktop systems can add up to an additional 4.2 GB. Deskside systems can add up to an additional 10.2 GB of disk capacity. The IBM 9334 Model 500 also provides for the attachment of the Internal CD-ROM Disk Drive, 150 MB Internal 1/4-inch Cartridge Tape Drive and the 2.3 GB Internal 8 mm Tape Drive.

Model 010 Drawer Expansion Unit

This rack-mounted, 4 EIA Unit high (171 mm), product includes a single 5.25-inch SCSI Disk Drive expandable to a total of four 5.25-inch SCSI Disk Drives giving a maximum capacity of 3428 MB of storage. It may only be installed in a 7202 Model 900 Expansion Rack. Each 9334 Model 010 requires one High-Performance SCSI Adapter in the attaching RS/6000 rack-mounted system.

Table 4.12. Disk summary

Drive	Type	Form factor	Average seek (ms)	Average latency (ms)	Rot. speed (rpm)	Data transfer rate (MB/sec)
160 MB	Fixed	3.5 inch	16.0	8.33	3600	1.50
320 MB	Fixed or portable	3.5 inch	12.5	6.95	4318	2.0
355 MB	Fixed or portable	5.25 inch	16.0	8.33	3600	1.875
400 MB	Fixed	3.5 inch	11.5	6.95	4316	2.0
670 MB	Fixed or portable	5.25 inch	18.0	8.33	3600	1.875
320/640 MB	Fixed	3.5 inch	12.5	6.95	4318	2.0
800 MB	Fixed	3.5 inch	11.5	6.95	4318	2.0
857 MB	Fixed	5.25 inch	11.2	6.02	4986	3.0

Model 500: Deskside Expansion Unit

This deskside product includes a single 5.25-inch SCSI Disk Drive expandable to a total of four 5.25-inch SCSI Disk Drives giving a maximum capacity of 3428 MB of storage. It may be attached to any desktop or deskside system. Each 9334 Model 500 requires one High-Performance SCSI Adapter in the RS/6000 itself.

Table 4.12 summarizes storage disks.

4.10   Memory

There are a range of memory adapters that can be used in the various RS/6000 models. These range from 8 MB cards to 64 MB cards. The maximum memory supported on RS/6000 at the moment is 512 MB but I would expect this to be increased from time to time in line with requirements. The architectural limits are 4 petabytes (2 to the power 52) for virtual address space and 4 gigabytes (2 to the power 32) for real address space. There is a discussion on the memory subsystem in Sec. 4.3.3.

4.11   Removable media

The various IBM tape drives are discussed here and summarized in Table 4.13.

Table 4.13. Tape summary

Name	Capacity	Data rate (KB/sec)	Tape Density	Media
8 mm	2.3 GB per cartridge	245		IBM 8 mm Data cartridge
1/4 inch	150 MB per cartridge	90		1/4 inch Data cartridge
IBM 9348 1/2 inch 9-Track Tabletop	154 MB(GCR), 42 MB (PE) per 2400 ft reel	200/781	1600 bpi or 6250 bpi	Standard 1/2 inch Tape Reel

8 mm Tape Drive

The 2.3 GB 8 mm Tape Drive is a streaming tape drive that uses the IBM 8 mm data cartridge or equivalent. The drive is primarily used for Save/ Restore, Archiving, and software and documentation distribution.

The internal drive can be used with all RS/6000 models, except Models 320 and 320H. One drive can be housed in the deskside units, while up to two can be housed in the rack-mounted SCSI Device Drawer. The internal drive attaches to the RS/6000 system unit using an internal cable to an IBM SCSI High-Performance I/O Controller.

The external drive is packaged in an 11 inches wide × 11.3 inches deep × 4.8 inches high self powered box. All RS/6000 models except Models 930 and 950 can use it. The external drive attaches to the RS/6000 by an IBM SCSI Controller Cable to an IBM SCSI High-Performance I/O Controller.

Characteristics
Capacity	2.3 GB per cartridge
Media	IBM 8 mm Data Cartridge or equivalent
Technology	Helical scan, rotating head
Operation	Streaming
Data transfer rate	245 KB/sec
Interface	SCSI (single ended) asynchronous

1/4 Inch Tape

The 150 MB 1/4-Inch Cartridge Tape Drive operates in a streaming mode. The internal drive provides data interchange and Save/Restore capabilities for Models 930 and 950, while the external drive provides data interchange and Save/Restore capabilities for all RS/6000 system units except Models 930 and 950.

The internal tape drive is housed in the Model 930 Processor Drawer and attaches to the RS/6000 system unit using an internal cable to a SCSI High-Performance I/O Controller.

The external tape drive is packaged in an 11 inches wide × 11.3 inches deep × 3.3 inches high self powered box. The drive attaches to the RS/6000 system unit using an IBM SCSI Controller Cable to an IBM SCSI High-Performance I/O Controller.

Characteristics

Media	1/4 inch Data Cartridge (P/N 21F8588) or equivalent
Capacity	150 MB per Cartridge (nominal)
Capacity with ECC	135 MB per Cartridge (nominal)
Compatibility	QIC-24 (read only, without EEC)
	QIC-120 (read and write, with or without ECC)
	QIC-150 (read and write, with or without ECC)
Data transfer rate	90 KB/sec
Interface	SCSI (single ended) Asynchronous

IBM 9348-Model 12 1/2-inch 9-Track Tape Drive Tabletop

The 9348 Magnetic Tape Unit Model 12 is an autoloading, auto-threading, tabletop model that can be used with all RS/6000 system units except Models 930 and 950.

The 1/2-inch Streaming Tape is attached to the RS/6000 system unit by an IBM SCSI Controller Cable to an IBM SCSI High-Performance I/O Controller.

Characteristics

Media	Standard 1/2-inch Tape Reel
Tape density	Selectable, 1600 bpi or 6250 bpi
Operation	Start/stop and streaming
Data throughput rate	781 KB/sec at 6250 bpi
	200 KB/sec at 1600 bpi
Interface	SCSI (single ended) asynchronous

Third Party Tapes

A variety of drives can attach to the RS/6000 using the SCSI connection, including drives compatible with IBM 3480 cartridge drives.

4.12   Communications hardware

4.12.1 Communications adapters

The ways in which the RS/6000 can communicate have been discussed earlier. This section describes in detail the various communications and I/O adapters that can be used in the RS/6000.

These include:

- 8-, 16- and 64-Port Asynchronous Adapters
- SCSI device adapter
- Ethernet adapter
- Token Ring adapter
- 3270 Connection adapter
- 4-port Multi-protocol adapter
- X.25 adapter
- System/370 Host Interface adapter
- 5085 and 5086 attachment adapters
- Serial optical Channel
- Block Multiplexor Channel adapter
- FDDI adapter

8-Port Asynchronous Adapter

This is a Micro-Channel adapter that takes up a single slot in the RS/6000. It will fit into any of the RS/6000 models. In the rack-mounted systems, it sits in the async expansion drawer. There are two versions, an RS232 one (RS232D) and an RS422 one (RS422A).

RS232 and RS422 are similar but have some slight differences. They both use the same 25-pin D connectors but utilize different pins for signalling. RS232 cabling can be safely used up to a distance of 200 feet, whereas RS422 can be used up to 4000 feet. However, RS422 does not have all of the control signals and is not always as 'foolproof' as RS232. Care must be taken in deciding which option to use and, if in doubt, I would normally recommend using RS232.

A multi-port interface cable is attached to the 8-port adapter. This multi-port cable has a connector box on the end which sits outside the RS/6000. The actual ASCII devices—screens or printers—are then attached to this connector box as shown in Fig. 4.11.

Up to eight devices, screens or ASCII printers can be attached via the standard 25-pin connectors. The RS232D 8-port adapter can be used for

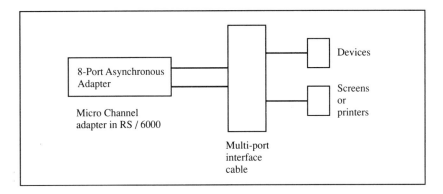

Figure 4.11. Connection of devices to the 8-port adapter.

attaching modems and remote devices which are to communicate over asynchronous connections. The maximum line rate of a single port is 38.4 KB per second. The 8-Port Asynchronous Adapter is available in three models, each supporting a specific asynchronous interface (EIA-232, EIA-422, and MIL-STD-188). The 8-Port Asynchronous Adapter provides support for attaching a maximum of eight asynchronous serial devices (terminals, printers, etc.) to an RS/6000. The optional 8-Port RS-232/RS-422A/MIL-STD 188 Cable Assembly connects to the 8-Port Asynchronous Adapter and provides the eight connectors for device attachment.

The 8-Port Asynchronous Adapter fits into a single I/O adapter slot. A maximum of seven 8-Port Asynchronous Adapters may be installed in an RS/6000 system, or eight in the Asynchronous Expansion Drawer of the rack models.

The 8-Port EIA-232/EIA-422A/MIL-STD-188 Cable Assembly allows up to eight separate devices to be attached to any of the 8-Port Asynchronous Adapters. An adapter can only be used with one cable assembly, no sharing is supported. The cable assembly features eight 25-pin male D-shell connectors. A wrap plug is supplied for testing.

Characteristics

Ports	Eight asynchronous
Data rate	Interchange rate up to 38.4 KB/sec
Connector	One 78-pin female output connector
	Eight signal/control wires per port
Buffering	16-byte buffering on transmit and receive per port
Compatibility	EIA-232, EIA-422, and MIL-STD-188 respectively

16-Port Asynchronous Adapter

Again, this a Micro Channel adapter that takes up a single slot in the RS/6000. It will fit into any of the RS/6000 models. In the rack-mounted systems, it sits in the asynch expansion drawer. There are two versions, an RS232 one (RS232D) and an RS422 one (RS422A).

As with the 8-port adapter, the 16-port adapter has a corresponding 16-port interface cable that sits outside the RS/6000 and has the 16 25-pin connectors. The actual ASCII devices—screens or printers are then attached to this connector box in the same way as in Fig. 4.11.

Some of the signals supported on the 8-port adapter (such as Ring Indicate) are *not* supported on the 16-port adapter, and therefore modem connections are not supported by the IBM. However, some modems will work quite happily over this adapter. Any particular modem connection that is required should be tested in advance, to determine whether it functions as expected. The maximum line rate of a single port is 38.4 KB per second.

The 16-Port Asynchronous Adapter is available in two models, each supporting a specific asynchronous interface (EIA-232 or EIA-422). The 16-Port Asynchronous Adapter provides support for attaching a maximum of sixteen asynchronous serial devices (terminals, printers, etc.) to an RS/6000. The optional 16-Port EIA-232/EIA-422A Cable Assemblies connect to the 16-Port Asynchronous Adapter and provide the 16 connectors for device attachment.

The 16-Port Asynchronous Adapter fits into a single I/O adapter slot. A maximum of seven 16-Port Asynchronous Adapters may be installed in an RS/6000 or eight in the Asynchronous Expansion Drawer of a rack model. A wrap plug for a 78-pin connector is supplied for testing.

The 16-Port EIA-232/EIA-422A Cable Assemblies allow up to 16 separate devices to be attached to any of the two 16-Port Asynchronous Adapters. An adapter can only be used with one cable assembly, no sharing is supported. The cable assembly features 16 25-pin male D-shell connectors. A wrap plug is supplied for testing.

Characteristics

Ports	Sixteen asynchronous
Data rate	Interchange rate up to 38.4 KB/sec
Connector	One 78-pin female output connector
Buffering	16-byte buffering on transmit and receive per port
Compatibility	EIA-232 and EIA-422 respectively

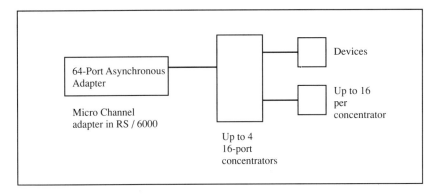

64-Port Asynchronous Adapter

Micro Channel
adapter in RS / 6000

Up to 4
16-port
concentrators

Devices

Up to 16
per
concentrator

Figure 4.12. Connection of
devices to the 64-port
adapter.

Cable length   EIA-232, up to 200 feet   EIA-422, up to 4000 feet
Surge protection   EIA-422, built-in circuitry on the adapter

64-Port Asynchronous Controller

The 64-port adapter works in a somewhat different way to the 8- and 16-port
adapters. Again, the 64-port card itself takes up one Micro Channel slot in
the RS/6000 or fits into the asynch drawer in the rack-mounted models. It is
only available as an RS232D version.

Up to four external concentrators can be attached to this adapter card.
Each of these four concentrators can attach 16 devices giving the total of 64
devices. The concentrators can be up to 2500 feet from the RS/6000 and the
devices can be up to 200 feet from the concentrator. They are attached as
shown in Fig. 4.12. Devices are attached to the 16 port concentrators using
RJ45 connectors. These are like telephone phone plugs but are slightly larger.

As with the 16-port adapter, some of the signals supported on the 8-port
adapter (such as Ring Indicate) are not supported on the 64-port adapter
and, therefore, modem connections are not supported by IBM. However,
some modems will work quite happily over this adapter. Any particular
modem connection that is required should be tested in advance to determine
whether it functions as expected. The maximum line rate of a single port is
38.4 KB per second.

The 64-Port Asynchronous Controller provides support for attaching a
maximum of 64 EIA-232 asynchronous serial devices (terminals, printers,
etc.) to an RS/6000. The 64-Port Asynchronous Controller fits into a single
I/O adapter slot. A maximum of two 64–Port Asynchronous Controllers may
be installed in a desktop system unit, four in a deskside system unit, or eight
in the Asynchronous Expansion Drawer of a rack-mounted system unit.

The 16-Port Asynchronous Concentrator attaches to the 64-Port

Asynchronous Controller and provides 16 connections for EIA-232 asynchronous devices. Up to four concentrators can attach to one 64-Port Asynchronous Controller.

Characteristics

Ports	Four (attaches up to four 16-Port Asynchronous Concentrators)
Data Rate	Interchange rate up to 38.4 KB/sec
Compatibility	EIA-232
Cable Length	Up to 2500 feet between the controller and concentrator
	Up to 200 feet between the concentrator and asynchronous device

SCSI Device Adapter

All RS/6000 systems can use the SCSI Device Adapter for control of fixed disks, CD-ROM, and other single-ended SCSI devices.

Up to seven SCSI devices can be attached using a daisy-chained cable (maximum of 6 m). There can be up to eight adapters per system.

Characteristics

SCSI data rate	4 MB/sec (synchronous protocol)
Streaming data mode	Memory I/O command and status transfer (100 ns cycle)
	First party DMA data transfer (100 ns cycle)
DMA rate	40 MB/sec peak burst
DMA burst length	Programmable, 4–128 bytes
I/O processor	80186 Microprocessor
Interrupt levels	Fully programmable
Vital product data	Machine-readable
Command support	Ability to accept multiple commands per device

Ethernet High-Performance LAN Adapter

The Ethernet High-Performance LAN Adapter is a high performance Micro Channel bus master adapter that allows the RS/6000 to attach to an Ethernet network. The adapter connects to any Micro Channel adapter slot.

The Ethernet High-Performance LAN Adapter is designed to provide a connection to a 10 MB per second Carrier Sense Multiple Access/Collision Detection (CSMA/CD) Ethernet network. This adapter supports the IEEE

802.3 and Ethernet V/2 external interfaces. To attach the RS/6000 to the network for connection to the standard 50-ohm (thick) coaxial cable, the user must supply the appropriate cable and external transceiver. To attach the RS/6000 to the network for connection to the standard 50 ohm or RF-58A/U (thin) coaxial cable, the user only has to supply an appropriate cable. The transceiver is included.

Characteristics

Interface	802.3 or ethernet V.2
Interrupt levels	Selectable
RAM addresses	Selectable
Cyclic redundancy check	32-bit
I/O processor	80186 Microprocessor

Token Ring High-Performance Network Adapter

The Token Ring High-Performance Network Adapter is a high performance Micro Channel bus master adapter that allows the RS/6000 to attach to 4 and 16 MB per second Token Ring Local Area Networks. The adapter connects to the Micro Channel adapter slot.

This adapter supports high-performance applications. The RS/6000 Token Ring Adapter is cable and network compatible with all existing Token Ring adapters. No new cables or network components are required. All adapters on a Token Ring Network must operate at the same speed.

Characteristics

Interface	IEEE 802.5
Protocol	IEEE 802.2 MAC/LLC
Hardware support	Up to 4 adapters per system
Interrupt levels	Up to 4 Address/Interrupt states supported
Connector	One 9-pin female D-shell Adapter Cable supplied to connect to IBM Cabling System or IBM 8228 Multi-Station Access Unit
I/O processor	80186 Microprocessor

3270 Connection Adapter

The 3270 Connection Adapter allows an RS/6000 computer to respond to a host system like the IBM 3278 or 3279 Display Station. This adapter allows a coaxial connection between an RS/6000 and a 3174/3274 Establishment

Controller, or between an RS/6000 and the integrated display/printer adapter of either the 4331 or 4361 processors.

The 3270 Connection Adapter connects to any Micro Channel adapter slot. The adapter for the RS/6000 is the same adapter as the 3270 Connection Adapter/A for the PS/2 system. No additional host system software is required.

Characteristics

Emulation	IBM 3278 and 3279 Display Stations
Mode of operation	Support for CUT and DFT modes
Data transfer rate	2 MB/sec maximum
Connector	One female BNC provided

4-Port Multiprotocol Adapter

The 4-Port Multiprotocol Adapter attaches an RS/6000 to synchronous communications networks using EIA-232, EIA-422, V.35, and X.21 physical specifications. The adapter prepares all inbound and outbound data, performs address searches, and in general relieves the system processor of many communications tasks. This card supports SDLC and BSC protocols at a full-duplex rate of up to 64 KB per second on all four ports simultaneously.

The 4-Port Multiprotocol Adapter connects to any Micro Channel adapter slot. The adapter has a 78-pin female D-shell connector to attach to the 4-Port Multiprotocol Cable Assembly; the cable assembly provides device connections. Up to eight 4-Port Multiprotocol Adapters can be installed in a RISC System/6000. Each adapter can support only one expansion box; no sharing is supported.

The 4-Port Multiprotocol Cable Assembly provides four 25-pin male EIA-232 connectors, two 15-pin male V.35 connectors, one 15-pin male X.21 connector, or two 25-pin male EIA-422 connectors for the Multiprotocol Adapter, Type F. The four ports can be configured with Port 1 as V.35, EIA-232, EIA-422, or X.21, Port 2 as EIA-232 or V.35, Port 3 as EIA-232 or EIA-422, and Port 4 as EIA-232 only.

Characteristics

Interface	EIA-232, EIA-422, X.21, and V.35
Memory	512 KB
Data transfer width	16-bit
Adapter form	Micro Channel bus master
Interrupt level	Two selectable, shared support

Surge protection   Built-in protection circuitry
Error checking   CRC generation and checking

X.25 Interface Co-Processor/2

The X.25 Interface Co-Processor/2 provides support for attaching an RS/6000 computer to an X.25 network. The X.25 Interface Co-Processor provides a single port that will accommodate three selectable interfaces: X.21, EIA-232/V.24, and EIA-232/V.35. The adapter connects to any Micro Channel adapter slot and has three cables which are optionally available (one for each interface).

This adapter allows an RS/6000 to attach to X.25 networks, and is capable of processing inbound and outbound data streams to off-load communications tasks from the system processor.

Characteristics

Memory   512 KB
Protocol   Full duplex synchronous or asynchronous
Interfaces X.21 at 64 KB/sec EIA-232/V.24 at 19.2 KB/sec
            EIA-232/V.35 at 56 KB/sec

System/370 Host Interface Adapter

The System/370 Host Interface Adapter is designed to work as either a high speed connection to the System/370 host for high speed file transfer or in conjunction with either the 5086 Attachment Adapter or the 5085 Attachment Adapter. The System/370 Host Interface Adapter (HIA) provides high speed file transfer between the RS/6000 and the System/370 through an IBM 5088 Graphics Control Unit. Only one System/370 Host Interface Adapter per system is allowed.

Characteristics

Number of adapters   Maximum of one per RISC System/6000
Buffers   64 KB RAM
Addressability   16 link addresses

5085 Attachment Adapter

The 5085 Attachment Adapter provides two functions for the RS/6000 system. The adapter provides a direct connection to the IBM 5085 Graphics

Processor from the RS/6000 processor so that the 5085 can utilize the RS/6000 based applications. The adapter also provides a switching capability that allows the 5085 to bypass the RS/6000 processor and utilize the applications that reside on the System/370.

One Micro Channel card slot is used by this adapter. Only one 5086 or 5085 per system can be attached.

5086 Attachment Adapter

The 5086 Attachment Adapter provides similar functions to the 5085 Attachment Adapter.

IBM RS/6000 Serial Optical Channel Converter

The RS/6000 Deskside and rack-mounted systems are enhanced with support of the RS/6000 Serial Optical Channel Converter. The Serial Optical Channel Converter provides two ports; each port can make a half-duplex optical link for communications by fibre-optic cable with an external IBM Business Partner router, utilizing standard AIX interfaces.

- The RS/6000 Serial Optical Channel Converter
    - Provides two ports on each Serial Optical Channel Converter
    - Provides unique data paths to system memory separate from the Micro-Channel interface.
- The Serial Optical Channel Converter supports the Transmission Control Protocol/Internet Protocol (TCP/IP), through standard AIX interfaces
- The converter provides connectivity for high performance heterogeneous networks, in conjunction with an IBM Business Partner router
- The converter utilizes Serial Optical Channel Architecture and extends the RS/6000 into technical computing environments where performance and heterogeneous connectivity is critical

Some important solutions areas, such as intensive applications, storage archiving, centralized data base access, client/server computing, and backbone networks, may now be possible.

The converter is designed for applications that require very high bandwidth, dedicated communications. The Serial Optical Channel Converter should not be confused with fibre optic-based technologies for local area networks (LANS), such as FDDI. IBM plans to support FDDI on the RS/6000.

The Serial Optical Channel Converter physically plugs into the RS/6000 processor system board and contains two independent 780 nanometer CD laser and PIN photo diode receiver pairs.

RS/6000 Block Multiplexor Channel Adapter

The RS/6000 Block Multiplexer Channel Adapter provides high-speed, parallel channel communications to a S/370 or S/390 mainframe in Block Multiplexer mode at data rates up to 4.5 MB per second.

This new channel connectivity allows the RS/6000 to communicate to a mainframe using the parallel channel protocol in block multiplexer mode. TCP/IP is supported and the IBM TCP/IP Version 2.2 for VM is required at the host. This allows the RS/6000 to be used as a gateway between the VM host and the downstream networks that consist of LANs or WANs. Therefore, distributed systems can access the VM resource, NFS and the TCP/IP applications resident at the VM host.

RS/6000 FDDI Adapter

The Fibre Distributed Data Interface adapter (FDDI) is a LAN communications technology that uses optical cabling designed for a line speed of up to 100 megabits per second. FDDI support is available for single attach stations (SAS) or, with an upgrade kit, for dual attach stations (DAS).

The FDDI adapter provides a single attach Station option and attaches to the FDDI primary ring of the network directly or via an external FDDI Concentrator. Connection via an external FDDI Concentrator isolates the work-stations from the primary ring and protects the network from routine station on/off cycles and individual station failures.

The adapter feature allows the RS/6000 to serve as a gateway between a lower speed LAN such as Ethernet or Token Ring, and a high speed FDDI backbone LAN. Fibre optic cable is designed to be immune to electromagnetic inference (EMI). Therefore, using fibre technology may prevent jamming by high power emissions. Additionally, since fibre optics do not emit electromagnetic radiation (EMR), use of this feature can enhance system security.

FDDI is designed to support the TCP/IP protocol, and supports NFS over TCP/IP. The implementation supports ANSI standard X3T9.5, although limiting Station Management (SMT) function to Agent support only. A programming interface (API) is provided for the device driver.

Adapters are summarized in Table 4.14.

Table 4.14. Connectivity adapters summary

Name	Compatibility	Operating mode	Transfer mode	Other
8-Port Asynchronous Adapter	EIA-232, EIA-422, and MIL-STD-188	Asynchronous	Up to 38.4 KB/sec	
16-Port Asynchronous Adapter	EIA-232 or EIA-422	Asynchronous	Up to 38.4 KB/sec	
64-Port Asynchronous Controller	EIA-232	Asynchronous	Up to 38.4 KB/sec	Use with up to four 16-Port concentrators
SCSI Device Adapter		Normal or streaming data	SCSI-4 MB/sec, DMA-40 MB/sec burst	Programmable interrupt levels
Ethernet High-performance LAN Adapter	802.3 or Ethernet V.2	CSMA/CD	Up to 10M bps	Thicknet or Thinnet attachment
Token-Ring High-performance Network Adapter	802.5	Token Passing	Up to 16M bps	Up to 7 cards per system
3270 Connection Adapter	3278 and 3279 Display Stations	CUT and DFT modes	2M bps maximum	
4-Port Multiprotocol Adapter	EIA-232, EIA-422, X.21, and V.35	SDLC and BSC	Up to 64 KB/sec	Up to 4 ports
X.25 Interface Co-Processor/2	X.21, EIA-232/V.24, and EIA-232/V.35	Synchronous or asynchronous	Up to 64 KB/sec	512 KB memory
System/370 Host Interface Adapter			2M bps maximum	16 link addresses
5085 Attachment Adapter			2M bps maximum	
5085 Attachment Adapter			2M bps maximum	

214

4.12.2 Modems

The models of IBM modems that can operate with the RS/6000 are discussed here.

5822

The IBM 5822-010 is a combined Data Service Unit/Channel Service Unit (DSU/CSU) that provides a means for interchanging data between an RS/6000 and a digital data transmission facility, and can also operate as a limited distance modem. It offers consistent Communication Network Management services to Netview users. The IBM 5822-010 offers end-to-end problem determination without requiring a DDS with a secondary channel and without affecting the user data bit rate.

The 5822 DSU/CSU attaches to the RS/6000 using a Serial Port Cable to an 8-, 16- or 64-Port Asynchronous Adapter Port or a Multiprotocol Adapter.

Characteristics

Operating mode	Multipoint or point-to-point as LDM
Compatibility	IBM 5821 DSU/CSU
Network	Digital Data System Channel Interface based on Bell System Technical Reference PUB 62310
Speed	Up to 56 Kpbs 19.2 Kbps as a Limited Distance Modem
Interfaces	EIA RS-232-D and CCITT V.35 connectors built-in RJ-48S eight-pin socket line interface
Diagnostics	Automatic self test and recovery Continuously monitors line signal quality Keeps track of abnormal line behaviours

5841

The 5841 Modem is a stand-alone device that provides a means for interchanging data between the RS/6000 unit and a voice-grade or equivalent communication line. The 5841 Modem transmits data in duplex mode using asynchronous transmission speeds up to 1200 bps and synchronous transmission speeds of 600 or 1200 bps.

The cable from the 5841 Modem attaches to the RS/6000 computer using a Serial Port Cable to an 8-, 16- or 64-Port Asynchronous Adapter port or a Multiprotocol Adapter.

Characteristics

Operating mode   Point-to-point
Compatibility   Bell 212A and 103
                        CCITT V.22A and V.22B
Network connection   Direct, by way of USOC RJ11 telephone jack
                        Through ROLM CBX analog line ending in an RJ11
                        jack
                        Through a Key System analog line ending in an RJ12
                        or RJ13 miniature jack
Speed   600 and 1200 synchronous
                        Up to 1200 asynchronous

5853

The 5853 Modem is a stand-alone device that provides a means for interchanging data between an RS/6000 unit and a voice-grade or equivalent communication line. The 5853 Modem transmits data in duplex mode using asynchronous transmission speeds of up to 300 bps; the modem transmits in synchronous or asynchronous transmission speeds of 1200 or 2400 bps.

The 5853 Modem attaches to the RS/6000 computer using a Serial Port Cable to an 8-, 16- or 64-Port Asynchronous Adapter port or a Multiprotocol Adapter.

Characteristics

Operating mode   Point-to-point
Compatibility   Bell 212A and 103
                        CCITT V.22A and V.23B
Network connection   Direct by way of USOC RJ11 telephone jack
                        Through ROLM CBX analog line ending in an RJ11
                        jack
                        Through a Key System analog line ending in an RJ12
                        or RJ13 miniature jack
Speed   Synchronous or asynchronous at 1200 or 2400—
                        duplex asynchronous at up to 300

5865

The 5865 Modem is a microprocessor-based device that provides a means for interchanging data between the RS/6000 and a voice-grade or equivalent communication line. The 5865 Modem allows synchronous data transmission in half-duplex or duplex mode and contains diagnostic features that enable you to differentiate between modem failures, line failures, and remote modem power loss.

The 5865 Modem attaches to the RS/6000 using a Serial Port Cable to a Multiprotocol Adapter.

Characteristics

Operating mode	Point-to-point
	Multipoint
	Multipoint tributary
Network connection	Direct by way of a cable with a 4-prong connector that fits a WE404B receptacle
	Direct by way of a cable that fits a modular 8-pin keyed (FJ48S like) receptacle
Speed	Synchronous at 9600

7861

The 7861 Modem is a stand-alone device that provides a means for interchanging data between the RS/6000 and a voice-grade or equivalent communication line. The 7861 Modem allows synchronous data transmission in half-duplex or duplex mode and contains advanced diagnostic and network management features. The 7861 has multipoint capabilities and a full speed range from 4800 to 19 200 bps, depending on the model. The 7861 also has switched network backup features and supports Trellis-Coded Modulation (TCM).

A cable assembly facility enables attachment of multiple systems or multiple communication controllers to one 7861 Modem. The modem attaches to the RISC System/6000 using a Serial Port Cable to a Multiprotocol Adapter.

The 7868 Modems are rack-mounted versions of the 7861, having all of the features and connectivity of the 7861 series.

Characteristics

Operating mode	Point-to-point
	Multipoint
Network connection	Direct by way of a cable with an 8-pin keyed modular plug
Speed	Synchronous from 4800 to 19 200

Table 4.15. Modem summary

Name	Operating mode	Data rate (bps)	Network connection	Compatibility
5822	Multipoint, or point-to-point as LDM	Up to 56 KB/sec on DDS and 19.2 KB/sec as LDM	RJ-48S eight-pin socket	IBM 5821 for data
5841	Point-to-point	600 and 1200 synchronous and up to 1200 asynchronous	Direct by way of USOC RJ11 telephone jack, or by way of a telephone system analog line ending in an RJ11, RJ12, or RJ13 miniature jack	Bell 212A and 103, CCITT V.22A and V.22B
5853	Point-to-point	Synchronous or asynchronous at 1200 or 2400 – Duplex asynchronous at up to 300	Direct by way of USOC RJ11 telephone jack, or by way of a telephone system analog line ending in an RJ11, RJ12, or RJ13 miniature jack	Bell 212A and 103, CCITT V.22A and V.23B
5865	Point-to-point, Multipoint, Multipoint tributary	Synchronous at 9600	Direct by way of a cable with an 8-pin keyed modular plug or with a 4-prong connector for a WE404B receptacle	
7861	Point-to-point or Multipoint	Synchronous from 4800 to 19 200	Direct by way of a cable with an 8-pin keyed modular plug	
7868	Point-to-point, Multipoint, Multipoint tributary	Synchronous from 4800 to 19 200	Direct by way of a cable with an 8-pin keyed modular plug	

7868

The 7868 Modem is a family of rack-mounted, microprocessor-based devices that provide a means for interchanging data between the RS/6000 and a voice-grade or equivalent communication line. The 7868 Modem allows synchronous data transmission in half-duplex or duplex mode and contains advanced diagnostic and network management features. The 7868 has multipoint capabilities and a full speed range from 4800 to 19 200 bps, depending on the model. The 7868 also has switched network backup features and supports 9600 bps operation with TCM.

A cable assembly facility enables attachment of multiple systems or multiple communication controllers to one 7868 Modem. The modem attaches to the RS/6000 using a Serial Port Cable to a Multiprotocol Adapter.

Characteristics

Operating mode	Point-to-point
	Multipoint
	Multipoint tributary
Network connection	Direct by way of a cable with an 8-pin keyed modular plug
Speed	Synchronous from 4800 to 19 200

See Table 4.15 for a summary of the modems listed above.

4.13   Miscellaneous hardware

3-Button Mouse

The opto-mechanical 3-Button Mouse allows users to point to and select items on a display. The cover on the mouse snaps off for routine cleaning of the roller ball. The mouse includes a 9 foot cable that plugs into the mouse port. The mouse adapter is built into the RS/6000 system unit.

Characteristics

Resolution	320 dpi
Features	3 Buttons on Mouse
Attachment	Built directly into RISC System/6000 unit

5083 Tablet

The 5083 is a flat-surfaced device that enables the user to interact with a displayed image by moving a cursor or a stylus on the tablet's active surface.

The 5083 Tablet is designed to be an easy-to-use input device for graphics applications. The tablet has a palm rest and a snap-on height adjustment, so that it can be used on a desk or on the user's lap. The Model 21 has an active surface area of 6.1 inches × 6.1 inches. The Model 22 has an active surface area of 10.25 inches × 10.25 inches.

The 5083 tablet requires either a cursor or a stylus as an input device. The 4-button cursor is a mouse-shaped device with four buttons for application use and a fine cross-hair for precise alignment and accurate digitization. The stylus is a pen-like device with a tip switch that is activated by pressing the stylus tip against the tablet surface.

The tablet attaches to the RS/6000 series using the standard tablet port. The tablet comes with a 7 foot detachable cable with 8-pin MINI DIN connectors on each end.

Characteristics

Features   Programmable resolution of up to 1279 lines per inch
                  Full sheet Menu-Holder Overlay
                  Support for either a 4-button cursor or a stylus
Attachment   Standard tablet port

5084 Digitizer

The 5084 Digitizer provides large-scale digitizing capabilities. Model 1 has a surface area of 24 inches × 36 inches. Model 2 has a surface area of 36 inches × 48 inches. Model 3 has a surface area of 44 inches × 60 inches.

The 5084 digitizer attaches to the RS/6000 unit using any EIA-232D port connection. The digitizer uses a 12 foot EIA-232 Interface Cable with 25-pin connector for attachment.

Characteristics

Features   Up to 1279 lines per inch resolution
                  Programmable command set
                  Support for both binary and ASCII output data formats
                  Support for use with the IBM 5083 Tablet
                  Cursor with 16 buttons and four indicator lights
                  Two programmable audible tones
                  Power supply/line cords
                  Teletype terminal (tty) driver in AIX supports programming to
                  the 5084
Attachment   EIA 232D port connection

6094-10 Dials

The 6094 Model 10 Dials is a compact, desktop unit with eight cone-shaped controls that allow the user to pan, zoom, and rotate dynamically two- and three-dimensionally displayed images. Manipulation of the dials becomes scalar input to the application program residing in the attached host.

The 6094 attaches to the RS/6000 system using the Graphics Input Device Adapter. The Dials connect to the adapter using a 7 foot cable with an 8-pin MINI-DIN connector.

Characteristics

Features   Eight potentiometer dials can be programmed for specific functions

Attachment   Graphics Input Device Adapter (6094 adapter)

6094-20 Lighted Program Function Keyboard

The 6094 Lighted Program Function Keyboard Model 20 is a 32-key desktop unit that provides interactive capability with graphics objects. The keys are controlled by the application and the functions the keys control are defined by the user.

The Lighted Programmable Function Keyboard attaches to the RS/6000 system using the Graphics Input Device Adapter. The Lighted Programmable Function Keyboard connects to the adapter using a 7 foot cable with an 8-pin MINI-DIN connector.

Characteristics

Features   32 easily viewed programmable keys

Attachment   Graphics Input Device Adapter (6094 adapter)

See Table 4.16 for a summary of the hardware.

4.14   High availability solutions

This section discusses the high availability options available for the IBM RISC System/6000. It discusses both High Availability RS/6000 (HA/6000) and Highly Available Network File System (HANFS). These are both software products that can be used in conjunction with standard RS/6000 hardware to provide high availability solutions along with high throughput by using clustered systems. HA/6000 can be used in various modes and these will be discussed in detail.

Table 4.16. Miscellaneous hardware—summary

Name	Features	Attachment
3-Button Mouse	Easy cleaning	Standard RS/6000 mouse port
5083 Tablet	Programmable resolution up to 1279 lines per inch; support for either a 4-button cursor or a stylus	Standard RS/6000 tablet port
5084 Digitizer	Up to 1279 lines per inch; supports both binary and ASCII output data formats; support for use with the IBM 5083 Tablet; cursor with 16 buttons and four indicator lights; two programmable audible tones; tty driver in AIX supports programming to the 5084	Any EIA-232D port
6094-10 Dials	Eight potentiometer; programmable dials for dynamic pan, zoom, and rotate of two- and three-dimensionally displayed images	Graphics Input Device Adapter (6094 adapter)
6094-20 Lighted Program Function Keyboard	32 easily viewed programmable keys	Graphics Input Device Adapter (6094 adapter)

The vast majority of system down-time is *not* due to hardware failure but due to other problems. HA/6000 takes into account all of these causes of failure, rather than just hardware failure.

This section also briefly discusses other aspects of the IBM RISC System/6000 and AIX that make it a very reliable system which will improve availability.

There is a comparison of the approach IBM has adopted with its high availability options for the RS/6000 with other approaches such as Fault Tolerant Systems and Symmetrical Multi-processors. This shows that the HA/6000 approach is a more complete solution in terms of price/performance and availability.

High availability

The subject of high availability is often discussed today. This should not be confused with fault tolerance which utilizes hardware replication to provide availability through specialized hardware circuitry and firmware.

High availability is a complex subject but it should be remembered that different customers will want different levels of availability. The very highest levels of availability can be achieved. Naturally, there will be a cost associated with this. In any specific situation where there is a need to make applications available to users, the following points should be considered:

- Which applications are critical?
- What data is critical?
- Which users/terminals are critical?
- What is an acceptable down-time?
- What is an acceptable recovery-time?
- What performance degradation can be afforded?
- What is an acceptable cost of providing high availability?

Having considered these points, a suitable system architecture can be designed to provide the required level of service. The design may well include components such as an Uninterruptible Power Supply (UPS), disk mirroring of data, operating system and applications, multiple network adapters and other components to provide 'no-single-point-of-failure'. HA/6000 and HANFS as described in this document can form part of this system design. Each design will clearly be specific for any particular customer and his requirements, but in the case of RS/6000 high availability solutions, only standard RS/6000 hardware and software products are used. HA/6000 uses software to provide no single point of failure within a clustered environment. HANFS provides for a highly available NFS (Network File System) server. It uses a similar 'no-single-point-of-failure' approach in that it pairs systems together with shared disks.

In high availability situations, the time taken to recover needs to be considered. HA/6000 can provide a much faster recovery time compared with alternatives in many situations.

Causes of System Down-time

Analysis of system down-time shows that:

- 1 per cent of system down-time is due to hardware failure.
- 99 per cent of system down-time is due to
    - *Hardware maintenance*   This includes scheduled down-time and tasks, such as upgrades to hardware, changes to hardware configuration, etc.
    - *Software maintenance* This includes scheduled down-time for applying new releases of software, etc.
    - *Software failures* This includes application bugs, operating system bugs and other software failures. These are clearly unscheduled failures and therefore cause most problems. Application problems are the most

    common source of system failure.
- *Operator error*   The complexity of UNIX can lead to operator errors if steps are not taken to minimize this.

Clearly anything that can be done to reduce scheduled down-time, reduce and simplify software maintenance, reduce operator errors and provide a more reliable software environment will be of benefit. IBM, through AIX Version 3 for the RS/6000, has provided added value in all of these areas.

The RS/6000 has specific hardware error detection and correction capabilities which are not typical for a system in this price range. There is extensive parity checking through the system. RS/6000 memory is of the Error Correcting Code (ECC) type. Memory scrubbing, bit scattering and spare bits are all used. More details on all of these areas are available from IBM.

AIX Version 3 has been rewritten, based on the original UNIX code and complying with all of the appropriate standards. However, the operating system has been made more reliable and stable. It is the first truly 'production' operating system available in the UNIX world.

AIX removes many of the traditional limitations within UNIX, meaning that the system rarely needs to be shut-down. In contrast, other UNIX systems often need to be closed down when performing simple administration tasks. For example, filesystems can be added, deleted and re-sized without re-booting the system. Also, the AIX kernel can be modified whilst the system is active. The kernel is dynamically scalable, allowing optimal tuning of system parameters at each instant. This means that the system does not require tuning, is always optimized, and reduces down-time—which would otherwise be needed both to carry out tuning work and recover from problems that might result from poor tuning. AIX uses a Journalled File System (JFS) to ensure integrity of the filesystems. All of these things make the RS/6000 and AIX more available than many other systems without even using any specific high availability options.

High Availability RS/6000 Functions

HA/6000 provides two basic functions: cluster management and distributed lock manager. Two or more machines are networked together (e.g. using Ethernet). These machines form a *cluster*. Each machine in the cluster runs a program called the *cluster manager*. This process starts automatically when the machine is powered on. The cluster manager on each system will periodically send a message to other nodes in the cluster to check that they are still up and running. If they fail to reply they are removed from the cluster. If and when a node fails within the cluster, programs are kicked off to enable users

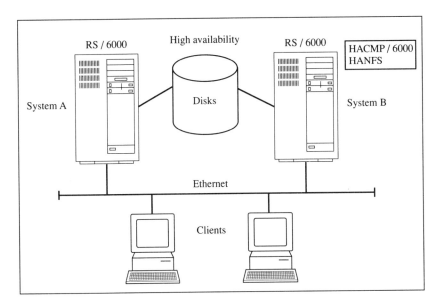

Figure 4.13. High availability options.

to continue using their application. The specific actions that will be taken can be defined by whoever implements the cluster. Typical actions would include the take-over of any shared disks and take-over of the network address of the failed machine. There are three modes of operation in an HA/6000 cluster:

- *Hot stand-by*   In this mode (mode 1), two systems (A and B in Fig. 4.13) are sitting side by side on a Local Area Network (LAN). They are sharing disks which are attached to both systems. One of the machines runs the application and the other machine waits in an idle stand-by mode.
- *Partitioned workload*   In this mode (mode 2), the systems are again sitting side by side with disks and other resources attached to both. However, in this case, applications are running on both machines. Applications running within this cluster can be distinct, different applications, or a single application that has been partitioned to operate in a distributed mode. Each machine acts as a backup to the other.
- *Full loosely-coupled multi-processing (LCMP)*   This mode (mode 3) is an extension to mode 2. Loosely coupled means that each system runs its own copy of the operating system independently but the systems are linked to run in conjunction with each other.

  In this case, the systems both have concurrent simultaneous access to the same physical disk drives. The application can run on both systems utilizing the full capacity of both.

Just about any application can be configured to run in HA/6000 modes 1 and 2. In mode 3, the distributed lock manager must be used by the application or Database Manager software to ensure consistency of the data.

Various combinations using the three modes are possible. For example, a simple extension is a three-way cluster with two active processors and a stand-by processor. Configurations do not have to be symmetric. A model 530H could be used as a standby for a model 550 for example.

In all cases, standard AIX functions can be used to provide a total solution. For example, AIX provides disk mirroring as part of the standard operating system. This can be used both for availability and performance reasons. In addition, the very advanced IBM 9333 high performance disk subsystem can be used for availability and performance. This allows the customer to add or change hard disks without affecting the running system.

Highly Available NFS (HANFS)

HANFS is an extension to NFS (Network File System) that is used for sharing data between machines.

Network File System (NFS) is commonly used for sharing data between machines on a network. It is a standard set of protocols that is supported by most UNIX systems. It runs in conjunction with TCP/IP, which is the network protocol. Any machine on the network can 'export' data that other machines can then 'import'. The data will then appear to be on the local machine, whereas it is actually elsewhere. The data is not transferred between machines, and so this is different to file transfer.

HANFS is an extension to the normal NFS facilities. HANFS provides a highly available NFS server. It uses a similar approach to HA/6000 in that it pairs systems together with a set of shared disks. The system will also have multiple network adapters for availability.

There is a 'heartbeat' to monitor server/backup status. HANFS supports the NFS protocol that runs on TCP/IP. It should be used if a highly available fileserver is required.

Fault tolerant, symmetrical multi-processors or HA/6000

There are three types of systems that are often considered when looking at systems to provide high availability.

- *Fault tolerant systems* These systems have two of every component in the system. In the event of failure, the stand-by component is brought into operation by micro-code of some kind. Although these can be very effective in terms of providing high availability, they tend to be fairly

Table 4.17. Comparing approaches

	Type of system		
	Fault tolerant	16-way SMP	HA/6000
Price	C –	C –	A
Performance	C –	A +	A
Availability	A +	C –	A

Note: The ratings range from A (good) to C (poor).

expensive and the 'spare' components are not used during normal use and therefore the full potential of the machine is not realized. IBM supplies the IBM System/88, which is a fault tolerant RISC system that runs the UNIX operating system.

● *Symmetrical multi-processors* These systems have a number of processors working together within the same system. They tend to be rather expensive, but often can provide good performance. However, these types of systems do not provide for high availability unless two systems are used. As discussed earlier, the vast majority of system down-time is due to hardware maintenance, software maintenance, operator errors and software failures. A symmetrical multi-processor system does not help in these cases.

● *High Availability RS/6000* High Availability RS/6000 or HA/6000 has been discussed in detail in this chapter. It can provide excellent price/performance along with high availability.

Table 4.17 can be used to position the IBM HA/6000 offering in comparison with fault tolerant and symmetrical multi-processor systems.

Summary

Experience with the HA/6000 and HANFS products has shown that customers believe this loosely-coupled approach is the only architecture that will meet their requirements for system uptime.

The HA/6000 approach is similar in concept, but more advanced in implementation, to that used with DEC VAX clusters and VMS systems.

Modes 1 and 2 have both been tested and proved with many applications and databases including Oracle, Ingres, Informix, etc. The mode 3 implementation has also been proved with various relational database products.

4.15   Examples of RS/6000 configurations

I have quoted a few sample configurations of RS/6000s here, with the corresponding list prices. Please be aware that, in many cases, discounts may be applicable. In addition, these prices are correct at the time of writing but are very likely to change in time. Therefore I would recommend that any prices are verified. The prices quoted are in UK sterling and are UK prices.

Entry Desktop RS/6000 model 220

Powerstation 220, LAN attached diskless mono workstation

- 220 System Unit
- 16 MB Memory
- SCSI Controller
- Ethernet Controller
- POWER Gt1 Graphics Feature

- Keyboard and Mouse
- IBM 8508 Greyscale Display (19 inch)
- AIX Version (1–2 users)
- AIXWindows 2D Environment/6000
- Total List Price = £4,864.00

Desktop RS/6000 model 320H

Powerserver 320H, Multi-port asynchronous system

- 320H System Unit
- 32 MB Memory
- 800 MB disk
- SCSI Controller
- 16-port asynchronous adapter

- Internal 3.5 inch diskette drive
- External 1/4 inch tape drive
- AIX Version 3 (1–16 users)
- Total List Price = £21 111.00

Deskside RS/6000 model 550

Powerserver 550, Multi-port asynchronous system

- 550 System Unit
- 128 MB Memory
- 7.0 GB disk (9333 High Performance Disk Sub-system)
- SCSI Controller

- 64-port asynchronous controller and concentrators
- Internal 3.5 inch diskette drive
- Internal 8 mm 2.3 GB tape drive
- AIX Version 3 (1–64 users)
- Total List Price = £116 008.00

These are just a few examples from a wide range of configurations that are available. IBM has advanced on-line tools to help size and correctly configure RS/6000 systems and networks. These tools help to ensure that customers implement a correctly sized high performance system suitable for its planned purpose.

5
Using the RISC System/6000

5.1 Getting started

This book is not intended to be a guide on how to use the RS/6000. There are other books in this series that describe this in detail and there are a number of IBM publications that describe particular aspects of how to use the RS/6000.

However, there are a few ways of getting started on the RS/6000. Each RS/6000 has an accompanying 'Getting Started' manual, and once a user logs into the system and performs a few simple tasks, he or she will soon be able to use the on-line documentation to learn about the RS/6000 and AIX.

5.2 IBM publications and manuals

There is a large range of documentation available from IBM relating to the RS/6000. This can be ordered from IBM as hard copy manuals, although many of them are shipped in soft-copy form with the on-line documentation.

Some of the most common manuals with their order numbers are listed below.

Hardware manuals

IBM RISC System/6000 7013 POWERstation and POWERserver Operator Guide   SA23-2621

IBM RISC System/6000 7013 POWERstation and POWERserver Installation and Service Guide   SA23-2622

IBM RISC System/6000 7012 POWERstation and POWERserver Operator Guide   SA23-2623

IBM RISC System/6000 7012 POWERstation and POWERserver Installation and Service Guide   SA23-2624

IBM RISC System/6000 7016 POWERstation Operator Guide   SA23-2625

IBM RISC System/6000 7016 POWERstation Installation and Service Guide
SA23-2626

IBM RISC System/6000 7015 POWERserver Operator Guide   SA23-2627

IBM RISC System/6000 7015 POWERserver Installation and Service Guide
SA23-2628

IBM 7208 2.3 GB External 8 mm Tape Drive Model 001 Setup and Operator
Guide   SA23-2639

IBM 7208 2.3 GB External 8 mm Tape Drive Model 001 Service
Guide   SA23-2640

IBM 7207 150 MB External 1/4-Inch Cartridge Tape Drive Model 001 Setup
and Operator Guide   SA23-2641

IBM 7207 150 MB External 1/4-Inch Cartridge Tape Drive Model 001
Service Guide   SA23-2642

IBM 7203 External Portable Disk Drive Model 001 Setup and Operator
Guide   SA23-2633

IBM 7203 External Portable Disk Drive Model 001 Service Guide   SA23-2634

IBM 7210 External CD-ROM Drive Model 001 Setup and Operator Guide
SA23-2637

IBM 7210 External CD-ROM Drive Model 001 Service Guide   SA23-2638

IBM Xstation Setup and Operator Guide   SA23-2656

IBM Xstation Service Guide   SA23-2657

IBM RISC System/6000 7015 POWERserver Async Expansion Drawer
Service Guide   SA23-2651

IBM RISC System/6000 7015 POWERserver CPU Drawer Service
Guide   SA23-2649

IBM RISC System/6000 7015 POWERserver SCSI Device Drawer Operator
Guide   GA33-3206

IBM RISC System/6000 7015 POWERserver SCSI Device Drawer Installation and Service Guide   SY33-0160

IBM 9348 1/2-Inch Magnetic Tape Unit Model 012 Operator Guide
SA23-2654

IBM 9348 1/2-Inch Magnetic Tape Unit Model 012 Installation and Service
Guide   SA23-2655

IBM 7204 External Disk Drive Model 320 Setup and Operator Guide
SA23-2658

IBM 7204 External Disk Drive Model 320 Service Guide   SA23-2659

IBM RISC System/6000 Problem Solving Guide   SC23-2204

IBM RISC System/6000 Quick Start Kit   SC23-2195

IBM Xstation 120 Service Guide   SA23-2657

IBM Xstation 120 Technical Reference   SA23-2661

IBM RISC System/6000 POWERstation and POWERserver Hardware Technical Reference—General Information   SA23-2643

IBM RISC System/6000 Hardware Technical Reference 7013 and 7016 POWERstation and POWERserver   SA23-2644

IBM RISC System/6000 Hardware Technical Reference 7012 POWERstation and POWERserver   SA23-2660

IBM RISC System/6000 Hardware Technical Reference 7015 POWERstation and POWERserver   SA23-2645

IBM RISC System/6000 POWERstation and POWERserver Hardware Technical Reference—Options and Devices   SA23-2646

IBM RISC System/6000 POWERstation and POWERserver Hardware Technical Reference—Micro Channel Architecture   SA23-2647

IBM RISC System/6000 POWERstation and POWERserver Hardware Technical Reference—SCSI Device Drawer   SA33-3207

AIX Family manuals

IBM AIX Family Definition Overview   GC23-2002

IBM AIX Family POSIX Conformance Guide   GC23-2159

General introduction manuals

IBM RISC System/6000 Technology   SA23-2619

IBM RISC System/6000 General Information and Planning Information Kit (kit includes following publications)   GK2T-0237

   IBM RISC System/6000 Software Offerings Overview   GC23-2189

   IBM RISC System/6000 Hardware Offerings Overview   GC23-2188

   IBM RISC System/6000 Communications Connectivity Overview GC23-2190

   IBM RISC System/6000 Planning Checklist   GC23-2191

   IBM RISC System/6000 Documentation and Training Offerings Overview GC23-2192

   IBM RISC System/6000 Quick Start Kit   SC23-2195

AIX manuals

Installation Kit for IBM AIX Version 3 for RISC System/6000 SK2T-0204

License Program Specification for IBM AIX Version 3 for RISC System/
6000   GC23-2194

Installation Instructions for IBM AIX Version 3 for RISC System/6000
SC23-2196

XL C Language Reference for IBM AIX Version 3 for RISC System/6000
SC09-1260

XL C User's Guide for IBM AIX Version 3 for RISC System/6000
SC09-1259

Assembler Language Reference for IBM AIX Version 3 for RISC System/
6000   SC23-2197

AIX Distributed Environments   GG24-3489

RISC System/6000 Technical Support Reference   ZZ61-0019

Multi-LP manuals

Task Index and Glossary for IBM RISC System/6000   SC23-2201

IBM RISC System/6000 Problem Solving Guide   SC23-2204

AIX Commands Reference for IBM RISC System/6000   SC23-2199

AIX Calls and Subroutines Reference for IBM RISC System/6000
SC23-2198

AIX Files Reference for IBM RISC System/6000   SC23-2200

AIX General Concepts and Procedures for IBM RISC System/6000
SC23-2202

AIX Editing Concepts and Procedures for IBM RISC System/6000
SC23-2212

AIX Communication Concepts and Procedures for IBM RISC System/6000
SC23-2203

AIX General Programming Concepts for IBM RISC System/6000
SC23-2205

AIX Communications Programming Concepts for IBM RISC System/6000
SC23-2206

AIX Kernel Extensions and Device Support Programming Concepts for
IBM RISC System/6000   SC23-2207

AIX Graphics Programming Concepts for IBM RISC System/6000
SC23-2208

AIX User Interface Programming Concepts for IBM RISC System/6000
SC23-2209

5.3   IBM education

There is a wide range of education available from IBM and third parties
related to AIX and the RS/6000. IBM has education centres that offer

standard training courses and workshops. These are published in education catalogues available from IBM. Standard AIX courses that are recommended for users new to UNIX, include the following:

AIX workshop

This course provides a working knowledge of the AIX operating system. Support staff and end-users of AIX who have no previous experience of using UNIX systems should attend this course. Participants should possess basic keyboard skills and should understand common computer terminology. On completion of this course, participants are expected to be able to:

- Start and log in to the RS/6000
- Manage AIX files and directories
- Execute AIX commands within the user shells
- Use the AIX editors and utilities
- Write and debug shell scripts.

The course has a high practical content and will be carried out using the RS/6000. The course can be attended at Education Centres or can be run on a customer site.

RS/6000 administration

This course enables the participants to administer AIX on a stand-alone RS/6000. RS/6000 support staff should attend this course. Knowledge of the basic operation of the AIX operating system is assumed. Participants should have attended the AIX Workshop or have equivalent knowledge. On completion of this course, participants should be able to:

- Install the AIX operating system and utilities
- Understand and use SMIT (Systems Management Interface Tool)
- Use AIX commands and SMIT to:
  - Manage users and system security
  - Add terminals and printers
  - Manage disk usage
  - Backup and restore data
  - Monitor system performance

The course has a high practical content and will be carried out using the RS/6000. The course can be attended at Education Centres or can be run on customer premises.

Other AIX courses

There is a wide range of further courses that cover specific AIX related topics. These include courses on subjects such as:

- Advanced RS/6000 Administration
- RS/6000 Asynchronous Communications
- RS/6000 SNA Communications
- C Programming for AIX
- AIX Device Drivers
- RS/6000 Performance Tuning

There are also many courses available for IBM business partners to help them learn about the RS/6000 and AIX and prepare them for the accreditation process required to market the RS/6000 and support customers. The TCP/IP communications course, for example, covers AIX TCP/IP Communications.

AIX TCP/IP Communications

This course enables participants to install and manage a TCP/IP network of RS/6000s and PS/2s using both Ethernet and Token Ring. Knowledge of the AIX operating system is assumed, such as that provided by the AIX workshop. Some AIX administration skills will also be useful. On completion of the course, participants are expected to be able to:

- Install and configure TCP/IP hardware and software
- Plan and customize a TCP/IP environment
- Use TCP/IP commands
- Install and customize NFS (Network File System)
- Install and customize NIS (Network Information Services)

The course has a high practical content and will be carried out using RS/6000s and PS/2s.

Education from other sources

IBM also supplies education and support through its VAR (Value Added Resellers) channel. Many of these companies, who sell RS/6000s on behalf of IBM, have specific skills and particular areas of expertise. These VARs will run appropriate courses covering such areas, or will provide education on particular applications.

In addition, there are numerous third party education suppliers that provide AIX education to users.

6
The RS/6000 and IBM

6.1   The changing face of IBM

IBM has changed dramatically over the last few years and has adjusted to the climate that exists in the computer market-place. This climate is one that is very competitive. The days of old when 'Big Blue' was in such a strong position have passed, and IBM finds tough competition in every area of its business from mainframes through to PCs.

In common with other suppliers, IBM now provides solutions, rather than just hardware and system software. Large numbers of skilled IBM employees are used to assist customers in implementing solutions and applications. IBM can provide Systems Integration support where IBM takes responsibility for solutions that involve products from a number of different organizations.

In the UNIX world in particular, competition is strong and because of the portability of applications, suppliers cannot afford to let their products lag behind. In contrast to days gone by, IBM has very high performance systems that are priced very competitively. It has not always been the case that IBM could win on price performance alone. IBM, of course, still strives to provide the highest levels of support and service to customers.

IBM throughout the world has re-structured and become more competitive and now finds that a lot of its business comes from software and services rather than hardware.

6.2   New marketing channels

IBM works with a number of business partners to provide RS/6000 solutions to customers. Customers may be familiar with IBM dealers and System Centres providing Personal System (PS/2) solutions, and IBM Agents providing AS/400 solutions. In the AIX world, there is a similar arrangement. RS/6000 Value Added Resellers (VARs) are qualified to provide

RS/6000 solutions to customers. Independent Software Vendors (ISVs) provide RS/6000 applications.

An IBM VAR has a number of people who have the necessary skills to market and support RS/6000 installations. A VAR must send staff on the relevant IBM courses and after successful completion will be accredited as an official IBM RS/6000 VAR. As the name suggests, the company typically will add value to the customer in some way, either through marketing and supporting particular applications, or through a specific area of expertise – for example complex communications. A VAR may sell other UNIX hardware and solutions in addition to the RS/6000.

IBM is also setting up agreements with companies who will act as Business Associates and act in a closer relationship with IBM to provide the very highest level of support and assistance to customers.

An ISV just sells applications and software and is totally independent of hardware platforms. IBM has marketing agreements with many ISVs and in many cases will sell software packages and support them.

Through these various business partners, IBM can provide high levels of support to customer organizations of all sizes.

6.3   Applications

Space availability

The IBMRS/6000 family with AIX Version 3 is an increasingly popular application platform which suits the needs of a wide variety of users. A large number of independent software vendors have developed a comprehensive set of technical and commercial applications. By year end 1990 some 1000 independent software vendors worldwide had provided more than 2500 major software applications for the RS/6000.

The power of the RS/6000 family and of AIX Version 3 ranges from extensive multi-user support to advanced technical workstation support. The level of support available to customers from IBM and its Business Partners is an added benefit for a UNIX operating system.

For the RS/6000 series, IBM has embarked on an extensive program to provide a variety of leadership applications from many different sources. This effort is supported by dedicated resources found in porting centres around the country.

The National Solutions Centre has the most current information on what applications are available. The applications available include packages for computational chemistry, electrical/mechanical design, geophysical analysis, computer-aided software development, as well as databases, languages, and office productivity packages. Information about the availability of a specific application can be obtained from IBM.

IBM publishes an application catalogue or directory in each country and this will list the applications available for the RS/6000. These directories have applications organized in sections including:

- Accounting and finance
- Business applications – general
- Computer aided manufacturing and design
- Distribution and associated trades
- Engineering, construction and architecture
- Government, health and police
- Industry specific applications
- Insurance, legal and professional services
- Scientific and technical applications
- Systems software

Database

A variety of third-party databases are supported on the RS/6000 including Pick, Informix, Mumps, Oracle, Ingres, Sybase, Unify and many others. IBM intends to market its own database product for the RS/6000. It is quite likely that this database will also be available on other UNIX platforms.

Application Pack/6000

In the UK, IBM markets a set of products under the title Application Pack/6000 or AP/6000. AP/6000 is a set of integrated and tested products based on the popular Uniplex Office Software and the Simdell Manager Series. IBM adds value by providing a complete package of software, hardware and one-stop systems support. With AP/6000, if anything does go wrong, there is only one number to ring. IBM supplies this support in the UK through the AIX Systems Support Centre.

Other software solutions will be added over time – a complete Image and Workflow application from Dorotech in the UK has just been added. All of these applications will be fully integrated and they will have the same 'look and feel'.

IBM services include:

- Application configuration
- Problem definition assistance

- Application loading/pre-loading
- Usability support
- Problem determination
- Problem source identification
- Problem management
- Required fix delivery

Uniplex products in Application Pack/6000 include:

- Uniplex II Plus Base
- Uniplex Advanced Office
- Uniplex Advanced Graphics System
- Uniplex Windows
- Uniplex Additional Dictionaries
- Uniplex Datalink

Simdell Manager products in Application Pack/6000 include:

- General Manager
- Authority Manager
- Minutes Manager
- Fax Manager
- Telex Manager

AP/6000 establishes an 'Open Systems' solution consisting of IBM Services and vendor software products. It is a corporate solution for the RS/6000 environment, providing a platform on which organizations can build their business applications. AP/6000 will be important in those enterprises that wish to take advantage of, and have made the decision to move into, the UNIX/AIX environment. AP/6000 reflects the way that businesses really work—not as a set of discrete functions, but as a sophisticated integrated whole.

Many other countries around the world have similar offerings that provide the same level of integration and support that AP/6000 can offer.

IBM porting centres

IBM has numerous Porting or Conversion Centres. The Conversion Centres assist third parties (ISVs, VARs and Business Partners) with the porting of applications so that they run on the RS/6000. This is a free service. Therefore, if an application has not yet been ported to the RS/6000 it can easily be achieved in many cases through the use of one of these centres.

The Performance Assurance Centre (PAC) provides benchmarking facilities for use mainly in customer situations.

It may be that the application does not yet run on the RS/6000. In that case bookings may be made at the Conversion Centre and PAC so that the third party will port the application immediately prior to the benchmark being run at the PAC. In addition to running benchmarks, the PAC will be able to provide reports of previous benchmarks so that a benchmark will not always be necessary.

6.4   RS/6000 support

When the chosen system isn't the right system, isn't installed correctly, is down, isn't working as designed, or the operation of it is totally confusing to users, it doesn't matter how good the application software is, or how fast the computer runs. That's why IBM has put an enormous emphasis on the reliability of its products and ongoing service and support.

IBM's support can be broken down into three categories:

- *Installation, preparation and implementation assistance*: Coverage here is comprehensive including turn-key solutions, multi-vendor integration assistance and conversion assistance. IBM's philosophy here is to avoid the problem upfront if at all possible.
- *Ongoing service*: If something *does* need to be fixed, it needs to be fast and effective. IBM Services have the tools and support to provide good coverage in this area.
- *Ongoing support*: Ongoing support is more than just service support. It consists of technical expertise on an ongoing basis for any upcoming customer concerns.

Installation and preparation assistance

- *Local support*: This is typically the first line of support. Local IBM Branch Offices or Business Partners will assign skilled technical people to help ensure that systems are properly configured, ordered and installed. Their job is to utilize not only their own skills, but to liaise with the customer for all other technical support available within the IBM corporation.
- *Documentation*: One area of direct customer support is good documentation. Good documentation can reduce support costs for customers and IBM. IBM softcopy documentation, distributed on CD-ROM, is available with IBM software. This distribution format removes the time-consuming and often dreaded task of manual updates because each new CD-ROM shipment is a complete replacement for the previous version. The documentation may be directly accessed with an optional CD-ROM drive, or placed on a server for rapid access by many LAN connected users. The IBM documentation goes beyond simple electronic copies of manual pages. The documentation is designed to work with IBM's hypertext help subsystem for rapid access and ease of use. Hard-copy documentation with extensive indexing is also available for a charge.
- *Education*: Knowledge of the RS/6000 and AIX Version 3 can be increased, prior to and after installation with IBM's educational

offerings. These may include self-study courses in local branch offices, classroom education or one company courses.

- *Configuration definition*: IBM Business Partners and account teams have access to advanced on-line configurators to ensure that all features ordered for machines are compatible and nothing that is required is forgotten. In addition, if one of the RS/6000 Standard Configurations is chosen, that configuration will have gone through extensive integration testing with a variety of applications in IBM's development facility.
- *Electronic product information*: IBMLink is an electronic support facility that can allow users to view much of the same product information that IBM account teams and Business Partners use, including the configuration definition tool discussed above.
- *Planning*: Although most RISC System/6000s will be easy to install, the potential impact of a problem during a major installation necessitates some preparation. IBM offers services which can assist you in assessing risk and developing plans to control it. These services are often made available without charge.
  - *System assurance reviews*: This meeting can be scheduled at an IBM facility or on-site location. It normally involves customer personnel, and an IBM Systems Engineer experienced in Systems Assurance. Other IBM personnel often attend with such skills as physical planning, network integration, capacity planning, etc. These reviews often uncover small items that have been overlooked, preventing potential problems before installation.
  - *Design Reviews*: For very complex projects, a structured design review may be appropriate. These are normally held in the early phases of project definition when investment is just beginning. The review is usually held at an IBM centre housing senior professionals with skills aligned with the key success factors for the project.

- *Tracking orders*: IBM maintains a national on-line database which is constantly updated by manufacturing and distribution facilities. Local branch office administrative personnel can access this information to answer customer queries about their order or to inform them of any improvements in shipping schedules.
- *IBM installation*: IBM Customer Engineers can assist with installation of an RS/6000.
- *Preloaded software*: Most RISC System/6000 configurations are shipped with AIX preloaded. This reduces complexity and time to bring up the machine.

- *Performance Evaluation Centre*: This centre puts out performance statistics that local IBM account teams and Business Partners can use to evaluate the load on your proposed system. In addition, in some selected cases, benchmarks can be performed here.
- *AIX Integration Centre*: This centre tests AIX products, including IBM-marketed and non-IBM applications, across appropriate platforms and network environments. Testing also includes other vendors' equipment, as applicable.
- *Conversion/Coexistence Centres*: One of these centres is available in every area. It may be utilized under complex conversion/coexistence situations.
- *Porting Centre*: This is a centre that may be used to assist with porting of applications to the RS/6000.
- *CAD/CAM Support Centre*: This can be utilized in reference to CAD/CAM related issues.
- *National Engineering and Scientific Support Centre*: This centre provides support for scientific and technical computing application.
- *Systems Integration*: IBM's Systems integration Division serves the needs of customers needing custom services. Examples of completed contracts include:

  - Systems conversions and migrations   - Project management
  - Systems integration   - Consulting
  - Systems programming   - Education
  - Application development

  Ongoing service

- *Comprehensive, effective hardware maintenance*:
  - Fast response: IBM's objective is for a customer engineer to respond within two to four hours whenever possible. This is due in part to the Advance Computer Dispatch System and Computerized Parts Logistic System.
  - Effective analysis tools: Extensive diagnostic aids are available to the local customer engineer.
  - Comprehensive support structure: This includes local customer engineers, product support specialists, installation planning reps, and systems management specialists. It also includes the area and national level support.
  - On site one year warranty: All RISC System/6000s are covered by a no-charge one-year warranty. This service is on site service rather than a carry in service.

- IBM services: IBM offers a wide variety of hardware service offerings. Customers can choose to sign up for extended maintenance option (at substantial savings) or choose a variety of other services like 24 hour-per-day 7 day-a-week service.

• *Software maintenance*: IBM software is supported without additional charge.

• *Additional services*:
  - Multiple vendor services: IBM coordination and management of maintenance and repair for IBM and non-IBM equipment. Problem management and resolution services are available for IBM and non-IBM networks, including trend analysis.
  - On-site customer engineer: Large installations may prefer the security of a dedicated on-site service person instead of IBM's lower cost dispatched service. This service can usually be arranged for an additional charge through a special bid process.

Ongoing support

• *Local support*: IBM account teams and Business Partners are there after the customer's installation to provide ongoing technical guidance and assistance.

• *Software updates*: IBM customers receive software fixes and corrections at no additional charge. This can be a substantial saving. When major new functions come out in a new software version, customers can choose to purchase the new version and continue support.

• *Electronic product information*: IBMLink can be used by the customer on an ongoing basis.

• *Question and answer database*: IBM maintains a database of technical questions and answers that is available to account teams and Business Partners. In many cases, another one of IBM's customers will have experienced a similar difficulty, and the solution will be recorded in the database. This database can significantly speed problem resolution for many customer difficulties.

• *Electronic submission of questions*: IBM Business Partners, account teams and many customers have access to facilities to submit questions. In most cases, questions will be answered within 24 hours. If the answers appear to be potentially useful to others, the questions and the answers go in IBM's question and answer database.

• *Support Hierarchy*: Beyond the above local support, IBM customers have an entire support structure available to them. Many of these vehicles have already been described in the installation and planning section.

• *Critical Situation Management*: In special situations, the local team has access to the AIX Integration Centre and to its Critical Situation Management process. Critical Situations are those problems affecting a customer's business which cannot be resolved quickly with local resources. The Critical Situation Management process brings an extensive network of specialists to focus on the problem. These resources can be invaluable in bringing a quick resolution to a problem.

Summary

IBM invests a significant amount of resource and energy into service and support organizations so that before, during and after a customer's installation, its customers are satisfied. Service and support have traditionally been one of IBM's strongest attributes and IBM intends to keep it that way.

6.5   Relationship between AIX and SAA

SAA and AIX are complementary and strategic IBM architectures delivering a broad set of customer solutions. IBM has announced products and statements of direction that demonstrate the intent to provide a significant level of interoperability between SAA and AIX. This will facilitate comprehensive enterprise solutions when both operating environments are required. Degrees of interoperability between SAA and AIX systems can be grouped into the following types of functions.

• Common: available on both SAA and AIX systems (e.g. database, OSI, OSF/Distributed Computing Environment)
• Bridges: perform data translation and conversion (e.g. mail interchange, NetView)
• UNIX function options: available on SAA systems when required for interoperability (e.g. TCP/IP, NFS, X Window System)

Figure 6.1 shows these functions.

SAA environment

IBM announced SAA in March 1987 as a framework for a complete enterprise information system across four IBM operating system environments: MVS, VM, OS/400 and OS/2 Extended Edition (OS/2 EE). SAA specifications promote development of consistent applications by providing standard-

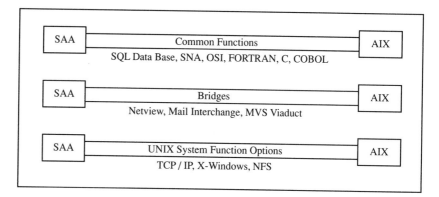

Figure 6.1. Relationship
between AIX and SAA.

ized interfaces for those SAA environments and by providing advanced
application development tools.

AIX operating system environment

The AIX Family Definition, first announced in March 1988, and enhanced
in February 1990, specifies a complete system environment which is based on
UNIX operating systems. It supports popular industry standards, and
includes IBM enhancements. It is a collection of interfaces, conventions, and
protocols supported across a broad price/performance range of IBM
computing environments. The AIX functions and interfaces are either
available or planned for the AIX family of products: AIX/370, AIX Version
3 for RISC System/6000, and AIX PS/2.

IBM interoperability

The areas of SAA/AIX interoperability announced by IBM are: sharing of
data, presentation services, selected communication protocols, network management and a selected common set of standards compliant languages
between the two environments. These capabilities will be provided on the
current or future product offerings. This demonstrates IBM's intention to
provide a significant level of interoperability between SAA and AIX systems.

Communications/connectivity

Connectivity is the basis for all interoperability. IBM has delivered products
(TCP/IP, LU 6.2 and OSI) in both SAA and AIX operating systems and
intends to expand protocol and physical connectivity support between
operating system environments. TCP is used by the Advanced Research

Projects Agency (ARPA), Internet and other networks following US Department of Defense standards for inter-network protocols. IP (Internet Protocol) provides the interface from higher level host-to-host protocols to local area networks or wide area network protocols. IP is used to carry packets to the next gateway or destination system.

Often, AIX systems and SAA systems need to be interconnected. It is IBM's goal to support SNA LU6.2, OSI and TCP/IP communications protocols on all SAA and AIX systems. These protocols will operate on physical connections such as IEEE 802.5 Token Ring, IEEE 802.3 and Ethernet and X.25. MVS, VM, OS/2 EE, and OS/400 (SAA systems) will support TCP/IP as an interoperability option.

Network management

Network management is one of the biggest challenges facing customers today. IBM provides products that give customers the ability to manage their networks by collecting information about the status of network components, using the network to transport this information to a centralized location selected by the customer, and then analysing the information and using it to control the network.

SNA, OSI and TCP/IP network management architectures each define different methods of collecting and transporting information. In OSI the Common Management Information Service/Protocol (CMIS/CMIP) defines information collection and transport. In TCP/IP the Simple Network Management Protocol (SNMP) defines information collection and transport. These architectures define both 'agent' and 'manager' functions. 'Managers' collect and analyse data sent by 'agent' functions residing on nodes in the network.

It is IBM's goal to provide network management for mixed SNA, TCP/IP and OSI networks with SAA and AIX systems.

In addition to the current available support, it is IBM's intention to expand support for SNMP agent function and CMIS/CMIP agent function to SAA and AIX environments. It is also IBM's intention to enhance NetView and AIX systems network management to provide manager function for both TCP/IP and OSI networks. MVS and VM users will then be able to manage mixed SNA, TCP/IP, and OSI networks from a single NetView focal point.

Distributed database

Relational database support is available on all SAA systems. Access to data distributed in remotely interconnected IBM systems is an increasingly common customer requirement. In recognition of this requirement, extensions to the capabilities of the SAA Relational Data Base Management Systems (DBMS) were announced in October 1988.

To support sharing of relational data between SAA systems and AIX systems, it is IBM's goal to provide AIX distributed relational databases. The AIX distributed relational databases will participate fully with SAA distributed database implementations (e.g. DB2, SQL/DS, OS/400 DBM, and OS/2 EE DBM). The SAA and AIX relational database managers will work together to support a distributed database capability, which allows both SAA and AIX users access to data in all environments. In this way, SAA and AIX users will be able to share common relational data.

It is IBM's intention to provide AIX distributed relational databases which conform to the ANSI SQL and FIPS standards and the X/Open SQL specifications in the X/Open Portability Guide, Issue 3.

Shared files

File sharing between applications executing on SAA systems and AIX systems is an increasingly common customer requirement. Today, file sharing between SAA systems and AIX systems is provided using Network File System (NFS). NFS Client support enables access to remote files on systems having NFS Server support.

The Open Software Foundation's Distributed Computing Environment will enhance distributed file sharing capabilities among heterogeneous systems. IBM executives have stated, in press releases and public speeches, that elements of the OSF Distributed Computing Environment will be supported in SAA and AIX environments. This will enhance our shared file support significantly.

Presentation services

Presentation services and user interface management for advanced applications on AIX systems are available through X Window System and AIXwindows. X Window System supports both local and distributed application access through its client/server support. X Window Servers directly manipulate the display screen, keyboard and mouse. X Window clients provide the applications accessed by X Window Servers. AIXwindows is based on the OSF/Motif graphical user interface offering and utilizes X Window System Version 11.3 Client support. Presentation services for applications on SAA systems are provided via the Presentation Manager

(PM). PM and AIXwindows, although different implementations produce similar user interface styles.

For customers requiring a consistent set of presentation services across SAA and AIX systems, it is IBM's goal to provide X Window System and AIXwindows support on all AIX systems, and as interoperability options on all SAA systems.

With this support, AIX workstations will be able to display local X Window System and AIXwindows applications and remote X Window System and AIXwindows applications executing on AIX and SAA systems.

Furthermore, it is IBM's intention that OS/2 EE workstations will also be able to access X Window System and AIXwindows applications which execute on remote AIX and SAA systems. Using PM support on OS/2 EE, SAA applications will also be displayable.

Mail exchange

AIX and other systems derived from UNIX operating systems support mail that meets the popular industry specification of RFC822 and RFC821 Simple Mail Transfer Protocol (SMTP) format.

IBM supports mail exchange between SMTP and OfficeVision networks via bridge functions which run on MVS, VM or OS/400. The bridges for MVS and VM are available through our IBM Business Partner, Soft-Switch. AIX systems support, or will support, the OSI mail protocol, X.400. It is IBM's intention to support X.400 mail exchange between these AIX systems and OfficeVision as well.

Common languages

Customers and software vendors may at times want to port applications between SAA environments and AIX environments. IBM provides a variety of common languages between SAA systems and AIX systems. FORTRAN and COBOL support the ANSI standards and C will fully support the draft ANSI C standard X3J11/88–159 of 12 December 1988, when adopted. FORTRAN, C and COBOL also implement the extensions of SAA CPI for those languages.

IBM intends to provide product offerings on all AIX platforms for C, FORTRAN and COBOL languages, which support the ANSI standards and implement the SAA CPI.

Summary of interoperability capabilities

IBM provides various levels of interoperability between AIX and SAA. Some capabilities are available now, whereas others are statements of direction. IBM can provide up-to-date information with regard to any of these aspects. These capabilities include:

- SNA LU6.2
- OSI
- TCP/IP
- SNMP
- CMIS/CMIP
- NetView

- SQL Database
- NFS Client
- NFS Server
- X-Client
- X-Server
- OSF/MOTIF

- SMTP-OV Mail
- X.400 Mail
- C
- FORTRAN
- COBOL

6.6   RS/6000 v AS/400

Many customers ask for comparisons between the RS/6000 and the AS/400. Both are mid-range computers sold by IBM, and some customers are confused as to which to choose to run an application. There is some overlap between the two systems, but I think it is very often a clear decision as to which system is the most suitable in any particular situation. This section will compare and contrast the two systems, and should help customers to make the right choice. Table 6.1 shows a comparison.

Table 6.1. RS/6000 v AS/400

RS/6000	AS/400
Open Systems – future governed by changing standards	Proprietary – future governed by IBM
Total solution – integrate chosen options	Total solution packaged
Choice of databases	Integrated database – single interface for applications
Portability of applications	Large application base (more than 8000)
Least technical support for UNIX systems	Designed for low technical support
Can be programmed at low level	Higher level of programming interface
Communications with IBM (SAA) and non-IBM	Communications with IBM (SAA) and non-IBM
Choice of application development tools	Good application development environment
ASCII system	EBCDIC system

The RS/6000 is an 'Open Systems' solution and its future will be governed by the emerging standards that we already see in the UNIX world. These standards are clearly beyond the control of IBM, and IBM will have to respond to these standards as and when they change.

In contrast, the AS/400 has a future that is governed by IBM, and IBM can protect its customers from unwelcome changes. IBM has a good record of protecting the investment that customers have made—for example, programs written to run on the very early (System/360) mainframes will still run on today's mainframes.

Although the AS/400 is proprietary, we have already seen IBM announce that the OS/400 operating system will conform with many Open Systems standards including POSIX, OSI, X25 and others.

There is a very large number of customers currently running applications on the AS/400, and IBM will protect the investment of those customers.

In the UNIX world there is more choice—choice of hardware, operating system (version of UNIX), database, applications, etc. One of the problems that this causes is the integration of the chosen components. Will they work together? Sometimes the answer is 'yes' and sometimes 'no'. Time-consuming testing and integration work often has to take place. This is one of the drawbacks of having such a wide choice.

In fact, once certain choices are made (for example, choice of a particular database product), the system is no longer 'Open', as many applications will not run with that chosen database.

In the AS/400 world, a database is shipped with the system. An advantage of this is that all applications written for the AS/400 tend to utilize this database. The look and feel of all AS/400 applications is similar. In addition, other applications can be easily integrated to use this data that is held in the database. Although the customer has less choice, this can be an advantage.

If we look at applications, the RS/6000 and the AS/400 are similar. There is a large pool of applications available for UNIX platforms. Many of these can be easily ported to the RS/6000, if they have not been already. Applications that are not highly graphical (writing to a specific graphics interface) can often be ported in a matter of hours. There is also a large pool of AS/400 applications available.

If we look at the support skills needed to run both systems, I think it is fair to say that the RS/6000 will often require a higher level of knowledge. UNIX is not an easy operating system to get to know, and although the RS/6000 is much easier to use than other UNIX systems, the AS/400 would probably win. In many cases, of course, an RS/6000 or AS/400 system can be installed and can sit in the corner running an application quite happily with very little support needed. The support skills would be needed in a more complex environment when changes to the system are constantly occurring.

There are a number of other areas in which the systems differ, but the choice of platforms should be made on one simple matter—application.

The key decision in choosing any solution is to choose the right software package or application. Having chosen this, the platform will follow. In some cases, in complex environments, where communications with other systems are required, it may be that one platform or the other is most suitable. However, the RS/6000 can communicate in an SNA (or IBM) environment as well as a UNIX environment. Equally, the AS/400 supports OSI and TCP/IP communications as well as IBM protocols.

Many customers perceive the AS/400 to be more expensive than UNIX solutions. This is not always the case. The hardware and operating system are often more expensive, but the AS/400 offers a packaged solution, and the overall cost of ownership is often comparable with the total cost of a UNIX solution. Customers purchasing a UNIX solution usually spend a large proportion of the total spend on services and consultancy in integrating the total solution.

6.7   The RS/6000 success story

The RS/6000 was announced in February 1990 and started shipping in the summer of 1990. It has already been a major success for IBM and is a major player in the UNIX market-place.

In the latter half of 1990, a total of 40 000 systems were shipped world wide, 25 000 to customers, and the remainder to IBM demonstration centres and business partners. Since then, it has continued to sell well across the world. IBM was initially surprised at the type of customers who were buying RS/6000s. It was expected that the major market would be for technical workstations, but in fact it has also been popular in the commercial market-place. It has sold around 50 per cent in each, but the commercial market is continuing to grow.

IBM intends to be the number one or number two supplier in the UNIX market-place by 1993/94. IBM has spent more than 40 billion dollars on research, development, and engineering over the last decade. Over the last four years, IBM has increased its budget for R & D by 25 per cent to 7 billion dollars in 1991.

The RS/6000 business is, however, already profitable for IBM and we will continue to see this level of investment. The revenue from RS/6000 products was more than one billion dollars in 1990 and more than 1.6 billion dollars in 1991. IBM shipped approximately 9 per cent of the total UNIX systems shipped in 1991. This puts IBM in third position in terms of market share. IBM is top in market share of commercial UNIX systems. This places IBM in a strong position to achieve its aims by 1993/94.

Appendix A. Other IBM systems

This book is primarily about the IBM RISC System/2000. However, IBM manufactures and markets a wide range of other computer systems. I will briefly describe these here for completeness.

System Application Architecture (SAA)

IBM has offered a range of system solutions over the years, each with its own unique strengths and advantages. These systems were developed to meet different requirements in the areas of performance, application environment (batch, interactive, transactional), and number of users.

Because of system differences, however, an application had to be tailored to the particular enabling functions of the system on which it would run. To use the same application on a different system required changing the application—an unproductive use of programming skills and time. System differences also meant that a company wanting to take advantage of a new system technology might lose a portion of its investment in existing applications. Another significant problem was how to enable new systems to communicate with older ones.

The need for greater user and programmer productivity and the importance of protecting information system investments demanded common application enablers, consistent applications and better connectivity.

System Application Architecture (SAA) meets these demands. Strictly speaking, SAA specifications are software interfaces, conventions, and protocols that programmers use to create common applications. SAA specifications provide a structure that enables consistent, transparent access to information resources across the SAA systems. SAA specifications and implementations fall into four areas:

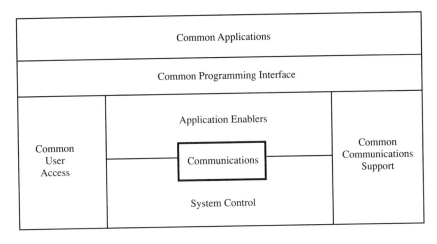

Figure A.1. System Application Architecture (SAA).

- *Common User Access (CUA)*   The design of screen elements and user interaction techniques.
- *Common Programming Interface (CPI)*   Languages and services that application programmers use to build and execute user software.
- *Common Communications Support (CCS)*   Protocols and conventions for connecting systems and software.
- *Common Applications*   Applications based on CUA, CPI, and CSS standard elements.

Figure A.1 shows the structure of System Application Architecture.

The SAA systems include:

- *MVS or VM systems*   MVS/ESA and VM are the operating systems that run on IBM mainframes. There are a variety of these available. The latest are System/390 systems. These include systems such as the ES/9000.
- *OS/400 systems*   OS/400 is the operating system that runs on the IBM AS/400 processors. The AS/400 is a very popular system that replaced the System/36 and the System/38. It is a mid-range computer that is widely used in commercial environments. It combines a wide range of power in terms of performance with ease of use.
- *OS/2 systems*   OS/2 is the SAA operating system that runs on the IBM Personal System/2 or PS/2. The PS/2 replaced the older IBM PC, PC XT and PC AT. Other operating systems such as DOS can run on the PS/2.

Glossary

A

ACE

Advanced Computing Environment. Consortium of vendors with the intention of providing a limited number of platforms on which binary compatibility could be achieved.

AIX

IBM's implementation of a UNIX-like operating system. It runs on IBM mainframes, the RS/6000 and the IBM PS/2 systems.

ANDF

An OSF initiative for shrink-wrapped applications based on a higher-level interface for applications, compilers, and tools.

ANS

American National Standard as defined by ANSI.

ANSI

American National Standards Institute.

Anti-aliasing

A graphics technique used to make diagonal lines (i.e. those that are not strictly vertical or horizontal) on a bit-mapped display appear more smooth. Diagonal lines on a bit-mapped display are jagged because the dots that make up the line can only be displayed at fixed positions on the screen, so a kind of staircase approximation is used. Anti-aliasing relies on a characteristic of human vision to make the staircase appear more like a straight line by reducing the intensity of dots that are off the 'true' diagonal.

ASCII

American Standard Code for Information Interchange. A standard specifying how characters and symbols can be encoded using various combinations of bits.

B

BitBLT

Bit-Block Transfer. The term for a graphics operation that moves a group (i.e. block) of dots from one location to another. BitBlt is usually implemented in hardware on the graphics adapter for mid-range and high-end work-station graphics. Many of these adapters also provide hardware assistance to modify the intensity or colour of the dots as they are transferred. BitBlt is extensively used by windowing systems.

Bit-mapped Display

Commonly called a graphics display in the PC world. The system has the capability to control individual dots (pixels) on the screen as opposed to being restricted to displaying characters.

Bit Plane

A graphics term used to refer to a portion of a frame buffer (i.e. block of video memory). One bit plane contains a single bit of memory for each potentially displayable dot on a screen. A single bit allows a dot to be turned on or off. Two bit planes enable a display dot to take on any one of four colours, three provide for eight colours, four for 16 colours, eight for 256 colours and 24 for 16.7 million colours. The colours are displayed as shades of grey on a non-colour monitor.

BSD

Berkeley Software Distribution, from the University of California at Berkeley.

C

CGI

Computer Graphics Interface: a 2D graphics standard spawned by GKS. Designed to be more efficient than GKS.

CGM

Computer Graphics Metafile: a standard for storing a graphics image in a file for archiving or possible exchange with another system supporting CGM.

CICS

Customer Information Control System. An On-Line Transaction Process-ing (OLTP) monitor.

CISC

Complex Instruction Set Computer.

Colour Lookup Table

The mechanism used to select a subset of colours from a larger palette. For example, a colour lookup table might be able to contain 256 different colours out of a palette of 16.7 million. This would allow up to 256 colours to be displayed on the screen at one time.

D

DASD

Direct Access Storage Device or disk.

DCE

Distributed Computing Environment. An OSF initiative to provide a comprehensive, integrated set of services that supports the development, use and maintenance of distributed applications.

Depth Cueing

A graphics technique that enhances the viewer's perception of depth by modifying the display intensity of objects based on their distance from the viewer. Distant objects are displayed with a lower intensity.

Dhrystone Benchmark

The Dhrystone benchmark is a small benchmark designed to measure integer instructions. Although the Dhrystone benchmark does a good job of measuring non-floating-point CPU performance and some types of compiler optimization, its small size allows it to execute entirely within most caches. Systems with fast CPUs but relatively poor memory subsystems can therefore report high Dhrystone ratings but perform much more poorly on many real applications.

Dithering

A graphics technique used to blur abrupt transitions in intensity or colour. Relies on a property of human vision that tends to 'average' the impression of very small adjacent points. A common application of dithering is seen in colour television sets which simulate all colours by controlling the intensity of small adjacent red, green and blue areas on the screen.

DME

Distributed Management Environment. An OSF initiative to provide a structure for the management of diverse systems and networks in a distributed environment. DME has two main components: a set of application services that provide some of the most critical system management functions, and a framework which provides the building blocks needed to develop applications to manage diverse systems.

DOS Server

Allows an AIX system to act as a file server, print server, and AIX host to PCs running the AIX Access For DOS Users licensed program. PCs do not have to be PS/2s. The PCs may be attached to the AIX system via Token Ring, Ethernet or ASCII asynch lines.

E

Ethernet

A common type of Local Area Network.

F

FIPS

Federal Information Processing Standard. A set of US Government published standards for Federal procurements.

Fixed Point

A particular way of representing numbers using a given number of bits.

Floating Point

A particular way of representing numbers using a given number of bits.

Frame Buffer

A block of memory used to hold a graphics image. Two independent frame buffers allow both the graphics display hardware, and the processor which is responsible for image creation, to operate at full speed. When the processor responsible for creating the image completes its task, it can signal the display hardware to address the new buffer which frees the old one for updates by the updating processor. This 'double-buffering' technique requires twice as much memory for graphics display, but can significantly improve graphics performance for applications that involve realistic simulated motion (i.e. animation).

Full Precision

An IEEE 64-bit floating-point number.

G

GKS

Graphical Kernel System: a standard for 2D graphics. GKS provides drawing capabilities for such things as lines, markers, text, and polygons filled with crosshatch patterns or colour. Interactive input from a variety of device types is also handled.

GKS-3D

Graphical Kernel System: a standard extension to GKS to three dimensions which rivalled PHIGS. PHIGS is generally considered the preferred choice.

GL

Graphics Library: an AIX Version 3 set of routines compatible with the highly regarded Silicon Graphics' library that excels at 3D modelling and imaging.

Gouraud Shading

Shading by interpolation of colour intensities at the vertices of polygon. Developed by Henry Gouraud of the University of Utah in 1971.

graPHIGS

An IBM 3D graphics library generally based on PHIGS with features from the proposed PHIGS+ and additional powerful extensions. Since graPHIGS was made available well before the PHIGS standard was

finalized, some minor differences are preserved to protect customer investments.

GSL

Graphics Subroutine Library. This is a low level 2D graphics interface
supported by IBM on the 6150 and AIX PS/2. It is supported under
AIXwindows.

GUI

Graphical User Interface – for example OSF/Motif with X Windows.

I

IEEE

Institute of Electrical and Electronic Engineers – a formal standards body.

IGES

Initial Graphics Exchange Specification: a standard for exchanging CAD
models from one system to another.

InfoExplorer

On-line documentation and help accessed using Hypertext on the RS/6000.

ISO

International Standards Organization.

L

LAN

Local Area Network – examples include Token Ring and Ethernet.

Linpack benchmark

A program written in FORTRAN based on floating-point intensive code.
The results of the Linpack benchmark are reported in millions of floating-
point operations per second MFLOPS. The results of this benchmark are
particularly valuable for unbiased engineering and scientific comparisons
because there is a single point of contact for source, updates, and results.
Dongarra has been tabulating the results for years and distributes them
widely (available on HONE's COMP in the performance section).

Livermore loops

A collection of floating-point intensive 'kernel' benchmarks distributed by
Lawrence Livermore National Laboratory (LLNL). The benchmark prints
out the MFLOPS rating for each of the tests as well as a number of
composite values calculated from the results of each of the tests. This
benchmark is primarily designed for comparing super computers but is also
used for high performance workstation comparisons.

M

Micro channel

Architecture of the I/O bus in the RS/6000 and the PS/2.

Mil standard

A US military standard.

MVS

IBM's mainframe operating system.

N

NFS

Network File System. Originally developed by Sun Microsystems to share data across networks of potentially different operating systems. Sun has published the interfaces and licenses the code inexpensively so NFS is widely used. NFS allows systems from different vendors to access remote files over a LAN as if they were on a user's local machine. Unlike many environments, this means that a user does not have to do anything special when a file is remote—no file transfer is required. For example, you can edit a text file that resides on another system with NFS support (e.g. a 3090 or a DEC VAX) in the identical way that you can on your own AIX system. In fact, you probably won't even know it's a remote file. Very large files (say, 10 megabytes) take a long time to transfer over the network. If you or your application use only a small part of the file (say a few records), only that small portion will be transferred by NFS. The net result is that you get more rapid access to data you need, and the overall network is not clogged by large file transfers. NFS is supported by virtually all open systems and an increasing number of proprietary systems (e.g. MVS and VM). AIX Version 3 supports NFS 4.0 and 3.2 protocols.

O

OSF

Open Software Foundation. An independent, non-profit development organization. Unlike most other standards related bodies, OSF actually implements specifications by developing and distributing software. IBM was an initial sponsor when OSF was first formed on 17 May 1988.

OSF/Motif

OSF's (Open Software Foundation's) windowing environment. Built on top of the X Window System, lends consistency to X by providing an interface that operates similarly to Presentation Manager and Microsoft's Windows. Also enables improved programmer productivity through a user interface toolkit that is based on the application programming interface for DECWindows.

OSI

A layered collection of standards developed under the aegis of the International Standards Organization for the interconnection of heterogeneous computer and communication environments.

P

Palette

A graphic facility used to reduce cost that enables a display system with support for a fixed number of colours to select each colour from a much broader range. For example, 256 colours from a palette of 16.7 million means that the graphics system can display no more than 256 colours on the screen at one time. Each of the colours can be independently selected out of a group of 16.7 million. This example would require 8 bits (1 byte) of memory for each dot potentially displayable on the screen. If 16.7 million colours were directly supported, each dot would require 24 bits (3 bytes). This technique is also known as a 'colour lookup table' or 'colour mapping'.

PEL

Picture Element. A single dot on a screen. Synonymous with PIXEL, neither being usually capitalized in documentation.

PHIGS

Programmer's Hierarchical Interactive Graphics System is an ANSI, FIPS and ISO standard for high function graphics programming.

PHIGS+

Proposed extensions to PHIGS to include additional capabilities such as hidden line and surface removal and shading produced by multiple simple light sources.

Phong shading

A method of calculating the shading for each pixel in a polygon based on interpolation of vertex normals. Developed by Bui-Tong Phong while working at the University of Utah in 1975.

Pipeline

A processor implementation technique designed to increase performance. Conceptually, pipelines are similar to an assembly line. Assembly lines divide work into small sequential stages that can be worked on in parallel by functionally specialized machines. Although an automobile may take some time to work its way through an assembly line, when viewed from the end, finished products are produced quite quickly. Computer pipelines operate on instructions in a similar manner. One stage may decode the instruction, setting up subsequent operations based on the instruction type. A second stage may move data from a general purpose register to the execution unit responsible for the desired operation. In the third stage, actual execution might occur and in the fourth, the result might be stored back into a general purpose register. Typically, each stage of a pipeline takes one cycle to complete. In this example, it takes four cycles for the first instruction to move through the pipeline, but after the first result is produced, subsequent instructions can be completed each cycle.

PIXEL

Picture Element. A single dot on a screen. Synonymous with PEL, neither being usually capitalized in documents.

POSIX

    IEEE's Portable Operating System Interface for Computer Environments. Note that a naming convention has evolved for open system operating environments. Most such environments include an 'X' within their name. In the case of the acronym POSIX, 'Computer Environment' was replaced by an 'X' in the acronym.

POWER

    Performance Optimization With Enhanced RISC.

     R

Rendering

    Construction of a computed image of a scene from a description of light sources, geometry of the constituent parts, and their surface properties, etc.

RISC

    Reduced Instruction Set Computing.

     S

SAA

    System Application Architecture.

SMIT

    Systems Management Interface Tool. Menu driven front end for systems managers on the RS/6000.

SNA

    System Network Architecture. IBM's network protocols.

SNMP

    Simple Network Management Protocol. Used in TCP/IP networks.

SPECmarks

    A composite measure of processor performance for engineering and scientific applications based on the SPEC series of benchmarks.

System Performance Evaluation Cooperative (SPEC)

    A group of workstation vendors committed to creating and distributing benchmarks designed to measure system performance for engineering and scientific applications. Most major workstation vendors are members including IBM.

System V

    ATC name for current versions of UNIX.

     T

TCP/IP

    Transmission Control Protocol/Internet Protocol. Communications protocols often used in a UNIX environment.

Token Ring

Type of Local Area Network.

U

UNIX International

An advisory group set up to advise AT&T on System V development.

V

VAR

Value Added Reseller.

W

WAN

Wide Area Network.

Whetstone Benchmark

A small benchmark originally published in 1976 designed to measure floating point performance including transcendentals (e.g. sine, cosine, etc.). Unlike the Linpack benchmarks, this test of performance is not managed by a single entity so multiple versions have proliferated. Although Whetstone results are still widely reported by the trade press, this benchmark is falling out of favour because quoted results may be based on different versions of the code.

X

X/Open

UNIX Standards Organization.

XPG3

Portability Guide produced by X/Open.

Xstation

System that runs X Windows linked into a UNIX host.

X Window System

The X Window System (informally known as X) supports device independent graphics across a heterogeneous network of computers ranging from simple PC clones to supercomputers. Unlike most windowing systems, X provides windows into the network. That is, each window can connect to any application written to X specifications (and almost all text based applications through a terminal emulator) on any machine in the network. X is divided into two parts:

- Server: controls the screen, keyboard and pointing device such as a mouse. Server code is run on a PC, workstation, or X terminal like IBM's Xstation.

- Client: interfaces directly with an application and communicates with servers.

Servers and clients communicate by passing messages to each other over a network or in memory if they reside in the same machine.

For example, a single workstation screen could have windows displaying a local text editor, a PROFs session from a 3081, a business graph being generated by a DEC VAX, and the graphical results of a weather model running on a 3090-600. This example would not require any special programming other than using the X Library calls.

X was developed as part of MIT's Project Athena (IBM and other vendors provided support for this effort). X is the most widely supported windowing interface for open systems. Further MIT enhancements are being supported by the X Consortium of which IBM is a member.

Index